D1180103

August Belmont

A Political Biography

John Q. A. Ward's bronze statue of August Belmont, situated next to the Belmont Chapel in Newport's Island Cemetery. (Courtesy of Mrs. Eleanor Robson Belmont)

August Belmont

A Political Biography

Irving Katz

Columbia University Press

New York & London 1968

E
410.9
.B45 K3

57376

To S. E. K., loving companion

and N. K. K., lovable distraction

Preface

DEMOCRATS ADDRESSING Jefferson-Jackson Day banquets proudly
date the party's genesis from the early 1800s. But how many
of those who extol the hallowed Democracy realize that
the party as a national organization nearly followed the Federal-
ists and Whigs into oblivion a century ago? The Democratic
President Buchanan had been repudiated; the party's young
northern champion, Douglas, lay dead; the southern wing had
seceded; and much of the northern branch had defected to the
rising star of Republicanism in the War for the Union.

Yet the Democratic Party did not disappear or become submerged in another political organization, but maintained its
identity thanks largely to the tenacity of August Belmont, an
international banker and American agent of the European
Rothschilds. Virtually unknown in political circles in the
1840s, he became a lively campaign issue in the 1852 presidential election and, soon after, a diplomat in Pierce's administration. He was on intimate terms with Buchanan even before
Buchanan entered the White House. In 1860 Douglas, the most
powerful Democrat in the country, singled out the forty-six-
year-old Belmont to run his presidential campaign by choosing
him as chairman of the Democratic National Committee. Belmont remained in this post for the next twelve years, a tenure
exceeded by no one else before or since. He resigned as national
chairman in 1872 but continued to mold party policy and to
champion his presidential choices. After Grover Cleveland's
election in 1884—the first such Democratic triumph in nearly
thirty years—the most powerful member of the Democratic

National Committee, Maryland Senator Arthur P. Gorman, acknowledged his debt to Belmont. "No man living," he wrote, "has rendered to his party so much service as you have. . . . The success [of 1884] . . . would not have been possible but for the foundation laid by you."

I believe Gorman was correct; his statement was not one of ceremonial rhetoric but an accurate evaluation. Yet, professional scholars have long been unfamiliar with Belmont's precise contributions to antebellum, Civil War, and Reconstruction politics. References to him are missing in many books which purport to be comprehensive accounts of his age, while inaccuracies pepper the pages of standard works which do mention him. That American historiography has lacked a book about this important man was due to the distressing fact that the files of the Wall Street banking firm, August Belmont & Company, together with much of Belmont's political correspondence, were destroyed by the Equitable Building fire in 1912.

The financial records are gone beyond recall, but, despite this frustrating knowledge, I tracked down enough material to convince me that his political career itself warranted book-length study. An ample number of Belmont letters were found in the manuscript collections of important contemporaries, such as James Buchanan, Stephen A. Douglas, Samuel J. Tilden, William L. Marcy, Salmon P. Chase, William H. Seward, Manton M. Marble, Samuel L. M. Barlow, and Thomas F. Bayard. Contemporary newspapers and periodicals, though never wholly reliable, supplied additional information. The greatest boon turned out to be the discovery of hundreds of Belmont's political letters, fortunately kept at home and preserved by his descendants and their families.

Gaps still remain in Belmont's story; yet I tried to avoid speculation where the available facts do not appear to support it. Where I yielded to the temptation of "creative" history, I did so out of confidence in the emerging picture.

I wish to acknowledge my gratitude to two members of the Belmont family: Mrs. Eleanor Robson Belmont (widow of August Belmont's son, August, Jr.) and August Belmont (great-grandson of my subject). Both made available the fascinating cache of letters and photographs that enabled me to explore a hitherto uncharted area of nineteenth-century Americana. For their hospitality, for their encouragement, and for the fact that they never asked me about the interpretations I would make of the material so generously offered, I am deeply indebted.

Several friends have aided me at various times during the book's genesis. Thomas P. Govan read a rough draft of the entire manuscript and made invaluable criticisms and suggestions. Vincent P. Carosso was the first to stimulate my interest in investment bankers. Herbert H. Kaplan provided intangible moral support, as did Martin Ridge, who also read the entire manuscript. Joseph J. Haywood showed me every consideration during my research in the private Belmont papers. Mrs. Ellen B. Doheny typed all the drafts of the manuscript. Bernard Gronert of the Columbia University Press made a number of thoughtful suggestions.

In the course of my research I received prompt and cordial assistance from a number of libraries and librarians, and I am especially grateful to the following: Miss Jean McNiece and Paul Rugen, Manuscript Division, New York Public Library; Mrs. Barbara P. Boucot, Department of Manuscripts, The Huntington Library; Manuscript Division, Library of Congress; Special Collections, Columbia University Library; Special Collections, University of Chicago Library; Special Collections, University of Rochester Library; Historical Society of Pennsylvania; New-York Historical Society Library; Indiana University Library; and Indiana Historical Society.

The Indiana University Graduate School helped me by generously providing two Grants in Aid of Research and two Summer Faculty Fellowship Awards.

By far the greatest contribution came from my wife, Sarah Elizabeth Katz. She alone knows how much of this book is really hers.

IRVING KATZ

Indiana University
Bloomington, Indiana
December, 1967

Contents

Illustrations

August Belmont

A Political Biography

1

★ ★ ★

From Alzey to Wall Street

On November 7, 1849, the most fashionable wedding of the year took place in New York's newly built Protestant Episcopal Church of the Ascension. August Belmont, a German-Jewish immigrant, exchanged vows with Caroline Slidell Perry, fourth daughter of Commodore Matthew C. Perry and descendant of an old and prominent American family. The "beautiful & well-bred Caroline," as Belmont described her in a letter home, displayed unusual broadmindedness for her day and upbringing; she unhesitatingly "put aside all prejudices in her esteem & love" and made no requests that he conform in any way to her religious beliefs.[1]

If, as Caroline did, one overlooked Belmont's religion, which he no longer practiced, and his foreign birth, he was undoubtedly a very suitable partner. Within a short time of his American arrival, contemporaries regarded him as the most distinguished Jew in New York business and social circles. By 1845 a metropolitan newspaper placed his worth at $100,000, and his acknowledged affluence opened doors to a world usually barred

[1] Perry Belmont, *An American Democrat: The Recollections of Perry Belmont* (New York, 1941), 4; Belmont to Elizabeth Belmont Feist, Oct., 1849, August Belmont Papers, private collection of Mrs. Eleanor Robson Belmont, New York City (hereafter referred to as "private Belmont collection"); Allan Nevins, ed., *The Diary of Philip Hone, 1828–1851* (New York, 1936), 888; G. T. Bedell to Belmont, Dec. 31, 1850, August Belmont Papers, New York Public Library. The Belmonts had six children: Perry, August, Jr., Frederika, Jane Pauline, Oliver Hazard Perry, and Raymond Rodgers. The children were reared as Episcopalians. Belmont attended the Church of the Ascension regularly, though he himself was never baptized. Conversation with Mrs. Eleanor Robson Belmont on Dec. 4, 1963.

Caroline Slidell Perry Belmont about the time of her marriage, circa 1849. (Courtesy of Mr. August Belmont)

to non-Christians. He set up a "splendid" country house in the northern, sparsely settled region of Manhattan Island, where he presented "fetes and soirees" and played host to famous visiting actresses and prima donnas. The exclusive Union Club, "the mother of clubs," admitted him to membership in 1848. Belmont became more and more conspicuous at the best fancy balls, in his choice box at the opera, and on lists of sponsors for worthy charitable events. Even his limp, a permanent souvenir from a duel he fought over a lady's "honor" in 1841, seemed to augment the romantic aura surrounding this parvenu with the exotic background.[2]

[2] [Moses Yale Beach] *Wealth and Biography of the Wealthy Citizens of New York City* . . . (6th ed., New York, 1845), 3; Robert G. Albion and

August Belmont about the time of his marriage, circa 1849. (Courtesy of Mr. August Belmont)

Though hardly a penniless refugee when he first arrived in the United States, Belmont had come a long way from his origins. He was born on December 8, 1813, in the Rhenish Palatinate village of Alzey, an old Imperial Free Municipality which had come under the jurisdiction of the Grand Duchy of Hesse-

Jennie B. Pope, *The Rise of New York Port, 1815–1860* (New York, 1939), 240; Arthur C. Cole, *The Irrepressible Conflict, 1850–1865* (New York, 1934), 127; Croswell Bowen, *The Elegant Oakey* (New York, 1956), 45–46. Belmont's adversary in the duel, fought at Elkton, Maryland, was Edward Heyward, a South Carolinian, who shot the banker in the left thigh. The two men later became reconciled. Belmont to Elizabeth Belmont, Sept. 15, 1841, Belmont to Simon Belmont, Nov. 10, 1841, private Belmont collection; Nevins, ed., *Diary of Philip Hone*, 558; Perry Belmont, *An American Democrat*, 6; *New York Herald*, Aug. 28, 30, Sept. 1, 3, 6, 8, 11, 15, 1841.

August Belmont's parents, Simon and Frederika Elsass Belmont. (Courtesy of Mrs. Rahel Liebeschuetz)

Darmstadt after the Napoleonic Wars. His parents were Simon and Frederika Elsass Belmont, and on the paternal side he was a descendant of Spanish Jews who fled the Iberian Peninsula during the reign of Ferdinand and Isabella three centuries earlier. August's father held a leading position in the Alzey community; he possessed a freehold estate and served for many years as president of the local synagogue. August's mother died when he was seven, and the boy went to live with an uncle and grandmother in Frankfurt, where he attended the Jewish Junior and Senior High School. When August was fifteen, his relatives prevailed upon their Frankfurt friends, the Rothschilds, to help train him for a business career.

The Rothschilds, whose reputation for financial acumen and success was gaining in western Europe, made Belmont an apprentice in their Frankfurt branch. There, amid much floor sweeping, errand running, and furniture polishing, the youth obtained a valuable close-up of the methods by which a prominent international banking house operated. The ambitious Belmont worked energetically at the Rothschild office, thereby hoping "to gain the confidence and good will" of his "esteemed employers by diligence and orderliness." When his father inquired about his morning punctuality, Belmont reassured him that not only was he always prompt at the office, but that, on the advice of Baron Carl von Rothschild, he arose daily at 5 A.M. in order to have a private tutor instruct him in French, English, composition, and arithmetic.

Belmont continued to gain his employers' trust. The Rothschilds rewarded him with a confidential clerkship in 1832. Two years later they singled him out again, designating him a traveling companion and secretary to one of the partners. This new position took Belmont outside Germany for the first time—to Paris, Naples, and the Vatican. Besides deepening his experience in international finance and giving Belmont insight into European politics, the trip developed and broadened his cultural horizons. He learned to speak Italian and visited numerous art galleries, laying the foundation for his lifelong devotion to and patronage of the fine arts.[3]

In 1837 Belmont embarked upon another journey which would prove to be his most significant one. The Rothschilds' Paris and London branches had become concerned with their

[3] Simon Belmont to August Belmont, Jan. 27, 1850, letter in possession of Mrs. Rahel Liebeschuetz, Liverpool, Great Britain, a great-granddaughter of August Belmont's sister, Elizabeth. Richard J. H. Gottheil, *The Belmont-Belmonte Family: A Record of Four Hundred Years* . . . (New York, 1917), 164-65, 171; Student Report Card, dated Nov. 11, 1827, Belmont to Simon Belmont, Sept. 22, 1828, June 17, 1829, Sept. 15, 1830, private Belmont collection; Henry Clews, *Fifty Years in Wall Street* (New York, 1908), 595-96; *Encyclopaedia Judaica: Das Judentum in Geschichte und Gegenwart* (10 vols., Berlin, 1928-34), IV, 34; *New York World*, Nov. 25, 1890.

immense interests in the Spanish Empire, whose stability was threatened by the Carlist War raging in Spain. The Madrid government constantly drew money on her Cuban possession, and the Rothschilds just as quickly took up these drafts. Needing a reliable agent on the scene in Havana to investigate the situation, the firm approached young Belmont, who readily consented to go. He stopped for briefings in Paris and London and sailed for Havana, via New York.

Belmont reached New York on May 14, 1837, and found a situation which his instructions did not cover. The United States had suffered a major financial crisis which struck at the roots of national prosperity and apparently threatened the very basis of American commerce. Two days after his arrival, he wrote home that "All banks have stopped payments and ⅞ of all business firms in the States have gone into bankruptcy. In New York alone there were counted more than 200." One of the casualties was the Rothschilds' American agent, the New York Stock Exchange firm of J. L. and S. I. Joseph & Co., which had gone under on March 17, with liabilities of 7 million dollars. Communications with the Rothschilds might take several months; yet the situation required an immediate decision. Acting on his own judgment, the Havana emissary delayed his departure for Cuba and remained in New York to superintend any jeopardized Rothschild interests.[4]

Belmont studied the new country while awaiting the Rothschilds' reply to his findings and comments. The more he learned of the tremendous possibilities opening up for the development of the still young United States, the more he resolved to make it his permanent home. He postponed his Havana de-

[4] Belmont to Simon Belmont, May 16, 1837, clipping from *Concord* (N.H.) *Independent Statesman*, Dec. 4, 1890, private Belmont collection; W. W. Craig and Challiss Gore, "House of Belmont: A Banking Family's First Hundred Years," unpublished manuscript in author's possession (New York, 1937), 4, 29; Fritz Redlich, *The Molding of American Banking: Men and Ideas* (2 vols., New York, 1947–51), II, 353; George Francis Train, *Young America in Wall-Street* (New York, 1857), xii, 308; Charles H. Haswell, *Reminiscences of an Octogenarian of the City of New York (1816 to 1860)* (New York, 1896), 326.

parture indefinitely, rented a little room at 78 Wall Street, and announced the establishment of August Belmont & Company. The Rothschilds eventually approved his decision and appointed him their new American agent. The new firm had an almost instantaneous success, and throughout the disturbed years between 1837 and 1842 the young banker helped straighten out the complicated Rothschild interests in the United States. In addition to serving as a disbursing agent, dividend collector, and news gatherer for the Rothschilds and their customers, the new house's activities included foreign exchange, commercial and private loans, acceptance of deposits, and the handling of commercial paper. Belmont's association with European capital attracted private corporations, railroads, and state and local governments to his services. By the time of the Mexican War, August Belmont & Company was sufficiently strong to underwrite a substantial portion of the United States Treasury loans.[5]

In another bid to strengthen his business position, the young banker accepted Austria-Hungary's offer to become its American Consul General. The firm gained additional facilities and prestige in international trade, and Belmont gained a convenient excuse "to get rid of Jury duty," which, to a single entrepreneur, could be "very irksome." He served in this capacity from 1844 until 1850, when he severed his connection with the Hapsburg regime, partly because he objected to Austrian re-

[5] August Belmont, *Letters, Speeches and Addresses* (New York, 1890), 5–7; [Joseph A. Scoville] *The Old Merchants of New York City* (5 vols., New York, 1864–70), I, 16; Alvan F. Sanborn, ed., *Reminiscences of Richard Lathers: Sixty Years of a Busy Life in South Carolina, Massachusetts and New York* (New York, 1907), 41; Redlich, *Molding of American Banking*, II, 347. The Rothschilds were "very upset" to hear of the 1841 duel and briefly contemplated taking the agency away from Belmont. The young banker assured them that all Rothschild funds had been placed under safe protection and insisted that there existed much support for his role in the "affair of honor" among "the most respected people here." Ultimately, he pacified his mentors and August Belmont & Company continued to handle their American business on into the twentieth century. Belmont to Simon Belmont, Nov. 10, 1841, private Belmont collection; John William Leonard, ed., *Who's Who in Finance and Banking: A Biographical Dictionary of Contemporaries, 1920–1922* (New York, 1922), 53.

August Belmont's residence at 109 Fifth Avenue, shown shortly after it was sold in 1893. (Courtesy of the Museum of the City of New York)

pression of Hungarian independence but also because of his burgeoning interest in American politics.[6]

Belmont, now wealthy and successful, might have settled comfortably into the harness of upper-class American life with no reproaches from any quarter. His peers probably expected he would do so, and to a certain extent he satisfied their expectations. He and his wife established residence at 72 Fifth Avenue, when the street was emerging as a fine boulevard. A few years later, Belmont purchased a Long Island farm which served as "a source of interest and relaxation" and as a training area for his race horses. In the late 1850s he acquired a mansion at 109 Fifth Avenue, on the corner of Eighteenth Street. He en-

[6] Belmont to George N. Sanders, March 21, 1853, George Nicholas Sanders Papers, Library of Congress; Craig and Gore, "House of Belmont," 6. It was not unusual in those days for merchants residing in large port cities to be appointed to such posts by foreign governments. William H. Aspinwall and Benjamin Aymar, both New York merchants, served as vice-consuls for Tuscany and Denmark, respectively. Albion and Pope, *Rise of New York Port*, 230–31, 240.

Interior of 109 Fifth Avenue, showing dining room, circa 1885. (Courtesy of Mrs. Eleanor Robson Belmont)

Interior of 109 Fifth Avenue, showing entrance hall, circa, 1885. (Courtesy of Mrs. Eleanor Robson Belmont)

larged and beautified it, added a stable and a superb art gallery, and made it in every way the nineteenth-century gentleman's ideal residence. There, he entertained his guests with an elegance and finesse rarely equaled in the city.[7]

But the restless Belmont could not be content with such a life, circumscribed as it was by conventional practices and responses. His wife's uncle, former Congressman John Slidell of Louisiana, was assuming importance in the Democratic Party by virtue of a strong state political machine, and he encouraged the banker to enter the ranks of "Young America" by open involvement in public affairs. From the security of Belmont's position, the uncertainties of political life challenged rather than intimidated him. Though he had never taken an active part in politics, he had voted for Democratic candidates ever since his naturalization in 1844. Belmont's earlier Democratic commitment, which had set him apart from most of his business acquaintances, who were active or nominal Whigs, now seemed particularly fortuitous. So, with boundless faith in his own ability, Belmont offered his services to "Uncle John" and entered the rough and tumble world of party politics.

[7] Eleanor Robson Belmont, *The Fabric of Memory* (New York, 1957), 117; Perry Belmont, *An American Democrat*, 3, 71.

2

★ ★ ★

Introduction to American Politics

SLIDELL WAS ONLY too happy to inherit such an able and enthusiastic protégé as Belmont, for he was deeply involved in an attempt to capture the 1852 presidential nomination for his friend, former Secretary of State James Buchanan of Pennsylvania. By the spring of 1851, Slidell confidently believed that most southern and southwestern Democrats would favor the as yet unannounced Buchanan at the Baltimore nominating convention, but that the key northern state of New York must be won if the overall Buchanan movement were to succeed. Thus, he and Buchanan, sensitive to the potential charge of "outside meddling" in local political affairs, chose the eager but inexperienced Belmont to manage the Pennsylvanian's preconvention campaign in New York.[1]

Belmont had no illusions about his task in the Empire State. The factious organization calling itself the New York Democracy had just experienced a typical internecine donnybrook, one which bequeathed such quaint, imaginative sobriquets as "Barnburners" and "Hunkers," and "Hards" and "Softs." In 1848 this fierce intraparty rivalry handed the state's thirty-five electoral votes to the Whigs, constituting a major factor behind Zachary Taylor's victory in the presidential canvass. The resultant scars were still visible, and an attempt at unity by a relatively neutral outsider seemed unlikely to succeed.

Belmont knew that every major aspirant for the party's

[1] There is no adequate biography of Slidell, but see Louis M. Sears, *John Slidell* (Durham, N.C., 1925). A good recent account of Buchanan is Philip S. Klein, *President James Buchanan: A Biography* (University Park, Pa., 1962).

nomination claimed some support within the New York organization. Buchanan's major competition included Senator
Lewis Cass of Michigan, the 1848 standard-bearer; General
William O. Butler of Kentucky, Cass' luckless running mate;
and Stephen A. Douglas of Illinois, a thirty-eight-year-old
freshman senator who had played a substantial role in the debates preceding the Compromise of 1850 and was the acknowledged leader of the expansionist "Young America" movement
within the party. Belmont also kept a cautious eye on William
L. Marcy of New York, a thrice-elected governor in the 1830s
and Secretary of War in Polk's cabinet, even though he had not
indicated an interest in the nomination. Belmont could not believe that the party would nominate Marcy, who would be past
his sixty-sixth birthday at the next presidential inauguration,
though the New York politician and his potentially large body
of supporters could well turn out to be the decisive factor in
New York.[2]

As early as March, 1851, fifteen months before the national
convention, Belmont wrote letters to James Gordon Bennett's
widely circulated *New York Herald* and to the *New York Na-
tional-Democrat* in which he successfully insisted that their editorials on possible nominees do "partial justice" to "Old Buck"
Buchanan. However, getting these and other Democratic newspapers to commit themselves to Buchanan's standard was another, more difficult undertaking. He felt caution was the best
approach for, as he reported to Buchanan, "they are very unreliable fellows & too much zeal might do you more harm than
good." He advised Buchanan not to worry over Tammany
Hall's recent endorsement of Cass or to take notice of any local
pro-Douglas noises. If anything, Belmont predicted, the Cass
designation might dissuade Marcy from throwing his hat into

[2] Valuable information on the New York Democratic Party in the 1840s and
1850s can be located in De Alva Stanwood Alexander, *A Political History of
the State of New York* (4 vols., New York, 1906–23); Ivor D. Spencer, *The
Victor and the Spoils: A Life of William L. Marcy* (Providence, 1959);
Stewart Mitchell, *Horatio Seymour of New York* (Cambridge, Mass., 1938);
and Alexander C. Flick, *Samuel Jones Tilden: A Study in Political Sagacity*
(New York, 1939).

the presidential ring and "make him more desirous to fight under your banner." [3]

In the summer of 1851 Slidell visited New York to give momentum to the Buchanan cause. First, he hoped to gain Marcy's aid for the Buchanan boom; in an interview he had found the "Governor sincerely friendly and cooperative." Second, Slidell approached a number of leading city Democrats about the possibility of establishing a "large and powerful" metropolitan newspaper, informative to commercial interests and profitably operated. Based on the "principles" of the *London Times*, the new paper would formulate national party policy and provide staunch backing for Democratic candidates. Belmont pledged $10,000 to the enterprise, and he and Slidell persuaded such prominent Democratic wirepullers as Charles O'Conor, Francis B. Cutting, and Theodore Sedgwick to become original subscribers. His major purpose apparently accomplished, Slidell returned to New Orleans to head up the Buchanan forces in Louisiana and other states of the Southwest.[4]

By the autumn, Marcy, urged on by the old Andrew Jackson group—the Van Burens (Martin and his son, John), Francis P. Blair, Sr., and his sons, and former Senator Thomas Hart Benton of Missouri—began talking and acting like a presidential candidate. He called in his friends O'Conor, Cutting, and Sedgwick and pointed out that the planned newspaper was taking on a distinctly Buchanan coloration. He suggested that the three consider withdrawing their pledges of support unless the Buchanan camp promised that the journal "would remain perfectly neutral on the subject of the Presidency," and that someone other than John W. Forney, Buchanan's personal choice,

[3] Belmont to Buchanan, April 3, 1851, James Buchanan Papers, Historical Society of Pennsylvania; Roy F. Nichols, *Franklin Pierce: Young Hickory of the Granite Hills* (2nd ed., Philadelphia, 1958), 218–19; Spencer, *Marcy*, 194–213.

[4] Slidell to Buchanan, Dec. 16, 1850, May 9, July 9, August 8, Sept. 5, 29, Oct. 9, 1851, Belmont to Buchanan, Dec. 6, 1851, Buchanan Papers; Sears, *Slidell*, 87; Allan Nevins, *Ordeal of the Union* (2 vols., New York, 1947), II, 12–13; Philip S. Foner, *Business & Slavery: The New York Merchants & the Irrepressible Conflict* (Chapel Hill, N.C., 1941), 82–83.

August Belmont, 1852. (Courtesy of Mr. August Belmont)

be brought in as editor. Belmont, the go-between, could not accept these conditions, and O'Conor, Cutting, and Sedgwick backed out. He realized that with Marcy's friends "not only not with us, but in all probability against us," any further time and energy expended for such a journal would be "worse than useless." Belmont did not give up a newspaper project altogether, but turned his attention toward collecting new subscriptions for a "Democratic Union" paper, one which would positively adhere to the Baltimore convention's choice and combat the "pernicious influence" of William Cullen Bryant's nominally Democratic, abolitionist-inclining *New York Evening Post*.[5]

Meanwhile, Belmont sounded out as many "influential" Democrats as he could in an attempt to manufacture a "judicious and effective" pro-Buchanan movement. What he heard indicated that many either were attracted to Marcy's candidacy or were "afraid to commit themselves at this early period." Such widespread indecision and cowardice paralyzed Belmont's initiative, and he could report to Buchanan nothing more concrete than that practically everybody acknowledged "Old Buck's" superior qualifications for the office of Chief Executive.

In January, 1852, Belmont asked Buchanan whether the time had come to announce his candidacy publicly. With Buchanan's assent, Belmont and other New York cohorts could organize some preliminary meetings, pass several strong pro-Buchanan resolutions, and then begin feeding propaganda to local Democratic newspapers. Marcy, of course, remained the unknown quantity. If his support were won over, Buchanan's declaration would gain strength within the Empire State Democracy. But should Marcy's antagonism be aroused, Buchanan might risk the combined opposition of Marcy, Cass, and Douglas. Buchanan was not prepared to go to war in New York before he had conquered his enemies at home. The Pennsylvania Democrats would be holding a convention in March to select delegates to Baltimore. Perhaps victory at home might scatter the opponents next door.[6]

Belmont could not sit by quietly awaiting the Harrisburg outcome. Marcy stopped over in the city for several days in late February, and Belmont successfully secured a "confidential interview" with him, hoping that some mutual arrangement could be worked out. Belmont at first allowed Marcy to do most of the talking. How was Buchanan feeling these days, Marcy in-

[5] Belmont to Buchanan, Dec. 6, 1851, Jan. 28, 1852, Slidell to Buchanan, Nov. 17, Dec. 27, 1851, Buchanan Papers; Buchanan to Cave Johnson, Dec. 22, 1851, in John Bassett Moore, ed., *The Works of James Buchanan: Comprising his Speeches, State Papers, and Private Correspondence* (12 vols., Philadelphia, 1908–11), VIII, 428–30.

[6] Belmont to Buchanan, Jan. 28, Feb. 24, 1852, Buchanan Papers.

quired, and was Belmont in constant communication with him?
Belmont answered that Buchanan's health was never better and
ignored the second half of the question. Then the "Governor"
turned to politics. Did Belmont know that the New York
"Barnburners" had given up on General Butler, in favor of
Marcy, and that a section of the "Hunker" wing had left Cass'
corner, also for Marcy's? Furthermore, Marcy's recent conversations with proslavery "ultras," such as Robert Barnwell Rhett
of South Carolina, indicated that of the major candidates only
he or Buchanan could obtain the support of the states' rights
extremists.

Now that the subject had been broached, Belmont proposed
a Marcy-Buchanan alliance to prevent Cass' renomination.
Clearly, the Democrats must carry New York and Pennsylvania in November to win the election. However, a Cass victory at Baltimore would trigger the identical Free-Soil defection in New York as in 1848, while Pennsylvania obviously
cared heart and soul for her native-born Buchanan. Belmont
also intimated that all the "strong news" from the South favored his man. Wouldn't it be a good idea for the "Governor"
to throw his influence behind Buchanan and support him in the
convention "fairly and firmly?" If, in such an event, the Pennsylvanian still failed of nomination, Belmont promised that the
Buchanan forces would rally to Marcy. Not surprisingly,
Marcy displayed no interest in the proposal and the conversation
ended.[7]

In the first week of March Buchanan triumphed at the Harrisburg convention. The Keystone State's Democrats endorsed
him by a three-to-one margin over his nearest rival, Cass, and
sweetened their "favorite son's" pleasure still more by giving
him a unit-rule control over his state's large delegation. Belmont
now pressed Buchanan to seek an understanding with Marcy
and even with young Senator Douglas, whose popularity was
broadly based. Buchanan tried, but Douglas reacted coolly,
while Marcy thought that if Buchanan came over to his side

[7] Belmont to Buchanan, Feb. 24, 28, 1852, Buchanan Papers.

first and if Marcy failed to obtain the convention's prize, then the New Yorker would deliver his strength to Buchanan. In short, preconvention negotiations bogged down in a stalemate, but Belmont remained undaunted and kept sending on to Buchanan the most glowing and optimistic predictions for Baltimore.[8]

Belmont's endeavors to provide Buchanan with journalistic assistance finally bore fruit in April, though not precisely in the fashion Slidell had envisioned. The banker unified the local Buchanan adherents into a "General Buchanan New York Committee" for greater efficiency in organization and fund-raising and then arranged, through the committee, to get control of a "small but widely circulated" paper, the *New York Morning Star*. Belmont prudently repressed his initial instinct to transform it into an avowedly pro-Buchanan mouthpiece; he thought it best to steer a neutral course to avoid incurring the hostility of the local Marcy and Cass groups, who might eventually have to be won over at Baltimore. For a while the *Morning Star* even assumed a posture favorable to Marcy, though Belmont simultaneously took care to insert in its columns, whenever possible, any evidence of Buchanan's strength in other states. He mailed the newspaper regularly to Buchanan, along with requests for suggestions and guidance, and reminded his chief that "our *only object* is to render ourselves useful to you. . . . You may rely upon my utmost discretion & that nothing can or shall be done by me which could compromise you in the remotest way."[9]

Belmont's expectations for Buchanan's nomination grew more sanguine as convention time neared. All the important Marcy men he had seen for weeks past named Buchanan as their second choice. One "warm admirer" of the "Governor" wrote a "very dispassionate" pamphlet which singled out Buchanan as

[8] Belmont to Buchanan, March 11, 18, 1852, Buchanan Papers; George F. Milton, *The Eve of Conflict: Stephen A. Douglas and the Needless War* (Boston, 1934), 89.

[9] Belmont to Buchanan, April 5, 15, May 27, 1852, Buchanan Papers; Roy F. Nichols, *The Democratic Machine, 1850–1854* (New York, 1923), 67–68.

the safest Democrat available. Belmont, at his own expense, sent copies to every Democratic congressman and to each delegate named to the Baltimore gathering.[10]

The presidential nomination proved as elusive for Buchanan as it was for Marcy. Belmont's supposition that the Marcy forces would turn to Buchanan was mere wishful thinking; Marcy's attempt to woo the Buchanan delegates was equally futile. Each too proud and stubborn to see the other adversary triumph, they released their delegates to the eventual winner, former United States Senator Franklin Pierce of New Hampshire, who had served as a Mexican War general. Slidell, the commander of the Buchanan camp at Baltimore, reported his observations and general impressions to "Old Buck" and noted that Belmont, who did not attend the convention, was "as much annoyed at your defeat as any of us." [11]

The banker's annoyance rested on a valid basis. He had placed all his political hopes on a Buchanan nomination in what had appeared to be the latter's best—and probably last—opportunity to grasp the party's most coveted prize. Still, candidates come and go, but parties usually exist for longer periods. Belmont, the loyal Democrat, now set out to show that he understood the political necessity of postconvention party harmony. He obtained his initial campaign credits when the Democratic National Committee, a party organization created in 1844 to raise funds for presidential nominees, faltered in its objectives. The committee originally hoped to amass more than $20,000 by assessing the Democrats in each Congressional district $100, but, as usual, partisan enthusiasm was not easily convertible into needed dollars. Belmont came to the rescue with a generous contribution. Later on, after Whigs leveled charges of anti-Catholicism at Pierce and the Irish-American (though Protestant) Buchanan delivered an address repudiating them, Belmont paid for and distributed over two thousand copies of the speech.[12]

[10] Belmont to Buchanan, May 27, 1852, Buchanan Papers.
[11] *New York Times*, May 31–June 7, 1852; Slidell to Buchanan, June 23, 1852, Buchanan Papers; Milton, *Eve of Conflict*, 89–92.
[12] J. Addison Thomas to William L. Marcy, July 31, 1852, Charles H.

Belmont's zeal in behalf of Pierce's candidacy brought mixed results. It put him into close association with the nominee's circle of Mexican War cronies, particularly General (now Congressman) Charles H. Peaslee of New Hampshire. But Belmont's activities made him a political issue, particularly in New York City, where the large recent influx of Irish and German immigrants had stimulated the omnipresent, if at times quiescent, xenophobia of many native-born Americans. When the October state elections in Pennsylvania, Ohio, and Indiana resulted in Democratic victories, local Whig newspapers saw a chance to profit from this latent prejudice and shifted the blame to Belmont, who furnished an inviting and conspicuous target. Horace Greeley's *New York Tribune* and Henry J. Raymond's *New York Times* devoted editorials to him, and their attack focused on two points: the banker employed "Jew gold" from abroad to buy votes for Pierce, and he still maintained his "un-American" ties with foreign kings by his tenure as Austrian Consul here. A typical *Times* smear noted Belmont's pro-Pierce stance and inferred that "the Rothschilds and the Emperor of Austria were both of them rather anxious for the election of Pierce and the consequent establishment of such a policy as would permit *them* to monopolize" the next administration. The *Tribune* reported, after a week-long "discussion" of the banker's "dual allegiance," that its "exposure of the Austrian Chargé d'Affaires [sic!] in favor of General Pierce has awakened the most intense indignation. . . . It explains where the thousands of dollars so lavishly used here were raised. The American people scorn the assistance of Austria and the Rothschilds." Greeley then called for an "indignation meeting" to protest the "Belmont affair." [13]

Belmont was "vexed and grieved" as Whig press attacks continued unabated, particularly in the *Tribune*, where Greeley

---

Peaslee to Marcy, May 9, 1853, William L. Marcy Papers, Library of Congress; Franklin Pierce to John E. Warren, July 16, 1852, quoted in *New York Herald*, Sept. 1, 1852; Belmont to Buchanan, Oct. 27, 1852, April 22, 1853, Buchanan Papers; Nichols, *Pierce*, 214.

[13] *New York Tribune*, Oct. 26–30, Nov. 1, 1852; *New York Times*, Oct. 29, 1852.

Horace Greeley (Library of Con-   Franklin Pierce (Library of Congress)
gress)

freely sprinkled anti-Semitic references in sarcastic, often vitri-
olic, editorials. The banker's activities were intended to be of
political value to the party. Would Greeley's "shameful appeal
to prejudice and ignorance" injure Democratic prospects? Worse
yet, would his own vulnerability to interminable character assassination by the opposition render him a permanent political liability? At first he was reluctant to enter a journalistic
tug-of-war, but when the *Tribune* asserted that he "poured
out" $2,000 to carry sparsely populated Richmond County for
Pierce he lost his patience. He called at the *Tribune* office and
demanded that the paper print his letter denying all of its editor's allegations. Belmont did not encounter Greeley, who later
refused the injured banker's request, claiming that the letter included an attack on General Winfield Scott, the Whig presi-

dential candidate, and was therefore nothing more than a political tract.[14]

A furious Belmont next turned to the pro-Pierce *Herald* and *Evening Post* for revenge. Both journals gleefully retrieved Greeley's gauntlet and flung it back by printing the letter. In addition, the *Herald* swung out at the "philosophers and socialists" of the *Tribune* who, in their "unwashed filthiness" stood "convicted" of having violated the "common decencies of society" by resorting to "desperate fabrications." The *Evening Post* labeled Greeley's assaults "gross and disgraceful falsehoods. . . . Pray what right has any editor to drag a private citizen before the public because he endeavors to aid in a just and noble cause? . . . Can the Tribune show by his acts or words that he [Belmont] has ever advocated the Austrian policy?" To the astute, pro-Whig lawyer and diarist, George Templeton Strong, "l'affaire Belmont" was "the last notable event of the campaign," though he thought it "a very silly business." Indeed, it was not only silly but, what was worse, ineffective.[15]

Belmont was jubilant following Pierce's easy victory over Scott. His first political action "under fire" found him on the winning side. In addition, he felt some degree of personal vindication, since the smears of the Whig press had no discernible effect on the New York returns. Perhaps the greatest satisfaction came in a congratulatory letter, dated the day after the election, from Buchanan who praised his efforts for the party. Belmont's reply speculated on whether Buchanan would accept a place in the new administration, noting that "no appointment would give so much satisfaction" to many Democrats as Buchanan's to the State Department.[16]

More than altruism underlay Belmont's "satisfaction"; he intended Buchanan's advancement to bring about his own. As a

[14] Belmont to Buchanan, Nov. 5, 1852, Buchanan Papers; *New York Herald*, Oct. 29, 1852.

[15] *New York Herald*, Oct. 27–29, 31, Nov. 1, 1852; *New York Evening Post*, Oct. 27–29, Nov. 1, 1852; Allan Nevins and Milton H. Thomas, eds., *The Diary of George Templeton Strong* (4 vols., New York, 1952), II, 107–08.

[16] Belmont to Buchanan, Nov. 5, 1852, Buchanan Papers.

reward for his services, Belmont hoped to be named to a diplomatic post. Realizing that his status as an original Buchanan man would put him at a disadvantage in the fierce struggle for one of the few prestigious foreign missions, he cast around for a way to convince the incoming administration that his unique position in international finance might promote some aspect of American foreign policy. The area in which he chose to advertise his competence was the Caribbean island of Cuba.

3

★ ★ ★

A "Grandiose Plan" for Cuba

For YEARS Cuba had seethed with discontent under Spanish rule, forcing an already impoverished crown to overextend itself by maintaining there an army of 25,000 men and a fleet of thirty-five ships. Such an unstable situation so close to United States territory led a growing number of Americans to favor Spain's ouster from, and American acquisition of, the island, though for widely differing reasons. Protestants, associating Spain with the dreaded Inquisition and religious authoritarianism, found their view bolstered by the bad press the monarchy generally received in the United States. Merchants and bankers believed Cuban possession would increase American commercial and financial strength. Military and naval spokesmen felt American installations in Cuba would enhance the nation's Atlantic defense system. Even antislavery organizations wanted American hegemony there in order to rid the island of its "peculiar institution," though in general the abolitionists were openly hostile to American pretensions in the Caribbean. On the other hand, it was taken for granted by proslavery southerners that Cuba's entry into the Union would swell the ranks of slaveholding states. Another group, known as the filibusterers, was more in favor of freeing the island than annexing her to the United States, insisting there would be time enough to think of annexation after Cuba gained her independence. Not confining themselves to oratory, they sailed regularly for Cuba to instigate and encourage revolution. Their expeditions, often outfitted in American ports, only stirred up an already volatile situation.

Given all these interests, Cuba naturally loomed large as an issue
in American political debate and diplomatic strategy.[1]

Belmont had his own ideas about Cuba, and in a letter to Buchanan soon after Election Day he unfolded a grandiose plan,
centering around himself, which he contended could not fail to
make the Pearl of the Antilles part of the Gem of the Ocean.
The banker did not doubt for a moment that the United States,
by force of arms, could seize Cuba, regardless of possible British
and French "blustering" over American expansion in the Caribbean. But why sacrifice American blood when more pacific
means—negotiation and purchase—lay at hand? Let the United
States continue to encourage Cuban insurrections and keep up
present Spanish apprehensions of an American invasion, thus
further depleting Spain's finances and increasing dissatisfaction
at the Madrid court. Simultaneously, Belmont could enlist the
aid of the French and English Rothschilds and other major
European banking houses. These financiers could warn Madrid
that present holders of Spanish government bonds felt uneasy
over that nation's approaching bankruptcy and threaten, by immediately unloading their securities, to ruin Spain's already
weak credit in the international money markets. Belmont foresaw a Spanish cabinet faced with rising discontent and subversion at home and "financial derangement" and declining prestige abroad. Madrid's only intelligent alternative would call for
a treaty with the United States and sale of Cuba to her for as
much as possible, especially as a refusal to negotiate might cause
the Americans to take Cuba from the mother country without
any compensation whatsoever.

Belmont explained how Pierce could create a climate favorable to Spanish capitulation. The new President must exercise
wisdom in choosing "clever diplomatists" to represent him at
London, Paris, and Naples, the latter then capital of the Bour-

[1] For a good introduction to American involvement in Cuban affairs at this
time see Basil Rauch, *American Interest in Cuba, 1848–1855* (New York, 1948),
and Amos A. Ettinger, *The Mission to Spain of Pierre Soulé, 1853–1855: A
Study in the Cuban Diplomacy of the United States* (New Haven, Conn.,
1932).

bon Kingdom of the Two Sicilies. Belmont specifically cited
Naples, rather than Madrid, as a key spot for manipulating
available influences. While America's emissary to the Spanish
court would find his official position an impediment, no such
obstacle would deter the movements of the plenipotentiary to
Naples. In addition, the King of Naples was a brother to Queen
Mother Maria Christina, "who is one of the cleverest & most influential persons in all Spain & has ever since her marriage kept
up the most intimate relations with the court of her brother."
Maria Christina would gladly part with Cuba, for she was
"avaricious . . . and has many large possessions in the island,
the value of which would be greatly enhanced by its cession to
the United States." Ideally, "our man at Naples" should speak
Italian, be familiar with the country's customs, and also have
close ties with principal Continental bankers. Here, Pierce was
extraordinarily blessed, for there actually existed a person with
these qualifications among his most fervent admirers.

Having resided myself at Naples some twenty years ago I think that by
my acquaintance with the place and knowledge of the language I could
be of infinitely more use to our government than any person the coming administration could find willing to take the place of Chargé
d'Affaires at that place, besides which my relations to and intimate acquaintance with most of the leading financiers of London, Paris, and
Madrid would also enable me to assist most effectually the efforts of our
ministers at these points.

Belmont concluded his letter with a plea. Would Buchanan,
confronted with such impressive qualifications, give Belmont's
application for the Naples post all the weight of his "powerful
influence?"

Buchanan wholeheartedly approved Belmont's Cuban proposal and promised to bring it to the President-elect's attention.
This he did in early December, but not quite in the manner Belmont anticipated. To Pierce he summarized the annexation plan
in a long paragraph, noting the significant role the Rothschilds
would have to perform and the necessity that "suitable ministers to Spain, Naples, England, and France" be chosen. But he
omitted mentioning Belmont's name at all and instead concen-

trated on pushing his fellow Pennsylvanian, Judge James Campbell, for a cabinet post.[2]

Belmont soon heard rumors that Marcy was slated to head the State Department. Not a man to take any chances, he began immediately to make overtures in that direction. He cornered Marcy's close political ally, W. J. Staples, and related the Cuban plan to him. Belmont spicily added for good measure that he stood on cordial terms with the Queen Mother's lover, who knew how to exploit her "lack of chastity and patriotism." Staples consented to pass all this on to Marcy, then vacationing in Savannah, Georgia, and even promised to include a strong recommendation that Belmont be tendered the Naples mission. Staples' subsequent letter touched on the banker's ability, patriotism, and zeal and noted that his affluence would obviate the need for financial assistance from Washington. Belmont was capable of maintaining the dignity of American diplomacy abroad from his own purse.[3]

Throughout December and January, as Pierce sought to round out his prospective cabinet and to fill other official positions, Belmont continued to remind Buchanan and Marcy—the one directly, the other through mutual friends—of his past and potential assets to party and country. Word reached him in January that Buchanan, following a chat with Pierce in Washington, would pass through New York City. The anxious Belmont guessed that Buchanan knew the composition of the incoming cabinet and dashed off an invitation which hoped against hope that "your numerous engagements will admit of your spending some days with us. . . . You must not for one moment hesitate in disposing always freely of my services." But Buchanan arrived and departed, leaving the news-hungry Belmont no wiser than before.[4]

[2] Belmont to Buchanan, Nov. 22, 1852, Buchanan Papers; Buchanan to Pierce, Dec. 11, 1852, in Moore, ed., *Works of Buchanan*, VIII, 493–99.

[3] W. J. Staples to Marcy, Nov. 26, 1852, Marcy Papers; Belmont to Buchanan, Nov. 30, 1852, Buchanan Papers; Rauch, *American Interest in Cuba*, 258–59; Nevins, *Ordeal of the Union*, II, 64–67.

[4] Nichols, *Pierce*, 357–58; Belmont to Buchanan, Jan. 7, 14, 1853, Buchanan Papers.

With Inauguration Day scarcely five weeks away, Belmont decided to move boldly. He boarded a train for the national capital and went straight to Pierce's old friend, Congressman Peaslee. He recalled his strenuous campaigning for Pierce and his financial contributions to the Democratic National Committee during its lean September days and then revealed his Cuban plan. Peaslee warmly assured his visitor that such generosity and loyalty had been remembered. He promised to do all in his power to advance Belmont's plan and appointment, adding that his nephew, Sidney Webster, now served as Pierce's private secretary. But Peaslee cautioned Belmont against depending solely upon intimates of Pierce, lest the latter lay himself open to charges of "favoritism." Why not get strong letters from influential Democrats outside Pierce's "immediate neighborhood," which could, along with the support of Peaslee and Webster, help further impress Belmont's talents upon the new Chief Executive? Peaslee also suggested that he act with haste and build up a strong case, before an incipient opposition, based on his foreign birth, had a chance to spread.

Belmont lost no time in requesting another letter from Buchanan. He tactfully reminded him of a standing promise to "serve me in this affair" and pledged to devote all his "feeble energies" toward getting Buchanan the next Democratic presidential nomination, "whatever may be the results of my present efforts." Belmont indicated that nativist pressure against his appointment could be countered by his sixteen-year residence in the United States and "an unwavering zeal & adherence for & to the Democratic party ever since." After all, "we have plenty of instances of adopted citizens . . . having served our country with great distinction." Belmont also hoped Buchanan would remind Pierce of the daily increasing German-American population in New York, Pennsylvania, and Ohio, whose combined electoral vote constituted a very important and, at times, indispensable element of party success. Thus, Pierce could gain enormous popularity among German-Americans by such a "direct refutation" of the Whig policy of barring the foreign-born from governmental posts. Finally, Buchanan's "own better judgment" could decide whether further allusion should be made to Belmont's Cuban plan. Buchanan complied with his friend's wishes, though he realized Pierce would not seriously consider such an application until the installation of the new Secretary of State.[5]

On March 5 Belmont learned that Marcy would be sworn in as the new head of the State Department. This disturbed him, for Marcy's friends in New York just as avidly pursued federal patronage. In desperation, Belmont again turned to Buchanan for succor. He dared not, in all humility and gratitude, ask anything more from him. But could another Pennsylvanian, the newly named Postmaster General James Campbell, "advocate my claims and qualifications in the Cabinet?" [6]

The next day's mail brought further news. Daniel E. Sickles, a wealthy, influential New York Democrat and a warm friend, wrote from Washington of an after-dinner chat with Pierce, in which the President criticized the careless foreign appointments of his predecessors. "Men have been selected without reference to their fitness for diplomacy or the particular place to which they have been accredited." Pierce had promised Sickles that he would take "great pains to secure the services of gentlemen who like Mr. Belmont possess the confidence of discerning men and who have [his] qualifications." Yet Belmont's excitement was not unalloyed. Practically every candidate for a chargé-ship, Sickles warned, requested Naples. In fact, each of the thirty-one states in the Union had at least one applicant for that city.[7]

Belmont, now satisfied that Pierce had been won over to his cause, reckoned Marcy as the final obstacle to success. There was no time to lose. He pleaded again with Buchanan, this time for a strong letter to the new Secretary. He even contemplated another journey to Washington to lay his case before Marcy and other New York Democratic officeholders there. However, on the eve of his scheduled departure, "a sort of monetary

[5] Belmont to Buchanan, Jan. 28, 1853, Buchanan Papers.
[6] Belmont to Buchanan, March 5, 1853, Buchanan Papers.
[7] Belmont to Buchanan, March 7, 1853, Buchanan Papers.

crisis" occurred on Wall Street, necessitating his presence in New York and compelling him to depend upon friends at the scene. George N. Sanders, a Democratic publicist also seeking a diplomatic appointment, wrote Belmont that those six years as Austrian Consul General had aroused opposition to the banker's application within Administration circles. Such a basis for denying him public office angered and exasperated Belmont, for it implied that as Consul General he had openly sympathized with the anti-republican regime of Austria-Hungary. "What is a consul," he complained to Sickles, "but a mere commercial agent . . . who is *in no ways* connected with the politics of the Government he acts for?" Did not the United States have more than twenty consuls in Europe and Asia who were not American citizens and, in fact, had never been in this country? Furthermore, Belmont asserted, the six Austrian Consuls and Vice Consuls currently in the United States were native-born Americans, "some of them, to my knowledge, staunch Democrats." The letter's conclusion made no secret of the banker's anger: "I do not mean to beg for the support of anybody. . . . Those who oppose me have my consent to do their d——est." [8]

April approached, and with no definite offer from the White House Belmont grew more pessimistic. Bad enough that Greeley's *Tribune*, in its usual unreliable fashion, publicized that "Mr. August Schoenberg, formerly of Hanau, Germany—better known in this country by his Frenchified alias of August Belmont" was an applicant for the Naples assignment. Worse still, the widely circulated newspaper approved Pierce's newly appointed Minister to Spain, French-born Louisiana Senator Pierre Soulé, as an example of "foreign born citizens who distinguish themselves by their brains . . . [and not] by their purses." But what irked Belmont the most was Marcy's ostensible opposition, for, after all the banker's efforts, what else could explain the lengthy delay? A sympathetic Buchanan ques-

[8] Belmont to Buchanan, March 14, 1853, Buchanan Papers; Buchanan to Marcy, March 8, 1853, Marcy Papers; Belmont to Sanders, March 21, 1853, Sanders Papers; Nichols, *Democratic Machine*, 195–96; Ettinger, *Mission to Spain of Soulé*, 144.

tioned Marcy's alleged "antagonism," but Belmont insisted he'd
heard "from undoubted source" that the Secretary of State
spoke "unfavorably" of his appointment.[9]

Belmont made one final assault on what he considered
Marcy's coolness. He asked New York merchants Isaac Townsend and Prosper M. Wetmore, both long-time Democrats, to
write their friend Marcy. Their letters presented Belmont's selection for the Naples vacancy as one which would gratify
many of the Secretary's personal friends, who remembered the
applicant's avid display of energy and liberality during the recent presidential contest, not to mention the scurrilous partisan
abuse he received for his pains. Belmont next notified former
Congressman Peaslee, just named Collector of the Port of Boston by his friend Pierce, that it was "now or never," and that
Marcy was the critical factor. The banker's appeal proved so
moving and persuasive that Peaslee, who had long ago sworn
never to "write a line or sign a petition for any candidate," felt
"compelled" in all honor to violate his pledge for Belmont's
cause. Even these endeavors failed to produce conclusive results. A weary, disgusted Belmont decided he had played "the
humble petitioner" long enough for his own self-respect. "If
the Governor [Marcy] feels pleasure in defeating me he is perfectly welcome." He requested Sidney Webster to withdraw
the application "at an early day," and thus put an end to his
part in the patronage race for Naples.[10]

Unknown to the impatient Belmont, the President had just
concluded his major ministerial appointments and turned to the
chargéships. Buchanan traveled to Washington to accept the
London portfolio, and while there he and Slidell pressed Belmont's application. The Chief Executive listened sympathetically. He was very much disposed to send Belmont to Naples,
but the presence of so many other prominent men in the same

[9] *New York Tribune*, March 22, April 10, 1853; Belmont to Buchanan, March
26, April 4, 1853, Buchanan Papers; Spencer, *Marcy*, 231-32.
[10] Isaac Townsend to Marcy, April 6, 1853, Prosper M. Wetmore to Marcy,
April 6, 1853, Charles H. Peaslee to Marcy, May 9, 1853, Marcy Papers; Belmont to Buchanan, April 4, 15, 1853, Buchanan Papers.

contest complicated matters. Still, something would be done for him.

Buchanan relayed the crux of the interview to his New York ally and expressed confidence that Marcy, out of regard for their long, personal friendship, would ultimately approve some foreign post for Belmont. Perhaps Belmont's agonizing wait could be avoided by choosing another location? In fact, now that Buchanan was off to London, Belmont's diplomatic services might prove even more useful in Brussels, which was, after all, but "short distances from Paris & Amsterdam, the principal money marts of the Old World and the only places upon which Spain relies to bolster up her decaying finances." Belmont accepted Buchanan's suggested alteration in plans graciously, even displaying a forced enthusiasm for the Belgian capital. But Belmont reminded his well-meaning go-between that the nature of his banking and business arrangements necessitated an imminent decision from Washington, "as I cannot remain longer a candidate." [11]

Five weeks later, the administration released the new diplomatic appointments. Marcy and Pierce terminated the Naples competition by naming the fifty-two-year-old New Yorker, Robert Dale Owen, known for his activities as a champion of labor and social reform. As for Brussels, the President selected his friend, J. J. Seibels, a Montgomery, Alabama, newspaper publisher who had served as a colonel on Pierce's staff during the Mexican War. But the chargéship at The Hague remained vacant. Would Belmont accept an appointment to the Netherlands? The banker did so with alacrity, for the failure to secure his first two choices could not nullify the fact that The Hague constituted an upward step. He would remember, for future reference, his experiences in political and patronage competitions, as well as the obvious advantage of belonging to the winning team from the very beginning. For the first time he had an

[11] Pierce to Buchanan, March 30, 1853, Buchanan to Pierce, April 2, 1853, Buchanan to Harriet Lane, April 7, 1853, Buchanan to Pierce, April 27, 1853, in Moore, ed., *Works of Buchanan*, VIII, 504–08; Nichols, *Pierce*, 256; Klein, *Buchanan*, 223–24; Belmont to Buchanan, April 22, 1853, Buchanan Papers.

official position in the American government. With the next
Democratic nominating convention scarcely three years away,
he would concentrate on two major tasks. Diplomat Belmont
would demonstrate conscientiousness, vigor, and imagination in
advancing the administration's foreign policy goals. More important, rising young politician Belmont would perform such a
large role in promoting Buchanan's candidacy the next time as
to hold a virtual carte blanche in the happy event of a Buchanan victory.[12]

[12] Belmont to Buchanan, May 12, 16, 28, 1853, Buchanan Papers; Marcy to
Belmont, May 28, 1853, private Belmont collection; William A. Swanberg,
Sickles the Incredible (New York, 1956), 90; *New York Tribune*, May 25,
27, June 2, 1853; *New York Herald*, May 26, 27, 1853.

4

★ ★ ★

Exercises in Diplomacy

BELMONT HAD NOT VISITED his native continent for fifteen years, and he welcomed the opportunity to appear before old friends as a fully accredited diplomat of his adopted land and as the husband of a girl whose antecedents made her as much of an aristocrat as a democracy could bring itself to acknowledge. In addition, Belmont confidently believed his tenure in the Netherlands would enhance American dignity and interests in Europe. His official task at The Hague would be to negotiate a new commercial treaty to open the Dutch East Indies to American consuls. But how much more impressive his diplomatic credentials would be if he could also forward his Cuban annexation scheme!

Belmont spent the early weeks of summer, 1853, in predeparture arrangements. He turned supervision of his financial affairs over to an experienced New York Stock Exchange broker, Charles Christmas, who, along with Belmont's bookkeeper, Erhard A. Matthiessen, would operate August Belmont & Company under the name Christmas, Matthiessen & Company. He also informed the Rothschilds of his new governmental position.

With high hopes and great anticipation, Belmont, accompanied by his wife, her unmarried sister, Isabel, two baby boys, Perry and August, Jr., and two nurses, sailed for Europe on August 20. They arrived in Liverpool ten days later and, thanks to Minister Buchanan's assistance, passed through customs without the usual lengthy examination. They spent the next ten days in and around London, entertained by Buchanan at the

American legation and by Baron Lionel de Rothschild at his country seat. From there Belmont and his entourage went to Paris, via "a most terrible passage" through the English Channel. Additional weeks were passed in Frankfurt and in Coblenz, visiting his father and married sister and renewing some childhood acquaintances. Finally, after "a delightful run down the Rhine," the family arrived at The Hague, seven weeks after leaving New York.[1]

The luxury-loving Belmonts missed the comforts of Gotham from the start. The old-fashioned Dutch capital, "where they are in everything about half a century behind the rest of Europe," contained no furnished houses for rent and only a few unfurnished ones. They spent the better part of two months "cooped up" in a second-rate establishment, the *Hotel du Vieux Doelen,* which Belmont found to be as costly as the most expensive West End hotels of London, but lacking any of their comforts. Eventually, the Belmonts acquired a house and came to appreciate the country and its cultural life, particularly the "rich galleries of magnificent paintings."

But the atmosphere at the court concerned Belmont more than his material surroundings. George Folsom, the retiring American chargé, warned the newcomer to expect "a very stiff" reception by the Dutch, who were "jealous" of other nations and exceedingly adverse to strangers. The gregarious Belmont soon learned the truth of Folsom's admonition. Peeved at the "foolish etiquette" prevailing at the capital, he complained to Buchanan that such treatment "is no joke and does not, I assure you, contribute toward making me more content with my situation." To Belmont's dismay, he found that a matter of the same "foolish etiquette" barred his formal presentation to King

[1] Craig and Gore, "House of Belmont," 7; Belmont to Buchanan, May 28, June 3, 15, Aug. 15, 1853, Buchanan Papers; Perry Belmont, *An American Democrat,* 29–51. Belmont's annual salary was set at $4,500, compared with the $50,000 to $75,000 he had been earning from his banking business. Belmont to Sanders, March 21, 1853, Sanders Papers. In 1854 Belmont was promoted to the rank of Minister-Resident. Marcy to Belmont, July 12, 1854, August Belmont Papers, New York Public Library.

Interior of the Legation at The Hague (painting by David Bles, c. 1854). From left to right: Miss Isabel Bolton Perry (Belmont's sister-in-law); August Belmont; Perry Belmont (4 years); Mrs. August Belmont; Mrs. Jane Slidell Perry (Belmont's mother-in-law), holding 3-month-old Frederika Belmont; Commodore Matthew Calbraith Perry (Belmont's father-in-law), holding 22-month-old August, Jr. (Courtesy of Mrs. Eleanor Robson Belmont)

William III, without which he could not begin his negotiations.[2]

Shortly before Belmont left for Europe, Marcy, aided by Assistant Secretary of State Ambrose Dudley Mann, issued a set of instructions to all Americans serving abroad, the most remarkable portion dealing with the clothing to be worn by the country's ambassadors. Marcy had attended a White House dinner

[2] Belmont to Buchanan, Nov. 18, 1853, July 8, 1855, Buchanan Papers.

in 1841 and had been repelled by the "truly ridiculous appearance" of diplomats decked out in "gewgaws." Now, he found
himself in a position to effect a change. Each head of a United
States mission received a circular encouraging "as far as practicable . . . his appearance at court in the simple dress of an
American citizen," along with the Secretary's regret that American emissaries had ever departed from the simplicity of that
ideal diplomat, Benjamin Franklin. The "simple dress" Marcy
had in mind was what "middle-class Americans" wore—black
dress coat and trousers with a silk top hat. Marcy's order was
discretionary and, as a consequence, threw his diplomats into
confusion. As one of them later complained, "Some go in dress
coats, others go in uniforms. These latter change from blue &
gold lace to blue embroidered with Stars & Eagles, & to black
velvet embroidered with lace ruffles & cuffs, all according to the
fancy of the wearer." Even Buchanan, the old Jacksonian who
proudly preached "Jeffersonian" principles, had to compromise,
the result being a ludicrous appearance before Queen Victoria
in a citizen's dress suit, a sword, and a three-cornered hat.[3]

Belmont also felt this quandary over attire keenly. He applied
to the Dutch Foreign Minister, Floris Adriaan Van Hall, for a
royal audience and indicated that, in compliance with instructions, he would wear a plain citizen's dress for the occasion as
well as all future ones. Van Hall objected and informed Belmont that King William preferred the established tradition of
the diplomatic uniform. As for Belmont's instructions, the Foreign Minister pointed to their discretionary loophole. Van Hall
further undercut the American's position by informing him that
the new Minister to Berlin, former Governor of New Jersey
Peter D. Vroom, had, after a two-month wait, finally agreed to
wear a "Gala Uniform." Belmont refused to yield, despite his
embarrassment at learning of Vroom's surrender. He insisted
that the spirit, if not the letter, of the Marcy circular had been

[3] Spencer, *Marcy*, 233–39; Ettinger, *Mission to Spain of Soulé*, 221–22; *New
York Tribune*, May 26, 1853; *New York Times*, Feb. 16, 25, 1854; Moore, ed.,
Works of Buchanan, IX, 75–77, 111–12, 142–43, 157–59, 361; Nevins, *Ordeal of
the Union*, II, 59–60.

approved by the American people and that, in point of fact, his own view of the proprieties fully coincided with those of his countrymen. The case of Vroom could easily be canceled out, Belmont countered, by the recent, distinguished reception of Senator Stephen A. Douglas in civilian attire before the emperors of Russia and France.[4] In the end, his persistence won out, and he was presented to the King and Queen in plain civilian dress. The fledgling diplomat continued to dispense with a uniform for all subsequent court and social functions, pleased that his actions did not lead to the slightest ostracism.

Belmont still had to overcome an additional hurdle, alleged American subversion in Sumatra, before Foreign Minister Van Hall would consent to discuss possible American consular privileges in the Dutch East Indies. Walter Murray Gibson, an erratic, thirty-one-year-old American sea captain, had been residing on the Dutch East Indian possession during the late 1840s. Early in 1851 colonial officials discovered that he was intriguing with a local chieftain, the Sultan of Djambi, their ultimate purpose being the overthrow of Dutch authority on the island. Gibson was arrested and then released pending a trial. Fifteen months later the colonial court, though convinced of his complicity, acquitted him on a legal technicality. The East Indian administration then appealed to The Hague, where the Minister of Justice reviewed the entire case, overruled the colonial court's decision, and sentenced Gibson to twelve years' imprisonment.

Gibson learned of the sentence and, true to his reputation for derring-do, evaded the authorities and fled the region. In the summer of 1853 he appeared at the State Department in Wash-

---

[4] Belmont to Buchanan, Nov. 18, 1853, Buchanan Papers; Belmont to Marcy, Nov. 8, 1853, Feb. 28, 1854, in Belmont, *Letters, Speeches and Addresses,* 8-9; Belmont to John M. Daniel, Feb. 5, 1854, Samuel L. M. Barlow Papers, Henry E. Huntington Library. The Prussian slighting of Vroom infuriated the easily angered Belmont. If Marcy's circular had been unqualified, "would Prussia have dared to refuse our Minister on that ground or kept him two months knocking at the door for the delivery of his credentials without admitting him? . . . They would not risk the cessation of a diplomatic intercourse." Belmont to Douglas, Nov. 15, 1853, Stephen A. Douglas Papers, University of Chicago.

ington and demanded government assistance in securing $100,-
000 from the Netherlands as an indemnity for his incarceration
and for the confiscation of his schooner, *The Flirt*. He related
his adventures to all who would listen, and his version of the
affair contained few points of tangency with the Dutch one.
The shipmaster insisted that he had been innocently arrested
and that a damaging letter allegedly delivered by Gibson's mate
to the Djambi chieftain was a forgery.

Marcy, impressed with Gibson's plausibility, asked Belmont
to resolve the dispute. The chargé d'affaires hastened to Van
Hall and requested him to show cause why Gibson's claim for
damages should not be met. The minister, asserting that the
treatment and losses suffered by Gibson in Sumatra were the
necessary consequences of his own revolutionary activities, produced several documents incriminating the sea captain whose
version he branded a complete fabrication. By way of summing
up, Van Hall declared that the last thing any foreigner who
had violated Dutch law on Dutch territory would obtain would
be indemnity. Both sides stood firmly. Belmont, considering it
useless to prolong his exchange of notes with Van Hall,
thought it best to terminate his part in the controversy. In the
summer of 1854 he wrote a last energetic note to the Dutch
Foreign Office and transferred the whole case back to Marcy.[5]

Belmont's hopes of avoiding further participation in the
"Gibson Affair," as the American press now called it, were
fruitless. That same summer the drama degenerated into farce.
Gibson, growing impatient with the disposition of his claim,
came to The Hague and told Belmont (falsely) that Marcy had
sent him as a special diplomatic agent. The captain's presence
embarrassed Belmont. First, the Dutch pro-government press
viewed Gibson's arrival as an indication of the American minister's weakness. Second, the anti-government press demanded
that if Gibson was a fugitive from Dutch justice he be arrested,

[5] Spencer, *Marcy*, 401–02; Belmont to Marcy, Oct. 8, 1853, Belmont Papers,
NYPL; Belmont to Marcy, June 24, 1854, Marcy Papers; *New York Herald*,
Nov. 3, 1853; Belmont to Buchanan, Nov. 18, 1853, Feb. 2, 1854, Buchanan
Papers; *New York Times*, Feb. 3, 1854.

and that if he wasn't guilty his claim for indemnity be accepted. Belmont, at this point, developed a sudden case of rheumatism from the damp Hague climate, and his physician advised a visit to mineral baths in Bohemia. Before leaving, Belmont assured Gibson, who kept badgering him unsuccessfully for a $500 loan, that the Dutch police would not dare arrest him in the American minister's absence.

Gibson, taking no chances, left for Paris but not before absconding with Belmont's complete dossier on him. On his arrival, he informed John Y. Mason, the American minister, that Belmont had not only advised him to leave The Hague but had also appointed him his special attaché. The sympathetic but unperceptive Mason graciously offered his visitor the run of the Paris legation, and the sea captain made the most of his advantage. Posing around the city as Mason's first secretary, he started feeding the Paris correspondent of Greeley's *Tribune* material with which to attack the Pierce administration's conduct of foreign policy. The most outrageous by-product of this *Tribune* "scoop" was the charge that Belmont had turned his legation into a banking house and from there was underwriting loans to finance Russia in the Crimean War.[6]

By this time Marcy, like Belmont, realized the nature of the man he had been working to help. Thereafter, Marcy ignored the chronically mendacious Gibson. But Belmont could not remain aloof so easily. Such a nerve-wracking experience cast a shadow on the beginning of his diplomatic career. True, Marcy and Pierce praised his handling of the episode. But the affair was seized upon not only by the *Tribune* but by Bennett's *Herald*, which had turned against the administration over a patronage dispute. Both papers reminded their readers for the duration of Belmont's diplomatic tenure how "this Austrian-born Jew banker" had "neglected" the "just cause" and claims of a "patriotic" American citizen.[7]

[6] Belmont to Marcy, Sept. 15, Oct. 7, 18, Nov. 14, 1854, Marcy Papers; *New York Times*, Oct. 12, 20, 1854; *New York Tribune*, Aug. 21, Nov. 10, 1854.

[7] Marcy to Belmont, Nov. 5, 1854, Belmont to Slidell, Dec. 28, 1854, Belmont to Marcy, March 12, 1855, private Belmont collection; Belmont to Marcy, May

Fortunately for Belmont, the press never learned of his initiative in the Cuban annexation plan, news of which leaked out at the same time the Gibson affair came to a head. Though his reputation was spared this additional blow, he found the Cuban episode equally depressing. For all his bustle and intrigue, both the Caribbean scheme and his self-appointed mission as an intermediary in it were doomed.

En route to The Hague in 1853, Belmont had stopped off in Paris to confer with "several gentlemen of influence in Spain" and passed on to Washington the portrait they drew of that nation's governmental instability. The Prime Minister in Madrid, Luis Jose Sartorius, found his position weakened by court intrigue and jealousy, and he would soon be replaced by General Ramon Maria Narvaez. Both Sartorius and Narvaez realized the royal treasury's desperate need to replenish its gold supply, as did Queen Mother Maria Christina, who reportedly advocated the sale of Cuba to the United States on the ground that the island would ultimately fall to the latter anyway.

The principal impediment to the project's realization lay in that intangible characteristic known as "Castilian pride," which "revolts against a direct sale to us." The more that Americans, either through filibustering expeditions or political and journalistic jingoism, spoke of "liberating" Cuba from the Spanish yoke, the more reluctant Spain would be to yield to pressure.[8] Belmont thought he saw an alternative to direct sale. Cuba could rise in rebellion and declare its independence, "which would be but the forerunner of its annexation by the United States." What was needed was a Spanish ministry of sufficient

24, 1855, Marcy Papers; *New York Tribune*, Nov. 3, 6, 1854; *New York Times*, Dec. 28, 1854. Gibson's career, much to the misfortune of those with whom he later came into contact, did not end here. In 1860, after failing to persuade Brigham Young to move his Mormon community to the South Seas, Gibson prevailed upon the church leader to appoint him a roving missionary. He went to the Hawaiian Islands, built up a thriving Mormon church, and then swindled it out of its lands. For the last half of the nineteenth century, Gibson was a prominent landowner in the island kingdom. At one point, he even became prime minister. Ralph S. Kuykendall, *The Hawaiian Kingdom, 1854-1874: Twenty Critical Years* (Honolulu, 1953), 102–04, 182, 190–95, 256–62.

[8] Belmont to Marcy, Oct. 18, 1853, Marcy Papers.

strength and support to take the responsibility for inaction by pleading exhaustion of government finances. Two of Belmont's Paris conferees, both "clever, influential & rich" Spaniards, gladly offered—for a fee—to go to Madrid and

prepare the way . . . by bribery & intrigue. . . . If a secret fund of $40,000 to $50,000 could be placed at my disposal or at that of our Minister in Paris I think that I could do more with so trifling a sum than the open offer of so many millions.

The "trifling sum" was not forthcoming, but Belmont doggedly pursued his goal. A May, 1854, dispatch to Marcy revealed that Spain's minister to The Hague, a Señor Bourman, turned out to be an old Belmont friend. In private talks Bourman confided a personal desire to sell Cuba to the Americans. Simultaneously, he warned of the potential dangers faced by any Spanish ministry that might propose such a measure.[9]

But nothing seemed to work properly for Belmont; the amicable era he had envisioned in Spanish-American relations, which was to ease Madrid's likely wounds on losing Cuba to the "yanquis," never developed. Pierre Soulé, the hot-headed American minister at Madrid, whose appointment Belmont had privately deplored, committed the gaffe of dueling with the French emissary shortly after arriving in Spain. Then, in February, 1854, Soulé's response to Spanish seizure of an American vessel, the *Black Warrior*, at Havana—an arrogant, peremptory demand for "satisfaction" within forty-eight hours "or else"—led to a further deterioration in relations.[10]

By mid-1854 Belmont suspected that Marcy no longer shared the general enthusiasm for American territorial expansion, much less the Cuban acquisition scheme. The Secretary's extreme caution annoyed Belmont, who believed he deliberately withheld late Cuban developments from Pierce. Belmont persuaded Slidell, now occupying Soulé's seat in the United States Senate, to bring the entire Cuban story to the President's attention. Then, on June 20, Belmont wrote Pierce a long letter, the contents of which he labeled so important as to necessitate immediate ac-

9 Belmont to Marcy, May 31, 1854, Marcy Papers.
10 Ettinger, *Mission to Spain of Soulé*, 227–40, 260–61.

tion. The diplomat's dispatch told of a communication, just received from a Parisian "on very intimate terms" with leading Frenchmen, revealing Louis Napoleon's attitude toward American interests in Cuba. The Emperor, worried over the Spanish-American rift, confided to advisers that in the absence of open or covert American violence against the island he would happily use his good offices to "induce Spain to sell it to us [the United States] at a good price." Belmont offered what he believed to be sound reasons for the communication's credibility: French fear that Cuban revolutionaries might be coming under English influence if, in fact, they were not already receiving English aid; and Louis' belief that American possession, "with its resources and powers of consumption," would prove more advantageous to French "commercial & financial interests." [11]

Belmont could not have been more wrong if he hoped that the information would hasten the long-anticipated breakthrough over Cuba. A military coup d'état (a week after Belmont's letter to Pierce) backed, it was rumored, by the French and English ambassadors ousted the Sartorius ministry and installed in its place a government headed by generals Baldomero Espartero and Leopoldo O'Donnell. The new leaders rejected outright any talk of selling Cuba and exiled the Spanish Queen Mother, the leading advocate of such a solution. Still, Belmont continued to press his Cuban plan upon the State Department, while Buchanan did likewise to Pierce and Slidell. Belmont also persuaded Sickles, now Buchanan's legation secretary, to write his good friend, Senator Douglas, and urge the Belmont scheme of economic pressure, bribery, and purchase.[12]

The combined weight from abroad as well as from nearby Capitol Hill proved too much for the essentially moderate

[11] Belmont to Buchanan, April 1, 1854, Slidell to Buchanan, June 17, 1854, Buchanan Papers; Buchanan to Slidell, May 23, 1854, in Moore, ed., *Works of Buchanan*, IX, 200–01; Belmont to Pierce, June 20, 1854, Belmont Papers, NYPL; Spencer, *Marcy*, 261–62.

[12] Ettinger, *Mission to Spain of Soulé*, 281–90; *New York Tribune*, Aug. 21, 1854; Belmont to Marcy, Sept. 15, 1854, Belmont Papers, NYPL; Buchanan to Marcy, July 21, 1854, Buchanan to Pierce, Sept. 1, 1854, in Moore, ed., *Works of Buchanan*, IX, 214–15, 251–53; Sickles to Douglas, undated, 1854, Douglas Papers, Univ. of Chicago.

Pierce to withstand. The President proposed to Marcy, who neither approved nor objected, that the three principal American diplomats in Western Europe—Buchanan, Soulé, and Mason—meet, utilize their collective wisdom to assess Belmont's plan, and, finally, draft a Cuban policy paper for Washington. Buchanan, contemptuous and distrustful of Soulé, foresaw no benefits resulting from such a consultation and advocated instead that Washington immediately begin to push the Belmont plan and give the minister at The Hague sufficient funds and instructions to pursue his ends. Still, Buchanan confessed, should Washington request him specifically to attend such a conference, he would reluctantly consent. Slidell, hearing of Pierce's proposal, suggested that Belmont be brought into the ministerial conference "on account of the Rothschild influence at Madrid & Paris." [13]

Ironically, Belmont, unaware that the fires he had tried to light were finally blazing, reassessed the situation and shifted to a more aggressive stance. Generals Espartero and O'Donnell were obviously unwilling to sell Cuba; nor did it seem likely that they would soon or easily be dislodged from power. Moreover, England, now joined by France, openly opposed Cuba's transfer to the United States. Still, both these powers were heavily engaged in military operations against the Russians in the Crimea at the moment. Perhaps the time was ripe for Washington to seize the apparent advantages presented by an all-out European war. Spain's procrastination in the still unsettled *Black Warrior* affair would give Pierce a fair excuse for reprisals. Direct negotiation being out of the question, the administration should now attempt indirect, unofficial talks with Madrid (but without Soulé's participation) for the purchase of Cuba. The anticipated negative answer from Spain should be rapidly countered with "action if we mean to obtain Cuba." Belmont's "action" was undoubtedly a euphemism for invasion.[14]

[13] Spencer, *Marcy*, 324–26; Nichols, *Pierce*, 365–66; Buchanan to Pierce, Sept. 1, 1854, in Moore, ed., *Works of Buchanan*, IX, 251–53; Slidell to Buchanan, Aug. 6, 1854, Buchanan Papers; Klein, *Buchanan*, 236–39.
[14] Belmont to Marcy, Sept. 15, 1854, Belmont Papers, NYPL.

The meeting of Ministers Buchanan, Mason, and Soulé occurred only one month after this latest Belmont dispatch to the
State Department. The conferees first met at Ostend, Belgium,
on October 9, 1854, but Buchanan's anxiety to escape unwanted publicity caused their removal to Aix-la-Chapelle three
days later. Belmont received no direct instructions from Washington and therefore did not attend, although he wanted to go.
Still, it comes as a surprise that his influence upon the subsequent "Ostend Manifesto" has been so minimized or overlooked
by historians dealing with the period. The document, dispatched to Marcy on October 18, virtually echoed Belmont's
long-cherished plan for purchasing Cuba, plus his most recent
bellicose statement. The essence of the Manifesto boiled down
to this: "If Spain should refuse to sell Cuba to the United
States, we shall be justified in wresting it from Spain, if we possess the power." [15]

The drafting of the Ostend Manifesto was as far as Belmont's
Cuban plan was destined to go, and his satisfaction, if any,
proved short-lived. The contents were leaked prematurely to
the anti-administration *New York Herald*, causing a furor
among both Pierce's enemies and the opponents of Cuban acquisition. Worse still, news of the Manifesto coincided with a
disastrous defeat for the Democrats in the fall congressional
elections. Thanks mostly to the Kansas-Nebraska Act of May
30, 1854, the opposition Whigs had been split asunder, serious
divisions and defections occurred within Democratic ranks, and
a new antislavery free-soil party, the Republicans, gained a plurality in the House of Representatives. This abrupt change in
Congress' political complexion ruined any chance that Cuba
could be acquired during the last half of Pierce's term.[16]

[15] Belmont to Buchanan, Sept. 25, 1854, Buchanan Papers; Belmont to Marcy,
Oct. 18, 1854, Marcy Papers; Belmont to W. S. Campbell, Oct. 18, 1854, Belmont Papers, NYPL; *New York Times*, Oct. 7, 16, 21, 26, 27, 1854. Good
accounts of the Ostend conference can be found in Rauch, *American Interest
in Cuba*, 256–65, 290–95; Nevins, *Ordeal of the Union*, II, 354–61; and Ettinger,
Mission to Spain of Soulé, 339–412. For the official transcript of the manifesto,
see Moore, ed., *Works of Buchanan*, IX, 260–66.
[16] Marcy to Peter D. Vroom, Nov. 4, 1854, Marcy Papers. A two-to-one
Democratic majority in the House was transformed into 108 Republicans, 83

The news of the Democratic defeat added substance to Belmont's growing frustration. The diplomatic post which had originally seemed an excellent way for an ambitious young man to prove his mettle had yielded little but the Gibson embarrassment and the Cuban disappointment. Belmont's early meetings with Van Hall over the treaty had appeared to go well, but not until he had been in The Hague a year did he get to see a copy of the proposed consular convention. His chafing at the pace of the negotiations was not so much a sign of restless temperament as of his anxiety to wrest some tangible accomplishment from his official assignment.

The proposed treaty itself was nearly as complicated as the circumstances delaying it. The numerous islands of the East Indian Archipelago offered an inviting field for American commerce. An 1839 treaty between the United States and the Netherlands promised "reciprocity of navigation and trade," but though American merchants looked hungrily at Netherlands India their ships still were barred from all but three ports in the entire Archipelago. By the late 1840s Yankee entrepreneurs stepped up their pressure on the Federal Government to "open" the Dutch East Indies to American trade. In 1851 President Millard Fillmore was successful in getting the Dutch to recognize "in principle" the posting of American consuls there. Nevertheless, American shippers continued to complain of restrictions.

Belmont's original instructions from Marcy called for persuading the Dutch to grant exequators, or written authorizations, to those Americans sent as consuls to the East Indies. Marcy even suggested that, should the Netherlands refuse to issue exequators, Belmont might intimate American abrogation of the 1839 treaty. In the opening rounds of negotiation, Van

----

Democrats, and 43 men unaffiliated with either major group. Still, Belmont could not shelve his grand Cuban design. When Augustus Caesar Dodge, Soulé's replacement at Madrid, stopped at The Hague in the spring of 1855 en route to his new post, Belmont presented him with letters of introduction to intimate friends in the Spanish capital, singling out in particular one who "has always been favorable to the sale of Cuba to our Government." Belmont to Marcy, May 24, 1855, Belmont Papers, NYPL.

Hall steadfastly refused to consider any abandonment of his
government's exclusionary East Indian policy. Basing his stubbornness on the necessity of preserving Dutch possessions, he
maintained that the entrance of foreign merchants and consuls
would be followed by foreign agents who would intrigue with
the natives to detach the colonies from the mother country.
Belmont, for his part, stressed the mutual benefits from free
Dutch-American trade in the Indies. He avoided, at least for the
time being, any mention of a possible treaty abrogation, for, as
he confided to Buchanan, the State Department "leaves a good
deal of doubt whether our government really intends to carry
the threat into effect, and I do not think . . . to bark unless
we mean to bite." [17]

Belmont's persistence and tact appeared to pay off, for by
March, 1854, only five months after his arrival at The Hague,
Van Hall assured him of imminent satisfaction. Despite these
promises, two months elapsed, and the Dutch Foreign Office
showed no alacrity in drafting a consular convention. Belmont,
eager to smother the irksome Gibson affair with more positive
accomplishments and not realizing that the episode must be a
cause of Dutch hedging, called on Van Hall. Urging the Foreign Minister to keep his word, Belmont cautioned him that
further delay in acting upon the American request might cause
Pierce to abrogate the 1839 commercial pact. Van Hall promised to think the matter over during a long weekend trip to the
countryside. He returned with the outline of a convention em-
bracing the American claim and assured Belmont he would submit it to the Minister of the Colonies for his consideration and
comment.

Belmont displayed little faith in Van Hall's promises; his dispatches to Marcy referred constantly to "proverbial Dutch caution." He continued to press the matter energetically and, when
convinced in June, 1854, that the Dutch were stalling, issued a
warning to Van Hall. If no convention were forthcoming by
April, 1855, the United States would give notice of intention to

[17] Belmont to Marcy, May 31, 1854, Marcy Papers; Belmont to Buchanan,
Nov. 18, 1853, Buchanan Papers; Spencer, *Marcy*, 401–02.

abrogate the existing Dutch-American commercial treaty. Van Hall reiterated that he intended to grant Belmont's request, but explained that even his powerful neighbors, England and France, possessed no trading privileges in the Indies. Consequently, the Dutch cabinet must move with prudence. To show his good faith, Van Hall swore that if Belmont refrained from any mention of the pending consular treaty in his dispatches to Washington, the preliminary draft would be sent over to the American legation within the week. Belmont, on the verge of a diplomatic triumph, begged Marcy to furnish the necessary power and credentials for the signing of such a convention "to enable me to bring the matter to a close." [18]

Not until the fall of 1854, after the Gibson case had come and gone, did Belmont again confer with Van Hall over the treaty. Though Belmont must have found it hard to believe, the scandal had worked to his advantage. The Dutch diplomat proved so pleased with Belmont's official apology for the earlier defense of Gibson that he allowed the American a major concession beyond the original draft. The United States would have permission not only to establish consulates in all free Dutch East Indian ports but in all other Dutch colonial ports open to foreign commerce. The proud Belmont signed the consular convention on January 22, 1855, and immediately received overwhelming congratulations from The Hague's diplomatic corps, many of whose members remembered their own futile attempts to accomplish such results. Marcy approved Belmont's work, and the Senate provided its ratification in March.[19]

Belmont had discovered, while ironing out the wording of the consular convention's articles on piracy, that no arrangements existed for the mutual extradition of criminals between his country and the Netherlands. The absence of such a compact struck him as serious, particularly because the United States had similar agreements with all major and most minor European powers and the increasing facilities for rapid trans-

[18] Belmont to Marcy, June 24, 1854, Marcy Papers.
[19] Belmont to Marcy, Oct. 7, Nov. 14, 1854, Jan. 23, May 1, 1855, Marcy Papers.

portation between the Netherlands and America "have unfortunately brought to our shores of late a great many criminals & fugitives from justice." The American diplomat lost no time in adopting this as his next project. He had already broached the subject to Van Hall while signing the final protocols of the consular treaty and found the Foreign Minister "perfectly ready & desirous" to pursue the matter. Marcy signaled the green light for undertaking official negotiations and sent Belmont the full presidential proxy to conclude an extradition treaty.[20]

Belmont's speed and thoroughness helped bring about a rough draft of the treaty only a few months after he'd mentioned its necessity to Van Hall. He submitted the draft to the State Department for scrutiny, and Washington's approval came quickly. But delays set in to irritate Belmont just when he was on the verge of consummating another diplomatic success. Marcy suggested some "simple modifications," Van Hall saw a "mountain in every molehill," and the Dutch Minister of Justice took several months for his assent. When Belmont returned the revised version to Washington in February, 1856, it met with additional "suggestions" from the Secretary of State and government lawyers. This diplomatic haggling, added to the inevitable fortnightly pauses during which the diplomatic pouches were in oceanic transit, put off the actual signing of the extradition treaty until May, at which time a provision was attached calling for nullification if both signatory governments failed to exchange official ratifications within a year. Marcy held on to the draft for two months before deciding to send it to Pierce. In August the President submitted it to the Senate, which ordered it to be printed. The following month the treaty returned from the government printers with a number of inaccuracies. Marcy, rather than allow the Senate to amend or reject the printed version, a course which he presumed Belmont

[20] Belmont to Marcy, Jan. 23, 1855, Marcy Papers; Belmont to Marcy, April 2, 1855, Belmont Papers, NYPL; Marcy to Belmont, April 30, 1855, private Belmont collection.

would disapprove, chose to have it reprinted, along with some "minor, technical alterations." [21]

The Secretary's action displeased Belmont, who was nearing the end of his tenure at The Hague and wanted full credit for concluding a treaty he had initiated and composed. He begged Marcy to resubmit the original May, 1856, convention to the Senate, but this proved impractical, for that body had meanwhile approved Marcy's newer version. Soon after, Van Hall's government fell on a parliamentary vote of confidence, and the new cabinet, an extremely weak one, demonstrated unwillingness to act decisively on anything that might risk its own dismissal.

The new Foreign Minister, Gevers de Endegeest, balked at portions of the Belmont-Van Hall extradition agreement, and Belmont, growing impatient, suggested to Washington six months before the May, 1857, deadline that it agree to accept any new Dutch version, for "to negotiate a whole new treaty would be very mortifying to me." This time Marcy consented, but the Senate, seemingly determined to have the last word, tacked on a few amendments. Belmont persuaded the Dutch to extend the deadline for another half year. More quibbling followed, but ultimately de Endegeest, the King, and the States-General accepted the extradition treaty with Senate amendments in August, 1857, just two months before Belmont's departure for the United States.[22]

The glow engendered by the treaty's successful conclusion helped mollify Belmont's pique at a letter received a few days before from Simeon Draper, a New York merchant and Whig. Draper reminded Belmont of an 1853 wager in which the banker had bet $500 that the United States would possess Cuba before Pierce left the White House.[23]

[21] Marcy to Belmont, July 14, 1855, Feb. 13, Sept. 5, 1856, Belmont to Marcy, May 9, 1856, Belmont Papers, NYPL; Belmont to Marcy, Jan. 22, March 27, 1856, Marcy Papers.

[22] Belmont to Marcy, Sept. 30, Nov. 13, Dec. 14, 1856, Belmont to Lewis Cass, May 4, June 21, Aug. 22, 1857, Belmont Papers, NYPL.

[23] Belmont to Charles Christmas, Aug. 10, 1857, Belmont Papers, NYPL.

5

★ ★ ★

"Malarious" Politics

BELMONT FOLLOWED domestic politics closely all during his diplomatic tenure abroad, commenting periodically on men and
events in his letters to Buchanan. He rarely passed up a chance
to criticize Pierce's "unwise" appointments, administrative fum-
bling, and injudicious policies. The administration's tolerance of
secessionists and free-soilers had exacerbated, not minimized, intraparty friction, and the tumult over Kansas and Nebraska
merely widened the unfortunate cleavage. Since his 1852 victory, Pierce's popularity had waned, and Belmont predicted
that the Cincinnati convention of 1856 would reject him in
favor of Buchanan. Considering the disrupted state of the Whig
Party, the Democratic nomination would be tantamount to
election. "With your name inscribed on our banner," he told
Buchanan, "we shall scatter the fanatics of Whiggery, Abolitionism, & Know-Nothingism to the winds." [1]

Belmont's correspondence also was intended to forge a closer
personal link with Buchanan. Letters from The Hague to London anxiously expressed the hope that Buchanan would visit the
Netherlands and partake of Belmont's hospitality: "When will
you come & see us? Your appearance amongst us would be
hailed with a good deal of joy by my family"; "I hope to have
the pleasure to take you once more by the hand"; and "We had
last month a visit from Ex-President Fillmore. They have now

[1] Belmont to Buchanan, Nov. 18, 1853, Feb. 2, 1854, June 19, Nov. 23, 1855,
Buchanan Papers.

seen at this court an American President, but I want them to see an American Statesman." [2]

The object of all this flattery kept his own counsel. Before accepting the diplomatic post at London, Buchanan had committed himself to no more than two years abroad, thus allowing ample time to prepare his bid for the coming nominating convention. In the interim Slidell kept him informed about political developments. Congressional Democrats were growing increasingly disenchanted with the administration, and Slidell himself was on the verge of an open rupture with the President. The Democratic Party, with no confidence in its nominal leader, behaved like an army without a general. "Say what they will of Nebraska & Know-Nothingism," Slidell scoffed, following the November, 1854, debacle, "the personal unpopularity or rather the solid want of consideration & influence of the administration has been the chief cause of our reverses." He urged Buchanan to declare his candidacy, but the seasoned, cautious Pennsylvanian refused. In the summer of 1855, when Slidell learned that Buchanan had asked Marcy for a letter of recall, he advised him to reconsider. "The political atmosphere [at home] is malarious (if there be no such word there should be) & those who are not compelled to inhale it had better keep away."

Buchanan heeded the warning and postponed his departure until the spring of 1856, while Slidell continued his usefulness. He rounded up enough powerful Democrats, North and South, including Senator Jesse D. Bright of Indiana, Governor Henry A. Wise of Virginia, Samuel L. M. Barlow of New York, a prominent corporation lawyer (among whose clients was August Belmont and Company), and William W. Corcoran, an important Washington, D.C., investment banker, to insure Buchanan's nomination. Yet, with all this campaign machinery set in motion, Buchanan's reluctance to declare openly for the nomination placed Slidell in an uncomfortable position. In January, 1856, the Louisiana senator pleaded with Buchanan to "make up your mind . . . that the cup will not be permitted to

[2] Belmont to Buchanan, Feb. 2, Sept. 25, 1854, June 19, Nov. 23, 1855, Buchanan Papers.

John Slidell (Library of Congress)   James Buchanan (Library of Congress)

pass from you." At last Buchanan acceded. He formally tendered his resignation, visited Belmont at The Hague during a short excursion on the European mainland, and sailed for the United States.[3]

After Buchanan's return to native soil, enthusiastic multitudes greeted him wherever he traveled, a fact that disheartened those opposed to his candidacy. When the convention at Cincinnati opened, it was clear that a majority of the delegates wanted Buchanan's nomination, but it took seventeen ballots to convince the Pierce and Douglas adherents that his lead was insurmountable, and that "Slidell and Company" meant to put him over. When Douglas released his delegates, Buchanan received the necessary two-thirds, marking the only time in American his-

[3] Buchanan to John W. Forney, Dec. 14, 1854, Buchanan to Marcy, April 26, 1855, Buchanan to Slidell, Dec. 28, 1855, in Moore, ed., *Works of Buchanan*, IX, 283, 346, 485–87; Slidell to Buchanan, Oct. 18, 1854, April 3, June 17, Sept. 2, 1855, Jan. 30, 1856, Buchanan Papers; Klein, *Buchanan*, 245–47; Sears, *Slidell*, 115–20.

tory that an elected President, who wanted another term in
office, failed of renomination. Slidell and other chief "Buchaneers" were so exhilarated by the realization of their long-
anticipated goal that, as their contribution to intraparty peace,
they placed Representative John C. Breckinridge, a Douglas
Democrat from Kentucky, in second place on the ticket.[4] In November, Buchanan emerged victorious over the Republican candidate, General John C. Fremont, as well as the American
(Know-Nothing) Party standard-bearer, former President Fillmore.[5]

Belmont's role in the campaign, though frequently alluded to
in historical literature, has not received careful and accurate
coverage. Major accounts imply he was in the United States,
contributing "thousands" and plotting strategy with other
"Buchaneers" to nail down the Cincinnati nomination, the October state elections in Pennsylvania, and finally the Presidency
itself. Here, Belmont is helping to lay "astute plans" to win the
nomination for his man. There, Belmont "is reported to have
given $50,000" for the Pennsylvania campaign. All of the
sources can ultimately be traced to an 1861 editorial in the
Albany Evening Journal, a Republican newspaper, published
by Thurlow Weed. Weed, a close friend of Senator Seward, a
power among New York Republicans, but hardly the last word
on Democratic campaign fund sources, claimed, five years after
the fact, that "James Buchanan was elected President . . .
simply because Messrs. [Cornelius] Wendell, [John W.] Forney, and Belmont raised $50,000 more money, to be expended
in Pennsylvania, than William A. Hall, Truman Smith, and the

[4] *New York Times*, April 24, 25, June 1, 1856; *New York Herald*, May 15,
16, 1856; *Official Proceedings of the National Democratic Convention, Held
in Cincinnati, June 2-6, 1856* (Cincinnati, 1856), 38-58. Douglas hoped the
result would be a harmonious party in the election campaign (and his own
nomination by the same united Democracy in 1860). Buchanan's backers, previous to Cincinnati, pledged that, if elected, their man would not consent to
a second nomination. Slidell to Buchanan, May 2, 24, 1856, Buchanan Papers.
[5] See Nevins, *Ordeal of the Union*, II, 452-514; Milton, *Eve of Conflict*,
230-44; Klein, *Buchanan*, 256-60; Roy F. Nichols, *The Disruption of American
Democracy* (New York, 1948), 19-50.

writer of this article could procure for the same object." [6]

Contemporary inaccuracy breeds historical myth. In point of fact, it was a physical impossibility for Belmont to have participated. After his 1853 departure for Europe he did not return to the United States until November, 1857.[7] Transatlantic communications at the time precluded his playing what, by any stretch of the imagination, could be considered a major role in the campaign. He undoubtedly contributed some money to the Buchanan coffers, but no evidence exists of an exact sum nor do the Buchanan Papers reveal any clues or references to a Belmont donation. In a letter to the secretary of the New York State Democratic Committee, Belmont referred to a recent contribution he had sent Slidell as the reason for his inability to help out the Buchanan campaign in the Empire State. But that is all.[8]

Belmont's absence during the campaign notwithstanding, he was remembered by journalistic detractors at home. Bennett's *Herald* attacked him early in the campaign and charged him with seeking the Paris mission in return for pecuniary contributions. The slander infuriated Belmont. To one such friend who had the bad taste to mention the rumor he retorted icily:

It may serve the purposes of that scamp Bennett to fill his columns with such absurd inventions, in order to injure Buchanan through me, but I

[6] Nevins, *Ordeal of the Union*, II, 456, 506; Foner, *Business & Slavery*, 135–36; Carl Sandburg, *Abraham Lincoln: The War Years* (4 vols., New York, 1939), I, 23–24; Alexander C. Flick, ed., *History of the State of New York* (10 vols., New York, 1933–37), VII, 86; James A. Rawley, "Financing the Fremont Campaign," *Pennsylvania Magazine of History and Biography*, LXXV (Jan., 1951), 25–26, 30–31. Thurlow Weed's statement in the *Albany Evening Journal*, Sept. 21, 1861, is quoted in [Charles Wright] *The Prospect* (Buffalo, 1862), 20.

[7] The Belmont Papers and Letterbooks in the New York Public Library contain letters written from The Hague during each month of the period April–December, 1856.

[8] "I should have most willingly sent my contribution to the good cause through your hands. . . . Before the receipt of your letter I had already some time ago requested Mr. Slidell at Washington to give to the Central Executive Committee on my behalf such a contribution as my means permit me to make towards promoting an event for which I have longed & labored for many years past. . . . I am therefore unable to comply with your request." Belmont to Richard Schell, Aug. 30, 1856, Belmont Papers, NYPL.

had hoped that *you* had too favorable an opinion of me to think me capable of enough egotism to have even a thought of such a post.[9]

Belmont forgot his annoyance in the face of extensive Democratic victories in October. This "glorious news," he wrote Buchanan, would turn the tide of secessionist and abolitionist fanaticism, silence the yells of sectional treason, and save the Union. Belmont's effusive letter read as if Buchanan's election were a foregone conclusion:

I have wished & worked & prayed for this happy event for many a year. . . . I pray to the Almighty, who has selected you for this great work, that He may give His blessings to the efforts of your patriotism & wisdom.

Belmont also touched on a more worldly matter. The incoming administration would need a trustworthy and skilled diplomat to represent it at Madrid and act effectively on the Cuban question, especially in view of an "imminent" change in the Spanish cabinet. He then mentioned that Mrs. Belmont suffered from the "damp & severe climate" of the Netherlands. The connection between these two last statements the banker left to Buchanan's perspicacity.[10]

The hopeful minister waited long enough at The Hague to dispatch post-Election Day congratulations to Buchanan—his last known letter to the Pennsylvanian—and then departed with his wife, children, and nursemaids for a four-month tour of the Continent. He returned to the Netherlands legation in April, 1857, expecting to find an offer of a new diplomatic assignment. The only Washington mail was a letter from the new Secretary of State, the veteran Michigan Democrat Lewis Cass. Cass expressed satisfaction with Belmont's record at The Hague and invited him to accept another four-year term there. Belmont's answer was his resignation. In it he did not once allude to a nostalgic desire to return home or to resume his banking opera-

9 Belmont to Richard Schell, Aug. 30, 1856, Belmont Papers, NYPL. In all fairness, Bennett's shaft fell not too wide of the mark. Soon Belmont would covet another diplomatic mission; but it would be Madrid, not Paris.

10 Belmont to Buchanan, Oct. 31, 1856, Buchanan Papers. Slidell's post-election comment proved more prophetic: "You are not to lie on a bed of roses." Slidell to Buchanan, Nov. 13, 1856, Buchanan Papers.

tions, but simply to the Dutch climate "which renders it unadvisable for the health of Mrs. Belmont to pass another winter at The Hague." [11] Cass replied that Buchanan "reluctantly accepted" his resignation and requested him to delay his departure until the fall, when a successor would arrive. Belmont graciously yielded and consoled himself by arranging for his personal belongings and recently purchased furniture, objets d'art, and wine cellar to be carefully packed into more than 250 crates for shipment.[12]

With a public reputation as banker, diplomat, and veteran Democrat, Belmont returned to the United States in November, 1857, in time to find the party embroiled in a major dispute. A Buchanan-Douglas feud, with roots in the early 1850s, had intensified after the 1856 election, when the new President (upon Slidell's advice) refrained from appointing Douglas men to top patronage posts. Then, on December 9, 1857, Douglas delivered a three-hour speech on the Senate floor denouncing the proslavery Lecompton Constitution that Buchanan wanted approved for the Kansas Territory.[13]

Belmont found many of his New York Democratic friends supporting the midwestern senator. He himself counted Douglas a personal friend and, in view of Buchanan's publicized disavowal of a renomination, thought him the logical Democratic standard-bearer in 1860.[14] But Belmont refused to be drawn

[11] Belmont to Cass, April 20, 1857, Belmont Papers, NYPL. Numerous letters in this period to Christmas, Matthiessen & Co. reveal Belmont's "desire" to lease a house in New York "for not more than two years," another indication that he expected to move back to Europe soon.

[12] John Appleton to Belmont, June 6, 1857, Belmont to Cass, Aug. 22, Sept. 23, 1857, Belmont Papers, NYPL.

[13] The Senate later approved the Lecompton Constitution, but Douglas Democrats and Republicans united to defeat it in the House. Milton, *Eve of Conflict*, 276–78; Philip G. Auchampaugh, "The Buchanan-Douglas Feud," *Journal of the Illinois State Historical Society*, XXV (April, 1932), 5–48.

[14] Belmont had entertained the Illinois Democrat back in 1853, at which time he had also gladly furnished him with letters of introduction to prominent European statesmen and financiers. Belmont to Baron Alphonse de Rothschild, May 13, 1853, Belmont to Douglas, May 14, 1853, Douglas Papers, Univ. of Chicago. In 1854, after having visited Belmont at The Hague, Daniel Sickles wrote Douglas that "In Belmont you have indeed secured a strong

into the controversy and maintained his allegiance to the administration. Though unsolicited, he appointed himself Buchanan's New York adviser, keeping the President informed through Slidell about the fierce Democratic bloodletting following municipal elections there. When the White House threatened to depose John McKeon, United States Attorney for New York, because of his role in a local primary fight against Mayor Fernando Wood, Belmont counseled a conciliatory approach instead. He urged Slidell to dissuade Buchanan from moving against McKeon, pointing out that the official's activities had had the full support of leading New York Democrats. "Though McKeon is no particular friend of mine & I have no personal interest whatever . . . , I think it my duty to warn the President" against alienating such influential local party members as John Van Buren and Daniel Sickles. "I have only one object in view: the good of the Administration & the Democratic party." [15]

Belmont's loyalty to Buchanan and his willingness to serve him assumed other forms as well. George Bancroft, the historian and oldtime Jacksonian, came to New York in February, 1858, at the height of Congressional debate on the Lecompton Constitution, and called on Gotham's citizens, particularly its merchants, to denounce the President's Kansas policy. Belmont responded by helping circulate a petition which endorsed Buchanan's actions and urged Congress to admit a slaveholding Kansas into the Union. The banker again defended the administration at an Independence Day party celebration at Tammany Hall, headquarters of the New York County Democratic organization, though here he was careful to attack only "Black" Republicans and Know-Nothings.[16]

In spite of these domestic interests, Belmont could not forget Cuba. This issue had occupied his mind for so long as to take

---

and a faithful friend." Sickles to Douglas, undated, 1854, Douglas Papers, Univ. of Chicago.

[15] Slidell to Buchanan, Feb. 14, Aug. 12, 1857, Aug. 8, 1858, Belmont to Slidell, Dec. 8, 1857, Buchanan Papers.

[16] Foner, *Business & Slavery*, 150; *New York Times*, July 7, 1858.

on an importance out of all proportion to its place in the total scheme of United States policy. His obsession with the island and with the role he imagined himself playing in its acquisition led him to push forward when political discretion should have dictated restraint.[17] Word reached Belmont in June, 1858, that Minister Augustus Caesar Dodge intended resigning his Madrid assignment in order to run for the Iowa governorship. Despite the fact that his pro-Buchanan activities had thus far failed to elicit any direct response from the White House, Belmont cornered Slidell in New York and offered his analysis of the latest events in Cuba and Spain. The senator, now the most influential man in Washington, promised to discuss the matter with Buchanan, but if he did so, he never reported the fact to Belmont.[18]

Ignoring the lack of response, Belmont wrote a long letter to Slidell in which, throwing protocol aside, he applied directly for the Madrid post. He reviewed the administration's repeated declarations favoring Cuban acquisition and again stressed that the time "has never been more ripe" to obtain the island. Spain was politically unstable and prone to sudden "revulsions" against constituted authority. Recent information from a "high-placed intelligent Spaniard" assured Belmont that if the United States kept the subject of Cuban purchase alive, more and more people within and without the Madrid government would come to accept its inevitability. Such an eventuality could best be stimulated by an American minister at the court who would at all times be prepared to "profit" from cabinet changes and to "shape them to our purpose." Belmont then got to the point:

I have heretofore spoken to you of the powerful friends I have at Madrid & also of the influence which my friends in Paris are ready & willing to place at my disposal if the President should think fit to confide me the Madrid mission. There is no man, whatever his talents & qualifications may be, who could be selected by Mr. Buchanan, who could in that regard secure the invaluable services which are at my disposal.

[17] Belmont to Buchanan, Oct. 31, 1856, Buchanan Papers; Allan Nevins, *The Emergence of Lincoln* (2 vols., New York, 1950), I, 446.

[18] Slidell had turned down Buchanan's offer that he head the State Department. Klein, *Buchanan*, 263.

. . . My appointment would be a popular one. . . . Almost every Democratic paper throughout the Union has connected my name with the mission, & my availability & fitness have been generally admitted & advocated.[19]

Slidell carried the Belmont letter to the White House, but Buchanan had already decided that Belmont was not the proper man to negotiate for Cuba.[20] Besides, the President hoped that Slidell would accept the Paris mission and knew Congressional opponents would complain if this appointment were followed by another to Slidell's "nephew." [21] Buchanan's solution to this sticky problem was to ignore it, leaving Slidell "under the impression that Belmont is out of the running" for Madrid.[22]

Belmont, of course, could not know of these developments. When Slidell came to New York City in December, Belmont called on him and expressed profound disappointment at not having heard from the President. Slidell attempted to apologize for Buchanan's neglect, whereupon the banker, losing his temper, inquired just how hard the senator himself had pushed the application. Slidell noted Belmont's increasing agitation, changed the subject, and soon bade him good day. The following morning Belmont visited Slidell's rooms, handed him a letter addressed to Buchanan, and requested that it be delivered in person. Slidell read its "disrespectful & offensive contents," per-

[19] Belmont to Slidell, June 5, 1858, Buchanan Papers.
[20] Buchanan did not write off the Caribbean project. His Annual Messages of 1858, 1859, and 1860 recommended Cuban acquisition from Spain "by fair purchase." See, for example, Moore, ed., *Works of Buchanan*, XI, 29. In January, 1859, Slidell introduced a bill in the Senate calling for an appropriation of $30,000,000 to facilitate negotiations for Cuba's purchase. The bill met with such strong opposition that the Louisianan soon withdrew it, and the issue was dead for the rest of the Buchanan term. Klein, *Buchanan*, 324-25; Sears, *Slidell*, 152-53, 158-59.
[21] Slidell, not wishing to trade a safe Senate seat for a temporary diplomatic assignment, never accepted the standing offer of Paris.
[22] Slidell to Buchanan, Aug. 22, 1858, Buchanan Papers. Louis M. Sears, Slidell's biographer, misinterpreted this letter to Buchanan to mean that the President *had* offered the Spanish mission to Belmont, and that it had not been accepted. Sears, *Slidell*, 152. Sears' error in turn led a biographer of Louisiana Senator Judah P. Benjamin astray on this point. See Robert D. Meade, *Judah P. Benjamin: Confederate Statesman* (New York, 1943), 113.

emptorily refused to be its bearer, and advised its writer to
burn it. This meeting ended abruptly and, as it developed, was
the last between the two men. This parting of the ways also signaled the final breach between Belmont and the Chief Executive for whose regime he had "longed & labored for many years
past."

Though the banker never sent Buchanan the intended letter,
the defection of the President's wealthiest ally in New York
could not remain a secret. The Chief Executive soon learned
that "our friend Belmont is a decided Douglas man." Slidell, not
in the least surprised to hear of Belmont's desertion, described
the December meeting to his chief, adding that he had since
"heard from others that he complains of me." The senator regretted the banker's conversion but assured Buchanan he would
not "take pains to conciliate him." [23]

From Belmont's standpoint the matter was beyond conciliation. Through his financial success and his political and diplomatic experience he had acquired a taste for being close to the
seat of power and leadership. Yet now he was unaccountably
barred from his accustomed confidences. Buchanan's sole ges-
ture, after all Belmont had done for him publicly and privately,
was merely a new appointment to the same mission he had held
under Pierce. And the first favor asked of Buchanan in five
years—the Madrid post—had not even been acknowledged,
much less granted.[24] Under the circumstances, a transfer of
loyalty from Buchanan to Douglas was inevitable. By switching
to Douglas, the strongest anti-Buchanan challenger in the Dem-

[23] Buchanan to Slidell, June 24, 1859, Slidell to Buchanan, July 3, 1859,
Buchanan Papers.

[24] Though Belmont failed to secure the Madrid post under Buchanan, his
oldest son, Representative Perry Belmont of New York, managed to get it
from the next Democratic administration. The son's autobiography recalls
that President Grover Cleveland sent his name to the Senate Foreign Relations
Committee in November, 1888. Chairman John Sherman, an Ohio Republican
who had entered Congress as a Whig during the Pierce administration, said
jocosely that he hoped young Belmont's instructions "were in no way intended to bring about the acquisition of Cuba." Perry Belmont, *An American
Democrat*, 378.

ocratic Party, Belmont forfeited nothing and had everything to gain.[25]

[25] Allen Churchill, author of a partly inaccurate sketch in the *Dictionary of American Biography*, has Belmont returning from The Hague "opposed to slavery as an institution" but nonetheless supporting Douglas' policies "rather than those of the abolitionists." Allen L. Churchill, "August Belmont," in Dumas Malone, ed., *Dictionary of American Biography* (22 vols., New York, 1928–58), II, 169–70. Belmont, as far as the record shows, never criticized slavery, either on moral or institutional grounds, throughout the entire antebellum era.

6

★ ★ ★

The "Douglas National Chairman"

BELMONT'S NEW POLITICAL ALIGNMENT did not signal any
change in his stand on the major issues of the day. He was sensitive to the ferment around him, but generally speaking what
concerned him were the practical effects of disunion, not the
moral and humanitarian aspects of human slavery. As a consequence, Belmont found the "dangerous" implications of southern secessionist oratory and the "irrepressible conflict" ideas of
New York Republican Senator William H. Seward equally upsetting. The banker felt the nation's stability could best be
maintained by convincing the South that most northerners were
hostile to the tenets of abolitionism.

In October, 1859, Belmont joined other like-minded New
York Democrats, including Barlow and Samuel J. Tilden, a rising railroad and corporation lawyer, to organize the Democratic Vigilant Association. This predominantly mercantile
group wanted to inform the South that New York's businessmen—especially those engaged in the "southern trade"—could
be relied upon to defend the South's legal and constitutional
rights, combat Seward's "atrocious disunion doctrines," and
purge all suspected free-soilers from important governmental
and party offices. Belmont was also one of the sponsors of a
mass meeting in the New York Academy of Music where numerous speeches underscored the need to save the Union at all
costs while simultaneously denouncing abolitionists, Republican
politicians, and John Brown's seizure of the Harpers Ferry
arsenal.[1]

[1] New York Herald, Oct. 1, 5, 6, 16, 1859; Foner, Business & Slavery, 155–56,
162–63; Milton, Eve of Conflict, 399.

But the semblance of unity mustered by the New York Democrats in support of the South did not hold true for matters closer to home. The Empire State Democrats still reflected the schism created by former President Martin Van Buren's 1848 third-party, Free-Soil candidacy. Most of the Free-Soil defectors supported Pierce in 1852, but their return to the regular fold met a mixed response. The state faction which welcomed them back was given the epithet, "Softshell," then "Soft"; in turn, the vehemently anti-Free-Soil wing received the title of "Hardshell," ultimately "Hard." The Softs were led by Tilden, former Governor Horatio Seymour of Utica, railroad magnate Erastus Corning of Albany, and Dean Richmond of Buffalo, chairman of the Democratic State Committee since 1850. The outstanding leader of New York's Hards was former Senator Daniel S. Dickinson of Binghamton who, along with most of the state's federal officeholders, was aligned with the Buchanan administration. Distinguishing between the groups

Stephen A. Douglas (Library of Congress)

was not always an easy task, for divisions on other issues tended to blur factional lines.[2]

New York City Democrats, typically more at war than at peace among themselves, had splits which often cut across Hard and Soft lines. Former Mayor Wood, a one-time leader of Tammany Hall (the popular name for the New York County Democratic organization), fought the regulars with his own local faction, Mozart Hall, which despite its name only added to party disharmony. In theory, Mozart Hall Democrats should have been Hard when Tammany was Soft and vice versa, but this was not a reliable guide to predicting their votes at state and national conventions.

Belmont had been careful to avoid identification with either side up to his break with Buchanan. Since Buchanan's administration consistently favored the Hards, Belmont became a nominal Soft.[3] Though he chose a side in the factional division, Belmont still worried over the unstable intraparty situation. In view of New York's importance in the national political picture, Belmont, Moses Taylor, another top Wall Street financier, and others advised Douglas that it would be wise to establish his national headquarters there. From such a base Douglas could not only coordinate his supporters' actions but, more importantly, demonstrate his strength to anti-administration Democrats who might be tempted to name a favorite son for the nomination. Douglas gave his permission, and in September, 1859, Belmont set the scheme in motion. He helped organize a Douglas campaign steering committee and collected a minimal campaign chest.

That the strategy succeeded became obvious when the State Democratic Convention met at Syracuse the following February. The leaders selected a slate of delegates to the national con-

[2] Sidney D. Brummer, *Political History of New York State During the Period of the Civil War* (New York, 1911), 24–31; Nichols, *Pierce*, 218–19.
[3] Roy F. Nichols dates Belmont's affiliation with the Softs as early as 1853, but I have found no evidence to support his contention. Nichols, *Disruption of American Democracy*, 84. Ivor D. Spencer claims Belmont was a Hard. Spencer, *Marcy*, 232.

vention at Charleston with the majority pledged to Douglas, and, over the bitter opposition of Dickinson and many of the Hards, Dean Richmond got the group to bind itself to a unit-rule voting system. News of the Syracuse results pleased Belmont, particularly his own designation as a Charleston delegate.[4]

Belmont next turned toward assisting the election of Douglas delegates and Democratic candidates in New England. On the evening of January 31, 1860, a large gathering of well-known New York Democrats met in Belmont's Fifth Avenue home, discussed the situation in the six states, and pledged funds to each of the Democratic State Committees. Several people joined Belmont in donating $500, and the conclave netted over $5,000. The banker toured New Hampshire, spent money for campaign literature, and made several speeches for candidates in the March state elections. Such activities earned Belmont the good will of influential party men there. Former President Pierce wrote that he would "never cease to remember with gratitude the substantial interest which you have manifested . . . in a little state with which you have no connection." The retired Chief Executive's best friend, Judge Josiah Minot, sent notice that the state organization felt "greatly indebted" for the banker's "timely aid." But for all Belmont's exertions in the Granite State the once predominantly Democratic New Hampshire voters elected the entire Republican state ticket. The "disastrous news" sobered Belmont; he realized how demoralizing the effect would be upon Democratic campaign workers and contributors in other states.[5]

The situation in Connecticut also called for outside help. Letters from Democrats there told a story of "immense sums" being spent by Republicans for the spring voting, buttressed

[4] Milton, *Eve of Conflict*, 384; Nevins, *Emergence of Lincoln*, II, 47; Brummer, *Political History of New York State*, 48–51. Edward Channing, the historian, said concerning the delegation: "Hardly a name of distinction appears except that of August Belmont." Edward Channing, *A History of the United States* (6 vols., New York, 1905–25), VI, 237.

[5] Belmont to Barlow, March 16, 1860, Barlow Papers; Pierce to Belmont, March 17, 1860, private Belmont collection; Milton, *Eve of Conflict*, 417–19.

with urgent appeals "to enable our friends to fight with equal weapons." Belmont made the rounds of the offices of "those firms engaged in the Southern and Southwestern trade"—that is, those whose fear of a Republican President was ostensibly greatest—and soon put together a subscription list totaling $25,000. Prominent among the names on the roster were those of Alexander T. Stewart, the "dry-goods king" with strong connections to southern planters, and Peter Lorillard, who was amassing a fortune in the tobacco trade. Belmont himself contributed $500. But in the end, Connecticut went the way of New Hampshire.[6]

Not all Democrats responded so positively or sympathetically to Belmont's vigorous political endeavors. Large placards were put up in Cincinnati informing the citizenry that "the Rothschilds have sent countless millions" to buy Douglas the presidency. Even more serious, Fernando Wood, angry at State Chairman Richmond for being excluded from the slate of Charleston delegates, led a movement of similarly discontented New York Democrats in an attempt to drive a wedge between Richmond and the local Douglas organization. Wood's followers spread rumors that Richmond planned to betray Douglas at Charleston and singled out Belmont as the prize traitor. After all, had not Belmont long maintained "intimate ties" with the Buchanan administration, and was he not a "nephew" of Slidell, the mastermind of the stop-Douglas coalition?

Wood's charges caused consternation among some long-time Douglas adherents. These men, such as Edward C. West, who had refused to switch his convention vote from Douglas in 1852 to make Pierce's nomination unanimous, were sensitive on the subject of treachery. They had been cheated earlier by men posing as "Douglas Democrats" and now wondered whether they had made the acquaintance of "another infernal scamp." West invited the unsuspecting Belmont to his law office where, in the company of two other Douglas friends, they discussed Douglas' prospects at Charleston.

[6] Belmont to Barlow, March 16, 1860, Barlow Papers.

The interrogation lasted over an hour, in the course of which Belmont angrily denounced Buchanan and persuasively disclaimed any connection or sympathy with Slidell. He did not deny his earlier associations with the two men, but he had been younger and less wise then. Just before leaving the trio, Belmont set forth his present political attitude in emphatic, straightforward terms: "I am the personal friend of Douglas, and the personal friend of his personal friends and will be with his friends at Charleston—besides all of which he is the only man in the country we can elect and this I have said to all of them." Belmont's words dispelled any lingering doubts among the Douglas men. West joyfully wrote the "Little Giant" of his satisfaction that "you have Belmont, heart and judgment." Ironically, the illness of Mrs. West prevented her husband's presence at Charleston, and Belmont now became recognized as "Douglas' man" in the New York delegation.[7]

Belmont looked forward to a hard but ultimately victorious struggle at the Charleston meeting and put no stock in southern threats of secession from the convention. Even a letter from the long-silent Slidell he found more amusing than disturbing, for it seemed to prove the growing despair among the anti-Douglas group. Slidell, having heard "with pleasure" of Belmont's coming trip to Charleston, expressed concern over not having gotten the news first-hand. What worried Slidell still more was the report, which he could not "believe for a moment," that "you go there with tendencies favorable to Douglas." Belmont, having received reports that Slidell was being put forward as Louisiana's favorite-son candidate for the presidential nomination, chose not to reply. He had every reason to suspect the ends to which Slidell would use *any* Belmont letter on the eve of the convention.[8]

[7] Sigmund Diamond, ed., *A Casual View of America: The Home Letters of Salomon de Rothschild, 1859-1861* (Stanford, Calif., 1961), 34, 36, Milton, *Eve of Conflict*, 415-16; Edward C. West to Douglas, April 16, 1860, Douglas Papers, Univ. of Chicago; Robert W. Johannsen, ed., *The Letters of Stephen A. Douglas* (Urbana, Ill., 1961), 216.

[8] Slidell to Belmont, undated [March, 1860], private Belmont collection; Sears, *Slidell*, 162-71.

On Wednesday morning, April 18, 1860, Belmont took leave of his wife, their five children, and a house guest, the young Salomon de Rothschild of Paris, at a Hudson River pier and boarded the *Nashville*, which was to transport the entire New York delegation to the Charleston meeting.[9] Had he been superstitious, he might have viewed an annoying waterfront incident as an evil omen for the political confrontation ahead. Just before sailing time, some of Fernando Wood's supporters among the large crowd of well-wishers maliciously pelted the handkerchief-waving delegation on board the steamboat with oranges. One such missile struck Belmont in the groin, forced him to go below, and caused him to miss the sight of Manhattan's skyline as the *Nashville* pulled out of New York harbor.[10]

The Democratic National Convention was called to order on Monday, April 23, at Charleston. The pro-Buchanan Democratic National Committee had chosen this site because it would provide a most unpropitious setting for a Douglas victory. South Carolina had conspicuously taken the lead in expressing extreme southern views, and her chief political spokesmen strongly opposed Douglas. Though most southern delegates were not agreed upon a specific candidate, they demanded that the party adopt the kind of campaign platform which Douglas had all but discredited in his verbal assaults against Buchanan's policies. Yet if Douglas, in the interest of raw political expediency, consented to run on a platform advocating free and untrammeled admission of slavery into the territories, his chances for success in the North would diminish considerably. To Belmont's way of thinking, a Douglas designation on a "Slidell platform" would completely nullify any value possessed by the convention prize.

[9] The banker's parting comment to the Frenchman was the prediction that if Douglas could not receive the nomination it would surely go to James Guthrie of Kentucky, a leading southern candidate who had served in Pierce's cabinet as Treasury Secretary. Diamond, ed., *Casual View of America*, 38, 42.

[10] Nichols, *Disruption of American Democracy*, 292; Mitchell, *Seymour*, 211.

Most of the opening day dealt with the seating of rival state delegations and jockeying for positions on various committees. The "immense deal of time lost by talking" bored the impatient Belmont, anxious for the main attraction of the convention. By Wednesday he confessed to his wife that only a willingness "to partake in the interesting work before us" could have induced him to spend a "most stupid time" in "such intense heat" with less cultured colleagues. His irritability showed through as he described a pro-Douglas party for delegates to which he felt obliged to go: "It was the most stupid of all stupid gatherings I have ever been at—there were about twelve ugly women with about sixty as ugly men." [11]

In his impatience Belmont underestimated the significance of the important business which had to precede the balloting, for a schism over the platform was to wreck the Charleston convention. The Committee on Resolutions submitted majority and minority platforms for convention consideration. The majority platform, referred to as the Yancey platform after former Senator William L. Yancey, a proslavery radical from Alabama, clearly avowed the national government's duty to protect slaveholders in the territories. The minority platform, put forward by Douglas men in committee, simply reasserted confidence in the 1856 Democratic platform, pledged support for Supreme Court pronouncements, and hedged over the rights of slaveholders in the territories. The convention, owing in good measure to New York's adherence to the unit rule, adopted the minority platform. An outraged Yancey delivered a highly emotional speech and then led the Alabama delegation from the auditorium. Slidell and the Louisiana contingent followed in Yancey's steps. When order was restored, six entire state delegations and parts of several others were missing from the conven-

[11] Official Proceedings of the Democratic National Convention, Held in 1860, at Charleston and Baltimore (Cleveland, 1860), 3–31; Alexander, Political History of the State of New York, II, 270–72; Belmont to Mrs. August Belmont, April 25, 1860, private Belmont collection. It is doubtful that Belmont ever became enamored of the plebeian pleasures of convention-going. But he managed to sublimate his snobbish views, at least for pragmatic reasons, sufficiently to attend the succeeding six Democratic national conventions.

tion floor. There was little chance to select a presidential nominee after these departures, and Douglas proved unable to garner
the necessary two-thirds support through fifty-seven ballots. In
view of the stalemate, the fifty-eighth ballot was postponed for
six weeks while the convention moved from the secessionist climate of Charleston to Baltimore, Maryland.[12]

Belmont telegraphed Douglas a brief version of the debacle
directly from Charleston. Back in New York he wrote his chief
a full and confidential account of the manner in which his
friends and enemies behaved. Douglas appreciated the information and requested Belmont to contact former Congressman
William A. Richardson, leader of the Illinois delegation, now in
New York for strategy sessions. Belmont conferred with Richardson and assured him that New York would hold together
for Douglas at Baltimore. But in a later letter to Douglas, Belmont thought he detected some wavering by "the timid
amongst us." He believed that Douglas' main threat in the delegation came from those who felt former Governor Seymour's
nomination would attract more southern sympathy. Fears of
these defections were probably exaggerated, though "nothing
can be lost by watchfulness. . . . All we want . . . is some
additional evidence of your strength at the South." A recent
pro-Douglas letter by Georgia Congressman Alexander H.
Stephens had been helpful, as would be a pending visit by Senator Thomas L. Clingman of North Carolina.[13]

Belmont solicited Douglas' opinion on plans to amend the
party platform at the outset of the Baltimore meeting. On the
final day at Charleston, a number of Kentucky, Virginia, and
New York delegates had drafted a resolution which forbade
Congress from destroying or impairing the rights of slaveholders in the territories. Belmont had been present and thought the
resolution might be tacked on to the platform as a concession to
the South. Other Douglas friends hoped this alteration would

---

[12] *Official Proceedings of the Democratic National Convention*, 31–91;
Milton, *Eve of Conflict*, 431–49.

[13] Douglas to Belmont, May 8, 1860, private Belmont collection; Belmont to
Douglas, May 18, 1860, Douglas Papers, Univ. of Chicago.

be performed immediately after seating the Baltimore delegates, but Belmont believed such a move unwise and urged no discussion of proposals until "after we have got through that important part of our business." Douglas not only agreed with Belmont but acknowledged that his value increased daily. Belmont wired Dean Richmond the Douglas strategy to "proceed at once to the 58th ballot without reconsidering the platform."

Late in May, Belmont once again discovered signs of unrest among some of New York's delegates. "The Seymour game is not abandoned," he warned Douglas, and Buchanan and Slidell "are moving heaven & earth in order to get this delegation away from you." Perhaps these wobbly New Yorkers needed a Douglas visit to bolster their loyalties. Could the senator consent to a short stay in "our good city of Gotham?" If he did, he could find hospitality at Belmont's house and do his cause immeasurable good as well. Illness in the Douglas household prevented acceptance of Belmont's "kind invitation." But Douglas doubted that the administration's "extraordinary efforts . . . to destroy the popular will" would succeed.[14]

Belmont tried to compensate for Douglas' absence by a burst of activity in the period between the conventions. He helped organize a "fitting and imposing" pro-Douglas rally at Cooper Institute on May 22, the like of which had never before been witnessed in the city. Then he persuaded leading Douglas men, such as West, George N. Sanders, former Congressman Cutting, and William B. Astor, to sit with him on a "self-constituted committee of seven" which would ask prominent and wealthy Democrats throughout the nation to help defray the senator's campaign expenses.

News of Belmont's yeoman service impressed Douglas, and in his last letter to Belmont before Baltimore he showed his appreciation:

I hope you will come to Washington a few days before the convention. I desire to see you & confer freely & confidentially. Your conduct toward me has been so honorable that I shall have no political secrets

[14] Belmont to Douglas, May 18, 31, 1860, Douglas Papers, Univ. of Chicago; Douglas to Belmont, May 22, June 4, 1860, private Belmont collection.

from you in the future. It is expected that our leading friends . . . will
meet here for consultation a few days previous to the convention. You
must not fail to be here.[15]

When the Democrats reconvened at Baltimore on June 18,
Belmont, Richardson, and others came determined to put their
man over, with or without the Charleston seceders, who, led by
Slidell, were just as determined to destroy the Democratic
Party rather than submit to Douglas' nomination. One Douglas
man, C. L. Ward, likened the arrival of the southern extremists
to Lord Byron's seventy virgins who, watching the siege of
Ismail, "were anxiously wondering when the ravishing will
begin." The "ravishing" began immediately. Those delegates
who had seceded at Charleston were excluded and replaced by
Douglas men, whereupon four additional southern states
walked out. This time the convention kept going, and on the
first ballot Douglas received 177½ of the 190½ votes cast. The
vice presidential place, reserved for a southerner, went to Senator Benjamin Fitzpatrick of Alabama, a staunch Douglas sup-
porter. Douglas, hearing of his nomination, wired Ohio delegate
Washington McLean, editor of the *Cincinnati Enquirer*, and requested him to thank Belmont and the New York delegation
for "heroic firmness & fidelity to principle" during the momen-
tous days at Charleston and Baltimore.[16]

The seceding Democrats held their own "Democratic National Convention" several days later in the same city and chose
Vice President Breckinridge and Oregon Senator Joseph Lane

[15] Milton, *Eve of Conflict*, 462; Sanders to Douglas, May 25, 1860, Douglas
Papers, Univ. of Chicago; Douglas to Belmont, June 4, 1860, private Belmont
collection. No record has yet revealed what transpired between Douglas,
Belmont, and their "friends" in Washington during the second week of June.
Murat Halstead, a Cincinnati newspaper correspondent, mentioned such a
meeting and reported hearing of Dean Richmond's presence there. Murat
Halstead, *A History of the National Political Conventions of the Current
Presidential Campaign: Caucuses of 1860* (Cincinnati, 1860), 159, 167.

[16] *Official Proceedings of the Democratic National Convention*, 93–174; C. L.
Ward to Douglas, June 20, 1860, Douglas Papers, Univ. of Chicago; Douglas
to Belmont, June 23, 1860, Stephen A. Douglas Papers, Illinois State Historical Library.

as their candidates. In addition to this dissident Democratic ticket, Douglas also faced competition from two other major groups. A National Constitutional Union Party, an amalgamation of old-line Whigs and Know-Nothings who had not gone over to Republican or Democratic ranks, nominated former Senator John Bell of Tennessee. The Republicans put forward former Whig Congressman Abraham Lincoln who had unsuccessfully opposed Douglas in a memorable 1858 senatorial campaign.

After Douglas' nomination, the convention's final task lay in the selection of a new Democratic National Committee, the organization charged with centralizing and directing the national campaign to follow. The New York delegation, at Douglas' request, chose Belmont for its seat on the committee, and as ex-

August Belmont during his chairmanship of the Democratic National Committee. (Courtesy of Mr. August Belmont)

pected, the new 29-member group quickly elected him chairman.

It has been assumed that the Wall Street banker gained the position of chief party fund raiser primarily on the strength of his financial standing. George F. Milton, Douglas' foremost biographer, guessed that by selecting Belmont "the Committee hoped he could smite the Manhattan rock and cause campaign funds to flow." But Milton simplified a highly important political decision. Belmont, in the nine months he had worked for Douglas, had gained the respect of many seasoned politicians for his organizing ability, his immense energy, his unswerving loyalty to the Douglas standard, and his efforts to diminish intraparty friction. Thus, for a variety of solid reasons, August Belmont became a "natural" for the national chairmanship.[17]

The new Democratic National Committee met at Washington on June 25 to discuss campaign plans. Its first task was to name another running mate for Douglas. Senator Fitzpatrick had allowed Slidell and other administration spokesmen to persuade him to yield his place on the Douglas ticket. Some committee members put forth the name of Georgia's Congressman Stephens, but Belmont opposed him. Instead, the new national chairman, backed by Douglas, succeeded in obtaining a majority endorsement of another experienced Georgian, former Governor Herschel Vespasian Johnson, who immediately accepted. Ironically, Johnson had told friends at the opening day of the Baltimore session that he personally preferred to drop Douglas in favor of Stephens.[18]

With the ticket settled, Belmont next tackled the job most vitally linked to a Douglas electoral victory. Money must be

[17] Milton, *Eve of Conflict*, 481; Nichols, *Disruption of American Democracy*, 334–35. Incidentally, President Buchanan characterized Belmont's selection as a major political blunder. "A man of the first consideration ought to have been selected . . . ; and, above all, he ought not to have been one of those who broke up the National Convention at Charleston." Buchanan to John B. Blake, Dec. 31, 1863, in Moore, ed., *Works of Buchanan*, XI, 353.

[18] *Official Proceedings of the Democratic National Convention*, 184–88; *New York World*, July 5, 1868; Herschel V. Johnson to Alexander H. Stephens, June 19, 1860, Herschel Vespasian Johnson Papers, Duke University.

raised to finance a propaganda and publicity campaign on the national, state, and local levels. At the outset, Belmont adhered to a common practice of his predecessors, that of calling upon the Democrats of each Congressional district to furnish the national committee with $100 for the canvass. A check a month later, however, revealed "not a single cent" of the anticipated $23,700 had been collected.

Belmont then concentrated on New York City and initiated a fund drive there. He established an impressive roster of prominent Democratic names for a pro-Douglas finance committee, launched with his own $1,000 donation, and waited for the "sinews of war" to arrive. Five weeks later a shocked national chairman discovered that nothing had been collected since his contribution. Belmont then made "a most *urgent personal* appeal" to wealthy businessmen, such as George Law and William H. Aspinwall, who had advocated Douglas' candidacy before Charleston. But Law "positively declined," and Aspinwall and the others "kept aloof." Things appeared gloomy, with no sign of improvement in sight.[19]

The beleaguered Belmont discovered that campaign funds raised in New York City were expected to be spent elsewhere, and he soon felt out-of-state repercussions from Gotham's famine. Ephraim K. Smart, the Douglas candidate for governor in Maine's September state election, requested both money and speakers to aid his cause. Belmont sadly informed him through Maine's national committeeman, Sylvanus R. Lyman, that the first commodity was simply not available, that the second was very scarce, and that Douglas, in fact, might not make a scheduled trip to the state. Smart, on hearing the deplorable news, "felt as if I could cry."

Henry H. Sibley, Minnesota's national committeeman, complained that though most Democrats and many Republicans in

[19] Belmont to Douglas, July 28, 1860, Miles Taylor to Douglas, July 29, 1860, Douglas Papers, Univ. of Chicago; Milton, *Eve of Conflict*, 488–89; Nevins, *Emergence of Lincoln*, II, 279, 292; Foner, *Business & Slavery*, 175; Belmont to George H. Thacher, July 27, 1860, Simon Gratz Collection, Historical Society of Pennsylvania.

his state favored Douglas' election, money was "absolutely necessary" to translate their support into votes on Election Day. "The people are very poor. Many voters living at a distance from the polls must be transferred thither by teams, and a thousand other *legitimate* expenses must be defrayed." All this was not helped, Sibley continued, by the "vast government patronage" in Minnesota which was being manipulated to stop Douglas. Belmont could not spare any national committee funds for Minnesota. Weeks later Sibley renewed his plea for "pecuniary assistance," as did his state's Central Democratic Executive Committee. As little as $10,000, Sibley swore, could bring Minnesota's four electoral votes into the Douglas column on Election Day. Belmont's reply was frank. Certainly every electoral vote was vitally important, but "it does not seem likely" that the national committee could collect in the entire nation "the $10,000 you require [for Minnesota alone]." Belmont did, however, send copies of the German-language Douglas biography he had prepared and financed, and referred Sibley to Louisiana Congressman Miles Taylor in Washington.[20]

Taylor, who had come to the capital late in July to take charge of the Douglas Congressional Campaign Committee, suffered a rude jolt himself and was in no position to offer succor. Upon arriving, he learned the dismal news that the "sinews of war, money, is absolutely wanting." Taylor wrote immediately to Belmont. He reminded the chairman that the national committee was responsible for much more important matters than the distribution of campaign documents, that it was "specifically charged with providing funds for the prosecution of the campaign," and he requested a quick shipment of party money to the nation's capital. Belmont's reply was terse. The only funds in the national committee's account were its chairman's own $1,000, and if the other committee members wouldn't assist Belmont's fund-raising effort, "the whole machinery has to stop."

[20] Smart to Douglas, July 26, 1860, Sibley to Douglas, July 16, 1860, Douglas Papers, Univ. of Chicago; Belmont to Sibley, Sept. 11, 1860, Henry Hastings Sibley Papers, Minnesota Historical Society; Milton, *Eve of Conflict,* 489.

Taylor refused to believe that, with the display of enthusiasm for the Douglas candidacy around the nation, the national committee could not easily finance a presidential campaign. He dashed off an angry letter to Douglas, accusing Belmont of "want of attachment" to the Douglas cause and of gross inefficiency, and even ventured so far as to hint of subversive intriguing between the national chairman and the Buchanan-Slidell crowd. "It will not do to have our chances of success . . . diminished by [Belmont's] . . . incapacity, inefficiency, or worse." Such, in Taylor's mind, was the "true state of this case," and he had already requested Horace F. Clarke, an intimate New York friend, to create a real Douglas campaign committee there, one "which is both competent and willing to perform what Mr. Belmont and his committee is either *unable* or *unwilling* to perform." [21]

Taylor's blistering attack failed to convince Douglas of Belmont's disloyalty. The nominee had just received a Belmont letter which, though pessimistic, had the ring of truth. The New Yorker had investigated "big business" apathy and penury. Prosperous merchants, hitherto heavy Democratic donors, were "afraid to lose their Southern customers by siding with us. . . . If we could only demonstrate to all these lukewarm and selfish moneybags that we have a strong possibility to carry the State of New York," the necessary funds would be forthcoming.[22]

Belmont knew he must find a way out of this impasse. He called a meeting of thirty-one leading New York Softs at his Fifth Avenue home to discuss methods "to save New York from the Republicans and to save the Union from the calamities of the election of Lincoln." Seymour, Richmond, Tilden, Corning, "Honest John" Kelly, Peter Cagger, and William B. and John J. Astor participated in the conference and heard Bel-

[21] Taylor to Douglas, July 29, 1860, Douglas Papers, Univ. of Chicago.
[22] Belmont to Douglas, July 28, 1860, Douglas Papers, Univ. of Chicago. Apparently the merchants, along with other observers of the political scene, were guessing that the normal Democratic vote in New York would be divided among Douglas, Breckinridge, and Bell, thus presenting the state's electoral votes to Lincoln on a golden platter. See, for example, Horatio Seymour to Samuel L. M. Barlow, July 26, 1860, Barlow Papers.

mont's presentation. New York State must be the battleground of the whole campaign; if the anti-Republicans could win all the southern states plus New York's thirty-five electoral votes, Lincoln would be denied an Electoral College majority, and the struggle would be thrown into the House of Representatives. Why not combine the Empire State's three anti-Republican slates and run instead a single "Union" electoral ticket in November? If the "Union" proved successful, each of the three coalition candidates could be awarded a proportion of the state's electoral votes, while Lincoln would be completely shut out. Nearly everyone present believed it worth a try, and some volunteered to broach the subject to the New York Hards.

Belmont, armed with the group's support, mounted a two-pronged attack to force the hands of the Bell and Breckinridge managers. On one front he began a series of personal negotiations with them. On another he mobilized several leading members of his Democratic Vigilant Association under a new name, the Volunteer Democratic Association of New York, and led them to issue a warning to the Douglas, Bell, and Breckinridge camps: "A union of the anti-Republicans must be effected before money can be obtained in New York City," and that "such a union once effected, the aid will not be wanting." [23]

In the midst of these financial concerns, Miles Taylor heard from his friend Clarke about the "difficulties" his would-be Democratic fund raisers faced in New York City. Taylor traveled to New York and talked to Belmont about the problem. After becoming "personally acquainted" with the chairman's efforts, he informed Douglas: "I did him [Belmont] a great injustice by my suspicions, and that I now believe him to be as sincere in the maintenance of the good cause as I am myself."

Taylor's benediction, pleasing as it was, produced nothing more tangible than all Belmont's efforts. The national chairman's earlier warning had not attracted contributions from

[23] Belmont to Tilden, Aug. 7(?) 1860, Samuel Jones Tilden Papers, New York Public Library; Flick, *Tilden*, 120; *New York Tribune*, Aug. 8, 15, 1860; *New York Herald*, Aug. 18, 1860; Nichols, *Disruption of American Democracy*, 347.

New York's moneyed men who, he was convinced, were either "in active sympathy with the Breckinridge movement" or stood aside from the contest. Consequently, Belmont continually dipped into his own pocket to print and circulate political pamphlets. He also paid the traveling expenses of campaign speakers to tour New York State, so as to "correct the false impressions" produced on voters' minds by hostile administration organs.[24]

Belmont's desperation made him propose to Douglas that he take the stump in his own behalf and speak around the country on the vital issues of the day. "I know that my suggestion . . . is not in accordance with what has hitherto been customary in presidential campaigns," but the reckless conduct of Buchanan, Slidell, and company rendered "exceptional exertions on our side necessary." Douglas was initially skeptical about breaking with the long tradition, but Belmont's compelling reasons, along with Douglas' love of a good fight and a good speech, won the senator over. For the next month people in New York and New England witnessed the unusual spectacle of a man actively requesting their votes for the highest office in the land.[25]

Even with Douglas' help, Belmont was not too sanguine about the New England prospect. He recalled unhappily having raised thousands of dollars for the March state elections in New Hampshire and Connecticut after assurances from top Democrats there that the money would "redeem" those states; the Republicans swept them both. In Rhode Island, Governor William Sprague, just elected on a Unionist ticket, hesitated to express sympathy for Douglas. As for Massachusetts, men like Caleb Cushing, Attorney General under President Pierce, and Benjamin F. Butler, a rising state politician, had joined with the "treacherous seceders" at Charleston and Baltimore.

The September state elections in Maine posed especially per-

[24] Taylor to Douglas, Aug. 13, 1860, Douglas Papers, Univ. of Chicago; Belmont to Sibley, Sept. 11, 1860, Sibley Papers; Belmont to George P. Morris, Oct. 18, 1860, New York State Library MS5393.

[25] Belmont to Douglas, July 28, 1860, Douglas Papers, Univ. of Chicago; Milton, *Eve of Conflict*, 490–96.

plexing questions for the Douglas organization. The Democratic State Committee, comprised mostly of party hacks,
looked to others to perform the burdensome chores of fund-
raising, document distribution, and campaign speeches. Besides,
Lincoln's running mate, Maine Senator Hannibal Hamlin, still
retained the statewide popularity he had known in his earlier
Democratic phase. For this reason, a Democratic victory there
two months before the November Election Day would provide
a tremendous psychological boost for the party and render pecuniary donations less difficult to extract. Miles Taylor frankly
admitted that *"everything* depends upon the election in
Maine." [26]

A Maine delegation visited Newport, Rhode Island, where
Belmont maintained a summer home, and got a commitment
from the national chairman to send both dollars and Douglas
there in a concentrated effort to put over the state ticket in
September. Belmont summoned the entire national committee to
meet him in New York City, but only two other members,
William N. Converse of Connecticut and Richard J. Haldeman
of Pennsylvania, showed up on August 9. Disgusted, the national chairman again appealed to his richest pro-Douglas
friends in New York, who listened patiently to the Maine proposition and finally consented to supply half the necessary funds
if New England Democrats would raise the balance. The plan
succeeded, but only because Belmont contributed most of the
New England portion. Douglas spoke in Bangor, Augusta, and
Portland, but Maine went the way of her sister states. Belmont
swore it would be years before he trusted "eastern gentlemen"
from New England again.[27]

These results pressed the national chairman to step up negotiations with the Bell and Breckinridge managers in other north-

[26] Belmont to Douglas, July 28, 1860, Taylor to Douglas, Aug. 13, 1860,
Douglas Papers, Univ. of Chicago.

[27] Ephraim K. Smart to Douglas, July 26, Aug. 4, 1860, Frederick O.
Prince to Douglas, Aug. 10, 1860, Sylvanus R. Lyman to Douglas, Aug.
11, 1860, Edmund W. Flagg to Douglas, Aug. 11, 1860, Douglas Papers, Univ.
of Chicago; Belmont to Erastus Corning, Sept. 13, 1860, Gratz Collection;
Milton, *Eve of Conflict*, 489–90.

ern states. In New York they reached an agreement under which the Empire State's thirty-five electors were apportioned as follows: Douglas 18, Bell 10, and Breckinridge 7. A Committee of Fifteen was set up to coordinate this coalition, and Belmont pledged $2,500 to its expenses. In New Jersey they established a joint slate though Douglas objected that "fusion with seceders merely added dishonor to defeat." Pennsylvania followed suit, but the strong Buchanan faction there secured a majority of the electors for Breckinridge.[28]

Belmont's great fear in the South was not Lincoln, whose following in the slaveholding states ranged from negligible to nonexistent, but Breckinridge. All signs indicated that Douglas and Bell, each campaigning as "Unionists," would divide the pro-Union vote and allow the Vice President, who also called himself a "Unionist," to carry most of that region. Douglas put Belmont in touch with an old Kentucky friend, journalist Blanton Duncan, who served as Bell's national chairman. The two men undertook to join Douglas and Bell electors on a single ticket in as many southern states as possible. To this end, Belmont requested Herschel Johnson "to effect a fusion in your state [Georgia] as well as in Alabama, Louisiana, Mississippi and North Carolina between our friends and the Bell men." [29]

Belmont also found time to organize several huge rallies of fusion Democrats at home. When Douglas came to New York City in September, accompanied by his running mate, "a monster mass meeting" honored them at Jones' Wood, a park in the East Sixties. Before the speeches, a hungry crowd estimated at twenty-five thousand was treated to roast steer, sheep, calves, and pigs, "so that every taste could be satisfied," and five hundred barrels of beer were provided to wash it all down. Belmont presided over this gala barbecue and, in a speech whose

28 New York Herald, Sept. 6–26, 1860; Brummer, Political History of New York State, 81–86; Milton, Eve of Conflict, 494; Belmont to Tilden, Oct. 5, 1860, Tilden Papers; Foner, Business & Slavery, 124.

29 Duncan to Douglas, Aug. 14, 1860, Douglas Papers, Univ. of Chicago; Belmont to Duncan, Aug. 19, 1860, John Bell Papers, Library of Congress; Belmont to Johnson, Aug. (?), 1860, in Percy S. Flippin, Herschel V. Johnson of Georgia: State Rights Unionist (Richmond, 1931), 140–41.

contents he would continually echo, warned that "our great republic" faced "the horrors of disunion and anarchy."[30] Five days later the national chairman spoke from a Cooper Institute platform on which sat "our richest bankers, largest merchants, and most eminent citizens" and predicted to the assemblage that Republican success would be detrimental to national peace and prosperity. Belmont reiterated these admonitions at subsequent rallies in October and right up to Election Day. He directed his fire at the "sectional" party behind Lincoln, "holding principles incompatible with the sacred obligations of the Constitution and arrayed in open and unrelenting hostility against the property and the institutions of the fairest portions of our common country."[31]

Belmont's unremitting efforts in behalf of his party and his total identification with the Douglas candidacy were a mixed blessing to his fellow partisans. His elevation in 1860 to the highest councils of the Democratic Party carried with it a serious drawback, for it again exposed his old vulnerability to partisan slanders. Republican newspapers printed highly exaggerated figures purporting to be Belmont's campaign contributions and then maliciously insinuated the source. Douglas' chairman, so the story went, represented the Rothschilds, those international Jewish bankers who manipulated European monarchs and governments and now "want to elect Douglas President, so as to control him."[32]

The "Douglas National Chairman," as opposition spokesmen dubbed Belmont, approached Election Day with a pessimism that belied his public pronouncements. The insurmountable difficulty of raising campaign funds prevented him from enter-

[30] A newspaper reporter depicted a famished, ill-mannered mob "pulling and hauling at greasy bones and gravy-soaked fibre . . . , tossing crackers, bread and meat hither and thither." *New York Times*, Sept. 13, 1860. For the text of Belmont's speech, see August Belmont, *A Few Letters and Speeches of the Late Civil War* (New York, 1870), 97.

[31] *New York Herald*, Sept. 18, Oct. 9, Nov. 3, 5, 1860; George N. Sanders to Douglas, Oct. 18, 1860, Douglas Papers, Univ. of Chicago; Belmont, *Letters and Speeches of Late Civil War*, 98–99.

[32] Reinhard H. Luthin, *The Real Abraham Lincoln* (Englewood Cliffs, N.J., 1960), 235; Milton, *Eve of Conflict*, 496.

taining serious thoughts about a Douglas majority in the Electoral College. His goal to run fusion slates was realized in only five states—New York, New Jersey, Pennsylvania, Rhode Island, and Texas. The most Belmont allowed himself to hope for was an election where no candidate received an electoral majority, throwing the entire result into the House of Representatives where, each state having one vote, Douglas' chances appeared more promising.

What stung Belmont was the magnitude of the senator's defeat in the Electoral College on November 6. Though Douglas received 29.5 percent of the popular vote (compared to Lincoln's 39.8 percent), he received only 12 out of 303 electoral votes. He won all of Missouri's 9 electoral votes. Only in New Jersey was a fusion slate victorious, and Douglas picked up 3 additional electors there. Lincoln won easily in New York, Pennsylvania, and Rhode Island, and Breckinridge scored a three-to-one majority over the Douglas-Bell ticket in Texas.

There is no denying that the Douglas Democrats were completely routed in the 1860 elections, and the superficial analyst will, by extension, lay much of the blame on national chairman Belmont. But this conclusion does not stand up statistically. If Belmont had been able to carry out fully his fusion plan of Douglas-Breckinridge-Bell tickets in the North and Douglas-Bell slates in the slaveholding and border states, the fusionists, in addition to Missouri and New Jersey, would have gained electoral votes in Virginia, Maryland, Georgia, Kentucky, Tennessee, Louisiana, California, and Oregon. Lincoln would have still maintained his majority in the Electoral College, but the Democratic defeat would not have been as disastrous as it appeared.

The "lame duck" session of the Thirty-Sixth Congress assembled on December 3, 1860, and the principal subject of discussion was a peaceful solution to the impending crisis. Belmont's attention focused on the Senate, where Douglas and John J. Crittenden, a seventy-three-year-old Kentucky Unionist, led the fight to establish machinery for a sectional compromise. At first, Douglas, despite a plan of his own, supported the older statesman's proposal, which hoped to "settle" the status of slavery in the territories by extending the old Missouri Compromise line westward to California. But Crittenden's idea failed to win majority approval in the special Senate Committee of Thirteen. Belmont "warmly commended" Crittenden for his "noble efforts" and "statesmanlike stand," though he feared that "no human power can stay the evil" of disunion. Douglas then called for constitutional sanction of his favorite "Popular Sovereignty" scheme, which would prohibit Congressional legislation for the territories but would protect "legitimate" southern rights.

Douglas indicated that he still had confidence in Belmont's political acumen by asking his advice on the measure:

Let me hear from you & your views on my propositions. . . . I am ready to make any reasonable sacrifice of party tenets to save the country. . . . However, I can never recognize or acquiesce in the doctrine that any state can secede & separate from us without consent.

Belmont read each of Douglas' resolutions carefully and assured him that they met with his

entire approval. The South could not ask for more & the dominant party of the North ought certainly to acquiesce in a plan of settlement, which in my opinion would not add a foot of slave territory to the Union.[33]

Before Belmont had sent off this answer, he received word that the Committee of Thirteen had rejected Douglas' resolutions as well. Because of the committee's decision, he begged the senator's indulgence in behalf of one suggestion, "dictated only by my warm attachment to you." Crittenden's desire to extend the Missouri Compromise line to California still loomed as the most feasible solution, and Belmont had "good reason to know that the conservative portion of the Republican leaders" favored it. But the Lincoln and Seward men in Congress would not accept the Missouri line for future territorial acquisitions, as

[33] Douglas to Belmont, Dec. 25, 1860, in Johannsen, ed., *Letters of Stephen A. Douglas*, 505; Belmont to Crittenden, Dec. 26, 1860, in Ann Mary Butler Breckenridge Coleman, ed., *The Life of John J. Crittenden, With Selections from His Correspondence and Speeches* (2 vols., Philadelphia, 1871), II, 317; Belmont to Douglas, Dec. 26, 1860, Douglas Papers, Univ. of Chicago.

"they say this would be holding out a premium for filibustering against Mexico & Cuba" in order to make new slave states. "If you could hit upon some plan of compromise by which to get over this difficulty, there might be some hope to save the country." A new Committee of Fourteen, formed early in January, 1861, with Crittenden as chairman, presented a plan paralleling Belmont's suggestions. It modified Crittenden's proposal by rendering future acquisitions of new territory almost impossible, while defining more clearly the probable boundaries of future slave states south of the "extended" Missouri line. This plan was also voted down. Douglas, convinced that the Republican Party favored southern secession to facilitate Senate approval of Lincoln's patronage appointments, saw further gestures as futile. To Belmont, the ship of state was sinking fast.[34]

Not content to supply advice and encouragement to the players on the Congressional stage, Belmont simultaneously engaged in a feverish postelection correspondence. His letters to leading southern Unionists and businessmen alternated between practical warnings against secession and impractical plans for compromise. The Democratic Party, and indeed the Union, he told everyone to whom he wrote, now stood on the precipice of utter disaster and ruin, and only staunch patriotism and total commitment to the idea of Union would save them. As the storm of secession neared, he repeatedly asked his correspondents: What went wrong? How could the situation be rectified? Often he answered the queries himself. The Democrats lost the White House because the country at large was disgusted with Buchanan's "misrule" and with the "disgraceful corruption" of his administration. "Many thousands of independent, conservative citizens" judged both northern and southern Democrats responsible for the President's misdeeds. Given this ardent desire for change, any nomination made at Charleston would have encountered rough sledding. To make matters

34 Belmont to Douglas, Dec. 31, 1860, Douglas Papers, Univ. of Chicago; Nichols, *Disruption of American Democracy*, 441; David Lindsey, *"Sunset" Cox: Irrepressible Democrat* (Detroit, 1959), 45; Albert D. Kirwan, *John J. Crittenden: The Struggle for the Union* (Lexington, Ky., 1962), 479; Milton, *Eve of Conflict*, 523–32.

worse, the seceding southern fire-eaters selfishly committed suicide to spite their party.

The derision that Belmont had always directed at the "abolitionist Republicans" he now leveled at the hotheads of the South. He chastised them for refusing to fight their constitutional battle within the framework of the Union and for betraying their northern Democratic colleagues. Is it manly, he asked, to withdraw from the contest when it becomes most fierce? Surely the southerners' reputation for generosity, chivalry, and character will not allow an abandonment of their northern defenders? Lincoln may enter the White House in March, 1861, but Democrats will still control the Senate and the Supreme Court. Will the South now forfeit those fields to the enemy as well? In letter after letter, Belmont utilized his talent for persuasion and flattery, concluding that southern and northern men of "conservative" spirit must unite against the "fanatical abolitionists of slavery" on the one hand and the "selfish and short-sighted abolitionists of the Union" on the other. He rejected the constitutionality or feasibility of secession. The very idea of two separate confederacies living side by side in peace and prosperity was really "too preposterous to be entertained" by any sensible man with a knowledge of history. "*Secession*," he warned, "*means civil war.*" As for Mayor Fernando Wood's threat to secede from New York State in the event of federal coercion toward the South, thus creating an independent city-state, Belmont had only scorn. What the naturalized financier wished for his young children was not the "gilded prospects of New York merchant princes [but] the more enviable title of American citizens."

Belmont was convinced that concessions could be made to mollify what he considered justifiable southern grievances. Why not sound the clarion call for a grand assembly of all the states to grant "the guarantees which the South has a right to demand?" The North must promise not to interfere with the South's "peculiar institution," and in return for such soothing syrup the would-be secessionists might attempt to improve sectional relations. Of course, the northern states would also have to repeal their personal liberty laws, which were so insulting to conservative, pro-Constitution, Union lovers. In his official capacity as Democratic National Committee chairman, Belmont wrote to every southern governor, urging each to refrain from any course which "must end in disaster for the South." He also prodded Herschel Johnson, John Forsyth and John C. Bradley of Alabama, and other Douglas Democrats and Unionists to grasp the reins of leadership in their communities and turn back the "demagogues."[35]

But the "demagogues" prevailed. South Carolina seceded on December 20, 1860, and the other six deep southern states followed suit in January and February. With such a desperate situation confronting the country, Belmont even tried to influence top opposition leaders in New York like Seward and Thurlow Weed. Seward was now the foremost Republican in Congress, destined to head the State Department in the incoming administration. Weed, leader of the New York Whig organization for over two decades, was an intimate friend and adviser of both Seward and Lincoln. Belmont's approach to Seward took the form of a warning: "Without wishing for a moment to defend the revolutionary proceedings" of the cotton states, Belmont insisted that only compromise based on the Crittenden resolutions would prevent the Upper South from following its sister states out of the Union. He reminded Seward of the senator's own recent statement: "Republicanism is subordinate to the Union, as everything else is & ought to be." Weed, ever scornful of abolitionists and other "extremists," had publicly asked for greater popular understanding of the southern dilemma. Belmont wrote him a grateful letter of appreciation, notwithstanding "I have fought to the last against the great party of which you have proved so formidable a leader."[36]

In addition to his unofficial role as chief party correspondent,

35 Belmont to John Forsyth, Nov. 22, 1860, Belmont to Herschel V. Johnson, Nov. 22, 1860, Belmont to Julius Izard Pringle, Nov. 26, 1860, Belmont to John C. Bradley, Nov. 28, 1860, Belmont to William Marten, Nov. 30, 1860, in Belmont, *Letters, Speeches and Addresses*, 23–29.

36 Belmont to Seward, Jan. 17, 1861, Belmont to Weed, Dec. 19, 1860, in Belmont, *Letters and Speeches of Late Civil War*, 18, 30–31.

the indefatigable Belmont took every chance for more direct action. He sponsored and participated in scores of meetings and rallies in New York City designed to halt the deepening political chaos. In personal and joint appeals, he called for reason, moderation, and justice. He attended informal assemblies where leading merchants and bankers of differing political persuasions were "unanimous in their voice for reconciliation." He signed "very strong" memorials, along with "leading men of both parties," to be sent to Congress as an indication of northern desire for reunion.

Belmont also printed and mailed out, at his own expense, hundreds of copies of John P. Kennedy's Unionist pamphlet, "The Border States," in which Fillmore's Navy Secretary "evinced great statesmanship and elevation of thought" in a conciliatory appeal to the South. When the New York State Democratic Committee announced an Albany "peace" convention, Belmont attended as the chairman of the New York City delegation, drafted a set of resolutions which warned against coercion of the southern states, and sent Douglas fifty copies to circulate "among your friends in & out of Congress." [37]

Belmont joined an impressive array of New York dignitaries in inviting the Bostonian Edward Everett, Whig statesman, educator, and lecturer, to deliver his famous oration, "George Washington," which, "at the present period in our history," might do the local citizenry some good. For a while Belmont was talked of as a possible New York delegate to the February 4 "Peace Convention," called by Virginia to "adjust the present, unhappy controversies." Although Belmont ardently supported the idea of such a meeting—referred to sarcastically as the "Old

[37] Nichols, *Disruption of American Democracy*, 419; Brummer, *Political History of New York State*, 112–23; Flick, *Tilden*, 130; *New York Times*, Dec. 17, 19, 1860; Belmont to William Sprague, Dec. 6, 13, 19, 1860, Belmont to John Forsyth, Dec. 19, 1860, in Belmont, *Letters, Speeches and Addresses*, 30–39; Belmont to Herschel V. Johnson, Dec. 11, 1860, Johnson Papers; Belmont to Johnson, Dec. 30, 1860, Belmont to Douglas, Feb. 11, 1861, Douglas Papers, Univ. of Chicago; Robert G. Gunderson, *Old Gentlemen's Convention: The Washington Peace Conference of 1861* (Madison, Wisc., 1961), 39; Foner, *Business & Slavery*, 237–38, 288–89.

Gentlemen's Convention"—he was passed over in the end.[38]

In February, Representative John Cochrane, a lame-duck Democrat from New York, introduced a bill authorizing federal seizure of all vessels entering and sailing from ports in the seceded states. Belmont protested vigorously to Douglas against the measure, which he feared would initiate a policy of coercion, alienate Virginia and the border states from the Union, and bring on war. "I hope you will use your powerful exertions in order to defeat it." Douglas' view paralleled Belmont's, and he helped kill the bill in committee.[39]

Belmont's peace activities came to a rude halt with the fall of Fort Sumter, South Carolina, in April, 1861. His worst fears were confirmed as Lincoln's call for 75,000 volunteers to quell the "insurrection" touched off the secession of Virginia, North Carolina, Arkansas, and Tennessee. There was time enough for Belmont to return to active politicking. Once war was declared and Fort Sumter's fall replaced such issues as slavery, states' rights, and nullification with the overriding one of national existence, he uncompromisingly backed a vigorous and relentless prosecution of the military effort. Belmont did not hesitate to lend his name and prestige to a variety of Union causes. On April 19, 1861, Belmont occupied a conspicuous seat on the platform while a New York Chamber of Commerce meeting roared its approval of President Lincoln's firm response to the

38 Belmont, et al., to Edward Everett, Jan. 25, 1861, Edward Everett Papers, Massachusetts Historical Society; *New York Tribune*, Jan. 30, 1861; *New York Herald*, Feb. 2, 1861. Only twenty-one of the thirty-three states sent delegates to the convention, which failed to accomplish its purposes. Gunderson, *Old Gentlemen's Convention*, is the standard work on the subject.

39 Belmont to Douglas, Feb. 11, 1861, Douglas Papers, Univ. of Chicago. The banker even lent his name to the organizing committee of an "American Society for Promoting National Unity," which at one point collected funds so that a New York rabbi's sermon finding slavery sanctioned in the Old Testament could be published and widely disseminated. The society constituted a rather naive attempt by "conservative" New York City businessmen to preserve peace by calling for the ouster of politicians and agitators from power and a nationwide popular referendum on war or peace. Foner, *Business & Slavery*, 273–74; *New York Journal of Commerce*, Jan. 12, 1861; Morris U. Schappes, ed., *A Documentary History of the Jews in the United States, 1654–1875* (New York, 1950), 683.

fall of Fort Sumter. Later that day, following a "Public Call" he had signed along with leading citizens like George Bancroft, Moses Taylor, James Gallatin, and Alexander T. Stewart, he joined in a mass meeting in Union Square at which concrete plans were formulated for the city's contributions to the Union cause, both in manpower and in money.

Belmont provided former Congressman Francis P. Blair, Jr., the Missouri Unionist and son of one of President Jackson's closest advisers, with funds and German-language material to assist him in equipping a loyal regiment which would be influential in keeping Missouri and other border states within the Union. Belmont's proudest wartime accomplishment was his leading part in raising and fitting out the first German-American regiment in the Union Army. On May 15, 1861, just before the entire outfit departed for the front, Belmont presented it with military flags and banners and in a rousing speech exhorted the soldiers to prove by deeds their loyalty to their adopted land.[40]

On June 3, 1861, Belmont's energies were forcibly pulled back into the political sector by still another calamitous event. The forty-seven-year-old Douglas suddenly succumbed to an "unidentifiable" malady. His death stunned Belmont. For the second time in his political career he found himself without a leader to serve, without a focus for his ambitions and ideas. Yet both events—the disillusioning break with Buchanan and the untimely death of Douglas—were the springboards that catapulted Belmont to the top of the party structure. His personal loss led, ironically, straight to his personal advancement.

The titular leader of the Democrats had died at a time when the party itself was gravely ill. No political next-of-kin ap-

---

[40] *New York Times*, April 20, 1861; *New York Herald*, April 21, 1861; Sandburg, *Lincoln: War Years*, I, 217–18; Belmont, *Letters and Speeches of Late Civil War*, 100. This First New York Regiment of Rifles, known as the "Blenker" regiment, after Colonel Louis Blenker, an exiled "Forty-eighter" from Germany, served with distinction in the early campaigns. The regiment received special commendation for covering the Federal retreat at the first Bull Run fiasco and earned Blenker a brigadier general's star. Perry Belmont, *An American Democrat*, 76–77.

peared to succeed him, and most of the veteran Democrats in Congress—southerners—had seceded with their states. What remained of the party in both chambers on Capitol Hill was further decimated by a division into prowar (Union) and antiwar ("Copperhead") factions. Altogether, there were never more than seventy-five Democrats in the House and ten in the Senate during the Civil War period, none of them outstanding personalities. Nor were there more than a handful of Democratic governors in this time.

Belmont, now forty-seven years old, picked up the baton of Democratic national leadership and sought to create some semblance of order out of the party's postelection disaster and postsecession chaos. He had already served the party for a decade. He knew every important member, and by virtue of his position he stood as the chief executive officer of the existing and continuing party organization. Perhaps, as some charged, the Wall Street banker moved into the commanding position for his own personal aggrandizement. But regardless of what motivated Belmont, few northern Democrats challenged his takeover of the party's reins.[41] Little could Belmont suspect that this assumption of real power for the first time in his political career would coincide, as he later recalled, with "the most disastrous epoch in the annals of the Democatic Party." [42]

[41] Nichols, *Disruption of American Democracy*, 511. A disillusioned former President Buchanan grumbled privately: "What can be expected from a party at the head of which is a speculating German Jew?" Buchanan to John B. Blake, Dec. 31, 1863, in Moore, ed., *Works of Buchanan*, XI, 353.

[42] Belmont to Henry D. McHenry, April 27, 1885, Eleanor Robson Belmont Papers, Columbia University.

7

Serving the Union

THE WAR YEARS were painful ones for Belmont. An activist by nature, he would have chafed at being on the losing side politically in any event. Given the extraordinary fact of a country at war with itself, his chances for political activity were temporarily circumscribed far beyond the traditional (and sometimes thankless) tasks of a loyal opposition leader. Though he contributed funds and attended rallies for the war effort, these were essentially collective gestures; they did not fulfill either Belmont's yen for action or his vision of his own uniqueness. Unfortunately, a military role was also closed to the exercise of Belmont's energies. In spite of his devotion to the Union, his lameness—dating from the 1841 duel—incapacitated him for the armed services.[1]

Other opportunities did exist to serve the Union. The North had two overriding concerns apart from the military sphere: to prevent European recognition of the Confederacy and to raise money through the marketing of securities at home and abroad. These goals, the one diplomatic, the other financial, touched upon areas of Belmont's particular competence. He had never been afflicted with false modesty, but in this case confidence in his own usefulness was justified. He had behind him the solid, if unspectacular, accomplishments of his years as official United States emissary at The Hague, his proven financial acumen as a

---

[1] Belmont was especially chagrined to see prewar Democrats like John A. Dix and Daniel E. Sickles of New York and Benjamin F. Butler of Massachusetts awarded generalships in the Union Army, for they no longer needed to prove their loyalty.

leading international banker, and a host of highly placed foreign contacts accruing from both these positions.

The immediate diplomatic danger was that the South might persuade Great Britain and France, natural commercial partners of the predominantly agricultural Confederacy, to break any attempted Union Navy blockade and compel Lincoln to come to terms. With this threat as a spur, Belmont initiated a massive foreign letter writing campaign. He had several purposes in mind: to sound out the depth of foreign sentiment toward recognition and to provide cogent arguments against such a course. At times the dense thicket of his rhetoric all but obscured the light of his reasoning. Yet, his sincerity overcame his flowery prose, and he became an eloquent proselytizer of the Union's goals and a convincing plaintiff of the Union's grievances.

Belmont launched his literary attack on the Confederacy within weeks of Fort Sumter's fall. On May 6, 1861, British Foreign Secretary Lord John Russell declared in Parliament his intentions to treat Confederate privateers operating against the Union blockade as "belligerents." Belmont interpreted this as "an initiatory step" by the Palmerston government toward recognizing the Confederacy, and retaliated with an angry, impassioned, and lengthy letter to his London banking associate, Baron Lionel Nathan de Rothschild, M.P., who, together with his intimate friend Russell, represented the City of London in the House of Commons. Did Lord John realize the possible consequences of his May 6 declaration? Suppose Ireland or Scotland should rebel against the Crown, or Canada attempt to dissolve her allegiance to the mother country? Would the British acknowledge American accordance of "belligerent rights" to those privateers fitted out by Irish, Scottish, or Canadian rebels? In a more soothing manner, Belmont conceded to his British correspondent that the United States "would never assume such an unfriendly position" to one of its "allies." But did it not have a right to expect the same treatment in return?

The British cabinet should be apprised on still another point. Loyal Americans hoped for English sympathy in the struggle before them. After all, British statesmen and newspapers had heretofore assumed a "most violent and uncompromising stand" against slavery. Did not Sir Lionel deem it "more than strange to see the British Government now give its moral countenance" to slavery? Confederate Vice President Alexander H. Stephens had recently declared slavery to be the basis of his government's fundamental strength, and who could doubt that this would "most probably require the reopening of the international Slave trade?" Did the Baron's good friend, Lord John, not comprehend that any British move toward strengthening the Confederates meant Her Majesty's Government's "consent to the nefarious traffic in human flesh?"

Belmont was also appalled by the Foreign Secretary's analogy between the Greek independence struggle four decades earlier and the southern rebellion. Because England had then recognized Greece as a belligerent, must the South also be accorded such recognition? "The simile of Lord John" was as unfortunate as his government's position in the present crisis. Every schoolboy knew that pre-1821 Greece was a "conquered & enslaved province of a semibarbarian Despotism . . . , a Christian people oppressed by fanatical Moslemism," and having the "warm & active sympathy of the whole civilized world on its side." But the southern states were

free & voluntary parties to a compact of Union . . . who cannot point to a single right guaranteed to them under the Constitution which has been violated & the only ground upon which they justify their rebellion is a *fear* that their peculiar institution may *hereafter* be interfered with.

Belmont followed up his argument with comparative statistics contrasting overall Union superiority in manpower, resources, and credit with Confederate "repudiation" of private debts to northern creditors. In closing, he requested the Baron to make one thing unerringly clear to Prime Minister Palmerston as well as to Russell. The whole North, even those who had opposed Lincoln's election in 1860, would stand by the administration to the end. Should those contemporary English leaders who referred to themselves by "grand labels" of "Whigs" and "Liberals" attempt to prolong the fratricidal war and bring down ruin "upon the material interests of the world" they will forever stand condemned before the judgment of history.[2]

But Belmont was never one to work in a vacuum. He sought to bring his private efforts to the administration's attention. Knowing that Thurlow Weed had a direct pipeline to Washington where his old friend and protégé, Seward, now headed the State Department, the banker decided to send Weed a copy of his recent letter to Rothschild, hoping that it would be brought to Seward's notice. Belmont surmised correctly; his enterprise was rewarded with an answer, not from Weed, but from Seward, who had found the letter "very able and interesting." The Secretary gratified Belmont further, saying he had taken "the liberty to submit it to the President who has authorized me to express his own satisfaction with it." Seward went so far as to ask the Democratic chairman's permission to retain a copy, for "it contains some suggestions which may prove useful to me."[3]

Belmont again reacted to Great Britain's "selfish, unwarrantable and unwise policy" several weeks later, when Queen Victoria, acting through Prime Minister Palmerston, proclaimed a strict neutrality toward both sides in the American struggle. He penned another long letter to Baron Rothschild attacking the latest proclamation as inconsistent with the British position during the Carlist Wars of Spain, the Hungarian revolt of 1848–1849, Garibaldi's independence movement in Italy, and the Crimean War. Belmont charged that a strict neutrality policy actually was an anti-Union one, as southern ports were already effectively blockaded.[4]

Encouraged by the administration's reception of his private diplomacy, Belmont sent a copy of this letter straight to Seward

2 Belmont to Baron Lionel Nathan de Rothschild, May 21, 1861, in Belmont, *Letters and Speeches of Late Civil War*, 32–35. This lengthy letter also appears in Schappes, ed., *Documentary History of Jews*, 451–56; and in the Abraham Lincoln Papers, Library of Congress.

3 Seward to Belmont, May 27, 1861, private Belmont collection.

4 Belmont to Lionel de Rothschild, May 28, 1861, William Henry Seward Papers, University of Rochester.

in appreciation of his "favorable considerations" of earlier views. Seward thanked him for a "very interesting and forcible letter," acknowledged its "peculiar value," and requested the banker to continue forwarding his opinions touching on the foreign situation. Belmont complied and sent copies of other germane correspondence. In one such letter to an English diplomat he had befriended at The Hague, Belmont sought to capitalize on a past association in order to disseminate some pro-Union sentiment where it might be most needed—the British Cabinet. This correspondent, known earlier as Sir Ralph Abercromby, 2nd, and now as Lord Dunfermline of Edinburgh, also happened to be brother-in-law to Foreign Secretary Russell. Belmont, remembering Dunfermline's underlying hostility to human slavery, emphasized how "the pro-slavery oligarchy, which had gained control of the Executive and Legislature of the Federal Government" in the Buchanan years, now sought to deceive English public opinion about the true state of their past grievances and present resources. Belmont then proceeded to refute southern "contentions" point by point and, in conclusion, suggested that the British Cabinet might not be aware of the facts. The letter's purpose was realized, as Belmont found out later. Dunfermline believed the "grave and serious questions" raised by his American friend to be of such importance that he forwarded the letter directly to Russell, citing it as an indication of how leading "American Anglophiles" viewed Her Majesty's stand on the Civil War.[5]

Several other letters to Seward condemned the protectionist Morrill Tariff of March, 1861, which adversely affected Manchester, England, cotton manufacturers. Their pressure, Belmont feared, would push the British Cabinet into recognizing the Confederacy. But Seward, even if he so desired, could not convince a tariff-minded Congress that Belmont's apprehensions might contain substance. On one occasion Belmont transmitted

[5] Belmont to Seward, May 29, June 6, 1861, Seward Papers; Seward to Belmont, May 30, 1861, Dunfermline to Belmont, June 21, 1861, private Belmont collection; Belmont to Dunfermline, June 3, 1861, in Belmont, *Letters and Speeches of Late Civil War*, 40–44.

delicate data regarding Franco-American relations to the State Department, at the same time imploring Seward "on no account to mention me as having imparted this information." According to the Rothschild agent in New Orleans, the French consul there was engaged in pro-rebel machinations. Washington promptly followed up this news by instructing the American Minister at Paris, William L. Dayton, to confer with French officials and persuade them to apply the proper remedy.[6]

The financial position of the Union was just as troublesome as the diplomatic. The Panic of 1857 had left the Treasury a legacy of deficits, and the secession crisis only made a bad matter worse. Uncertainty over the country's future clouded the money markets to such a degree that even the prospect of up to 12 percent interest and enticing discounts failed to start a stampede among investors for federal securities. Such a situation called for a strong hand at the Treasury's helm. Instead, for reasons of political expediency, Lincoln chose Senator Salmon P. Chase of Ohio, a lawyer by training who knew little of finance. The outbreak of armed hostilities, while ending doubts about what course the North would pursue, opened a new set of uncertainties. Not only was the Union's need for money multiplied, but, as financiers like Belmont knew, it would be competing with its own dismembered self for the available funds in the foreign markets. Belmont estimated that the South's revenues also were woefully inadequate to finance a major war and that the rebels were "longer on cotton than on capital." The Richmond government, too, would have to resort to Europe.

As a businessman and as a Unionist, Belmont naturally hoped the North would be the one to succeed in raising the needed funds, but neither hard-nosed business sense nor patriotism could completely account for this stand. He had to face the distinct but dreadful possibility that the Rothschilds would invest in Confederate securities. His political position—that of the Democratic National Chairman cooperating with the primarily

---

[6] Belmont to Seward, June 6, 18, 24, July 16, 1861, Seward Papers; Seward to Belmont, June 19, 1861, private Belmont collection.

Republican North—was tenuous at best. To have the firms of
which he was the American agent subsidizing the formerly
Democratic South would have spelled his political ruin.[7]

Five days after Fort Sumter, the Confederate Congress authorized a 50-million-dollar loan, to be raised in part by a sale
of 8 percent bonds and in part by the issuance of non-interest-
bearing Treasury notes. A worried Belmont lost no time in ridiculing this ambitious undertaking to the conservative, property-
minded Rothschilds. "Who will loan a dollar," he asked, "to a
confederacy of States, of which four have already repudiated
their debts, while the remaining five will in less than three
months be in default of their semi-annual dividends?" Certainly
the Rothschilds would not lend money to a regime headed by
Jefferson Davis, who had even advocated repudiation in his presecession days! Belmont predicted—accurately—that in less
than a year the Confederate state governments would pay their
obligations in Treasury warrants, "which will have the same ultimate value" as the now worthless "assignats" of Revolutionary France. The banker persistently pressed home to the Rothschilds, who heeded his advice, that Confederate securities
would be shortly depreciated and eventually worthless. When
Richmond succeeded in floating its only bond issue abroad, in
1863, the Erlanger banking firms of Paris and Frankfurt under-
wrote it. The Rothschilds, already large investors in Union
bonds, would not cooperate with the Erlanger agents, and Belmont expressed his gratitude for their faith in his judgment.[8]

The banker's first conspicuous contribution to the Union's financial affairs came shortly after war broke out. The United
States Treasury had been unsuccessfully trying to procure subscriptions for the 8-million-dollar balance of a bond issue authorized in the last month of the Buchanan administration. On
April 19 Belmont joined with other financial and commercial

[7] Foner, *Business & Slavery*, 297–98; *New York Herald*, March 5, 1861.
[8] Redlich, *Molding of American Banking*, II, 86; *New York World*, Nov. 25,
1890; Belmont to Lionel de Rothschild, May 21, 1861, in Belmont, *Letters and
Speeches of Late Civil War*, 32–35; *Harper's Weekly*, VII (April 25, 1863),
258.

William H. Seward (Library of Congress)   Salmon P. Chase (Library of Congress)

leaders in forming a committee to advertise and sell this balance. The banker also wrote to Chase and sent him a list of prominent Democrats and Republicans who had recently subscribed to a large foreign loan. Chase was pleased to hear from Belmont and to have evidence that, though money was tight, it could be tapped, given favorable terms. Again, as with Seward, Belmont's enterprise was rewarded with his favorite balm—an acknowledgment of his "kindness" and an indication that his advice would be welcome. Did Belmont have any suggestions on the "proper mode" to approach a new, larger bond issue? Did the financier feel that a 50-million-dollar subscription at 7 percent could be obtained at home, along with one twice as large at 6½ percent in Paris or London?

Belmont approved the domestic loan but felt its success

hinged on a downward revision of American tariff policy. He was less confident about the feasibility of a foreign issue under existing conditions. From the vantage point of Wall Street, it was impossible to predict the effect of an American loan on European capitalists. He feared they might be suffering from the same delusion affecting their governments, "that by withholding all aid from us, they may force us into a settlement of some kind with the Southern states." Yet, sending an official Treasury agent abroad to discuss such a loan would be bad policy, for the possible failure of such a negotiation, if generally known, would undoubtedly depress present American securities.[9]

Belmont, however, was in a position to help Chase get a more direct reading of the European financial pulse without the risks incumbent in sending an obvious suppliant. The banker himself intended sailing for Europe to spend several months with his wife and five children, who had gone ahead. If the Treasury Secretary were still disposed by then to negotiate a foreign loan, he could privately inform Belmont, who would "be very happy to devote my best energies toward the futherance of your views." If Belmont saw that terms were possible, Chase could empower him to negotiate the loan. Should it prove impossible to accomplish anything concrete, "no harm would have been done because nobody would know of the failure." In the same vein, Belmont offered his European services to his other administration correspondent, Secretary Seward.

Both men approved the banker's plans. The advantages of a Belmont mission must have seemed obvious to them. His acknowledged ease of access to top European circles, coupled with his lack of formal administration connection and the smoke screen furnished by the presence of his family, could easily mask his semiofficial status. On June 17 Belmont boarded the steamer *Persia*, en route for England and, as the press solemnly reported, a reunion with his vacationing family. In real-

[9] *New York Tribune*, April 20, 1861; Chase to Belmont, June 19, July 1, 1861, private Belmont collection; Belmont to Chase, July 3, 1861, August Belmont Papers, Library of Congress.

ity, he considered himself the eyes, ears, and mouthpiece of the two most important members of Lincoln's cabinet.[10]

Belmont's initial report to the Treasury Department followed a month of conversations with British, French, and German bankers. The time and prospects for a foreign loan were "not at all propitious." As the banker had warned Chase, the loan market was decidedly unfavorable, and major capitalists were disposed to keep back their funds in the hope of forcing a cessation of American hostilities. Belmont's efforts were impeded by "mischievous" gossip published in the *New York Daily News*. The paper, edited by Mayor Fernando Wood's brother and fellow "copperhead," Benjamin, circulated reports that Belmont came to Europe as a "Treasury agent for foreign loans" and "these rumors having found their way to England . . . , I found myself assailed by questions on all sides." Still, some cause for optimism remained.

France and Germany, as far as Belmont could ascertain, seemed friendly to the Union, and if the Union army and navy could be placed upon a more efficient footing and the supremacy of their strength demonstrated in combat, "there will be no difficulty in negotiating very large amounts of our securities on the Continent." But early military reverses led Belmont to conclude, by October, that not even a remote chance existed for negotiating an American loan abroad. Any indirect attempts by Chase to do so "would be worse than useless." In fact, the administration had better forget all about a foreign flotation and concentrate instead on a domestic one. Belmont's opinion became the official one; Secretary Chase abandoned all possibility of approaching the European investment market.[11]

Belmont's letters to Seward, particularly those dealing with British and French attitudes toward recognition of the Confed-

[10] Belmont to Chase, July 3, Belmont Papers, LC; Belmont to Seward, June 24, July 16, 30, 1861, Seward Papers; Chase to Belmont, Aug. 10, 1861, private Belmont collection; *New York Times*, June 18, 1861.

[11] Belmont to Chase, Aug. 15, Oct. 31, 1861, Salmon Portland Chase Papers, Historical Society of Pennsylvania; Chase to Belmont, Sept. 13, 1861, private Belmont collection.

eracy, were more extensive. He made it a point, upon his arrival in London, to arrange a number of personal interviews with high-level officials. The American minister there, Charles Francis Adams, prompted by a strongly favorable letter of introduction from Seward, went out of his way to open still other doors. From these sources Belmont gathered that the general English situation was somewhat less favorable than it might be. Queen Victoria, her consort Prince Albert, and the great mass of Englishmen sided with the North.

But Prime Minister Palmerston, some of his close advisers (such as Chancellor of the Exchequer William E. Gladstone), and the influential *London Times* leaned to the South in misguided or malicious sympathy. Through the good offices of Baron Rothschild, Belmont secured a private, hour-long interview with Palmerston. The banker felt that if he could be made to see the North's position, the whole climate would take a turn for the better. Palmerston questioned Belmont closely on a wide range of topics: slavery as a cause of the war, the Union's military strength, popular attitudes toward English neutrality, and the meaning of recent Congressional legislation touching on maritime commerce and the blockaded southern ports.

Belmont responded to all these inquiries authoritatively, asserting the nation's determination to crush the rebellion at all costs. He was pleased by Palmerston's interest in American affairs, though one statement disturbed him: "We do not like slavery, but we want cotton and we dislike your Morrill tariff." [12] The American sensed the import of the remark. He notified Seward that the English government and people could not accept the North's justification for fighting the Confederacy as

[12] Belmont to Charles Francis Adams, July 28, 1861, Adams to Belmont, undated (probably July 28, 1861), private Belmont collection; Belmont to Seward, July 30, 1861, Seward Papers. *Punch*, the constantly delightful British humor magazine, satirized the prime minister's declaration:

> Though with the North we sympathize
> It must not be forgotten,
> That with the South we've stronger ties,
> Which are composed of cotton.

Quoted in John W. Foster, *A Century of American Diplomacy* (Boston, 1901), 373.

long as "this war is not carried on for the abolition of slavery in the Southern states." Perhaps English sentiment, which showed a potential disposition toward improvement, could use the tonic of a reduction in the "objectionable" Morrill tariff? Nothing else could contribute so effectively toward disproving widespread southern assertions that the war was merely a contest between free trade and protection. Further, a tariff reduction would tend to increase the revenue and improve the trade of America's great commercial cities, whose response to the demands of patriotism surely entitled them to the administration's sympathetic consideration.[13]

Belmont's next stop was Paris. Though unable to meet Louis Napoleon, he tried to convince influential members of the Emperor's inner circle that it would be bad politics and worse morals for the French even to consider recognition of a government whose chief cornerstone was human slavery. Belmont found the French situation more reassuring than the English one. He believed it was certainly in France's best interest to maintain the Union's strength and prosperity as a growing maritime power and as a check upon English predominance in the Atlantic.

Belmont then traveled to the German-speaking states, and the region's "warmth and sympathy" for the Union pleased the Rhenish-born visitor. "The whole population," he wrote Seward, "is strongly for us & the warmest wishes are expressed for our success." Even the German press, but for one exception, "universally denounced" the southern rebellion. The pro-Confederate newspaper was the French-language *Journal de Frankfurt*, which published daily long letters, purportedly written by its New York correspondent, that "for their views & impartiality . . . might claim the archtraitor Jeff Davis as their author." Belmont suspected the American Consul General there, one Ricker of Louisiana, whose appointment had been

---

[13] Belmont to Seward, July 30, Aug. 16, Sept. 25, Oct. 21, 1861, Seward Papers; Seward to Belmont, Sept. 2, 1861, private Belmont collection. In fact, Belmont deemed repeal of the Morrill law as worth more to the Union cause than the most brilliant military victory.

pushed by Slidell and granted by Buchanan, of "manufactur-
ing" the pro-secessionist articles right in Frankfurt. He warned
Seward that Confederate leaders would pass up no chances to
place themselves and their cause in a favorable light and that
Washington must not neglect to counteract the machinations of
their busy agents and spies on the Continent.[14]

Belmont originally intended to return to the United States in
the autumn of 1861, but his wife's illness caused a postponement to the following spring. He continued to receive up-to-
the-minute information from "reliable quarters" in London and
Paris and to pass it on to the State Department. In September
Belmont noted several indications of Great Britain's readiness to
intervene in American affairs, particularly the daily attacks on
the United States by the *London Times* and *Post*, which were
"undoubtedly intended to prepare the popular mind" for Palmerston's contemplated "outrage." Belmont had even more painful news of French intentions the following month. "Well informed parties" told him of Emperor Louis Napoleon's anxiety
to recognize the Confederacy at once, notwithstanding all the
friendly assurances of the French Minister, Mercier, at Washington. French manufacturers and chambers of commerce were
also said to be very strongly in favor of interference in the
American war. A Balkanized America would be unable to
thwart France's newly hatched plans to dominate Mexico. Besides, the appointment of two Orleans noblemen to Union General George B. McClellan's staff had angered the Emperor, always sensitive to any rise in Bourbon prestige.[15]

In November an incident occurred which Belmont feared
would weaken further the already fragile Anglo-American link.

[14] Belmont to Samuel L. M. Barlow, Oct. 30, 1861, Barlow Papers; Belmont to Chase, Oct. 31, 1861, Chase Papers. Interestingly, Belmont, while in-
timating the necessity to recall Ricker, felt compelled to deny any aspirations
of his own for the post. He could neither expect nor accept "any office of
emolument at the hands of the party for the defeat of which I did my utmost."
Belmont to Seward, Aug. 16, 1861, Seward Papers.

[15] Belmont to Seward, Sept. 25, Oct. 21, 1861, Seward Papers; Belmont to
Barlow, Oct. 30, 1861, Barlow Papers. The two Frenchmen were the Count of
Paris and his uncle, the Prince de Joinville.

Ironically, one of the principals involved was the banker's former colleague and relative, Slidell.[16] Reports reached Belmont that Jefferson Davis had designated Slidell and James M. Mason his emissaries to Paris and London, respectively, their main purpose being to secure favorable attention and perhaps even diplomatic recognition of the Confederacy. Belmont knew the two men. Mason, a Virginian, "would do no wonders" in London; Slidell, however, was a different case. He had proved himself a crafty politician, and that he "should at this juncture represent the rebels" was "a great pity." Still worse from the Union standpoint, Slidell was "fully master of the French language, while our worthy minister, Mr. Dayton, has to have an interpreter at all his interviews with [French Foreign Minister] Thouvenel." Belmont hoped that the vessel carrying the two men would be caught by the Union Navy's blockade. "Would it be right for me," he wrote jocosely to a New York friend, "to wish my venerable uncle comfortably lodged at Fort Lafayette?" [17]

Ultimately, Slidell did wind up in a Union prison, though not in a manner which the punctilious Belmont approved. The Confederates, on board the *Nashville*, successfully crashed the Atlantic blockade and landed at Havana, where on November 7 they took passage on a British merchant ship, the *Trent*. On the following day, the Union warship *San Jacinto*, commanded by Captain Charles Wilkes, halted the *Trent*; the two commissioners were removed and "comfortably lodged" in Fort Warren, Boston Harbor.

Northerners generally praised the incident and acclaimed Captain Wilkes a hero. But to Belmont, well-schooled in the do's and don't's of international diplomacy, it constituted a blunder of the first magnitude. All his admonitions to Baron Rothschild and other English leaders about "Southern" disre-

16 Belmont had not seen the Louisianan for over two years, although as recently as May, 1861, Slidell requested the banker's good offices in the event southern-owned property in the loyal states was confiscated. Slidell to Belmont, May 2, 1861, Barlow Papers.
17 Belmont to Barlow, Oct. 30, 1861, Barlow Papers.

spect for law and order appeared absurd in the light of this northern breach. "Not a dozen battles lost," he wrote Chase from Nice, France, "could have damaged our good cause as much as the ill-judged & over-zealous act of Capt. Wilkes." And to what ends? "Neither the violent & clumsy representations of the demagogue Mason nor all the energy & astuteness of . . . Slidell" could have persuaded Great Britain and France to support the South if it were not in their own best interest. Interning the rebel commissioners was not of sufficient importance to Union survival to risk war with the most powerful nation in Europe. Their imprisonment would not contribute one one-thousandth as much to the Union's ultimate victory as would "the sword of McClellan & the broadsides of our navy against the Southern forts." England, it was true, had frequently done as bad or worse in the War of 1812, but that afforded no excuse for an honest man to adopt the methods of a rogue. Belmont realized that to surrender the commissioners, when public opinion dictated otherwise, would be risky for the administration. Still, the two rebels were not worth the price of a war. "As Captain Wilkes acted on his own responsibility & not under the instructions of the Government, the President has every opportunity to get in an honorable & dignified manner out of the difficulty."

Leading men on both sides adopted similar positions toward the matter, and after several weeks of diplomatic discussions, Slidell and Mason were released to British custody. After Seward assured the Palmerston ministry that Wilkes had acted without authorization, a detente in Anglo-American relations followed.[18]

Though the diplomatic crisis proved short-lived, Belmont's annoyance at the incident did not subside as rapidly. The banker had been angry at Slidell since the futile attempt at the Madrid appointment, but this was a small matter compared to

[18] Sears, *Slidell*, 180–84; Belmont to Chase, Dec. 8, 1861, Chase Papers; Belmont to Barlow, Dec. 10, 1861, Barlow Papers. A standard account of the Trent incident can be found in Thomas L. Harris, *The Trent Affair* (Indianapolis, 1896).

Belmont's utter contempt for Slidell's disloyalty to the government in which he had once participated. That Slidell, "a northern man"—he was born in New York City—the "stout advocate of the Monroe Doctrine," was now bent on "using all the resources of his ingenuity & cunning to bring a foreign enemy to invade his native soil" was beyond Belmont's belief. He also despised Slidell's hypocrisy in complaining publicly to European newspapers of ill treatment at Fort Warren, while confiding to friends that he had enjoyed every comfort during his imprisonment. "I hope & trust that I may not meet him, because I could certainly not extend to him the ordinary recognition of civility among acquaintances." Belmont was to be spared such an unwanted experience. Though he and his family spent weeks in Paris during the winter of 1861–1862, the two old "Buchaneers-in-arms" never crossed paths.[19]

While in Paris, Belmont met Thurlow Weed. Weed had just arrived from England, where he had been publishing newspapers, circulating pamphlets, and delivering speeches abusing the slaveholding Confederacy. One day the two had breakfast with Edward Ellice, a prominent Whig M.P. Ellice, in the course of conversation, warned the Americans that the Civil War would become so financially "onerous to the northern people that they would force the government to make terms with the South." The unlikely combination, Belmont and Weed, controverted these assumptions, the former insisting that so long as foreign nations maintained strict neutrality "our government & people were strong enough in men & money to preserve the Union."[20] When William W. Corcoran, the southern-leaning banker who had once been a power in Democratic Party circles, later asked Belmont to explain his collaboration with their old enemy Weed, Belmont replied unequivocally: "My own views on our national trouble have never changed. I have looked upon seces-

[19] Belmont to Barlow, Feb. 10, 1862, Barlow Papers; Sears, *Slidell*, 235.
[20] Weed to Seward, April 21, 1862, in Frederick W. Seward, *Seward at Washington as Senator and Secretary of State: A Memoir of His Life, with Selections from His Letters, 1861–1872* (New York, 1891), 87; Thurlow Weed Barnes, *Memoir of Thurlow Weed* (Boston, 1884), 407–08; Perry Belmont, *An American Democrat*, 114–15.

sion as a great political blunder & crime. . . . I shall always remain uncompromisingly opposed to it." [21]

Now that Belmont had established rapport with Seward,
Chase, and Weed, he felt emboldened to accord Lincoln the
benefit of his opinions and advice as well.[22] For a start, the
banker shared some thoughts on international commerce with
the White House. Great Britain's textile workers suffered badly
as a result of the successful Union blockade against southern
ports. The possibility still existed that for this reason alone
Palmerston's government might consider recognition of the
Confederacy justified. The Union government, Belmont confided to Lincoln, could act to ease the pressure on Palmerston
and at the same time stimulate subversion within the enemy lines.
Federal naval and military units now controlled some of the
best Atlantic and Gulf ports, nearly all of which "are very well
adapted as outlets for cotton & other Southern produce." Why
not use Congressional authority to appoint collectors at these
ports, opening them again to commerce under current tariff
laws? Cotton planters would be allowed to bring their crop and
exchange it against "foreign production of gold & silver." The
Confederacy, in retaliation, would probably enact laws forbid-
ding cotton to be sent into the reopened ports and thus fall
squarely in the Union trap. This in turn would create an "intense feeling of dissatisfaction" among both the British textile
manufacturers and Dixie's beleaguered cotton growers. At the
very least, the Confederacy's refusal would give her a black eye
in Europe "and might even sow the seeds of a rebellion in reb-
eldom powerful enough to throw the whole Richmond Cabinet overboard."

The banker, unaware that such a policy had just been im-
plemented by Washington, received Lincoln's "sincere thanks"
for the advice "as a *justification* of the course which it was in-

[21] Belmont to Mrs. August Belmont, Oct. 23, 27, 29, Nov. 13, 1863, Belmont
to Corcoran, Feb. 8, 1864, private Belmont collection.

[22] Belmont had met the President only once—for a brief moment in July,
1861—and had come away with the belief, shared by others, that Chase and
Seward would dominate the administration. By the spring of 1862 Belmont
realized that the Chief Executive was master in his own house.

tended to *suggest*." Belmont's chagrin on learning that his plan lacked originality was offset by the President's closing words: "You will not neglect to give . . . [me] the benefit of your large sagacity and experience as often as you have occasion and opportunity." [23]

The first anniversary of Fort Sumter came and went, and an impatient Belmont, appalled by the continued carnage on the battlefield, grew restive at what he considered slow progress toward military victory. Now back in the United States, he added military counsel to his diplomatic and financial arsenal. He outlined suggestions for a war policy in a letter to Thurlow Weed, who had also returned and who he knew would pass them on to Washington.

Belmont found no other solution "to our present difficulties" than a reconstruction of "but one Government over all the states." Reviewing the Union's military progress to date, he proposed two alternatives to effect such an end, both presenting difficulties "of the gravest nature." Lincoln could negotiate with the leaders of the rebellion to determine the existence of any possibility "to reestablish a Federal Union"; or he should "crush the rebellion" by an energetic and unrelenting prosecution of the war effort. Should the White House wish to consider the former alternative, it might designate "one or two conservative men," perhaps Weed and former Governor Seymour of New York, who, without holding any official position, yet possess sufficient weight and influence with the North "as to inspire confidence in their statements to the leading men of the South." These commissioners, under specially defined presidential authority, could proceed to Richmond and attempt to restore the Union by offering several conditions: amnesty for "political offenses" during the war; a national convention to "reconstruct the federal compact with such modifications in the constitution as our late sad experience has demonstrated to have become necessary"; the assumption of war debts by respective sections or, better still, by the Federal Government; and the

[23] Belmont to Lincoln, May 9, 1862, Lincoln Papers; John Hay to Belmont, June 2, 1862, private Belmont collection.

strict enforcement of the Monroe Doctrine throughout the hemisphere.[24] Such concessions, Belmont went on, would be "very distasteful" to northerners—"to no one more than myself"—but every sacrifice must be made, every prejudice and conviction yielded, if by such means peace and prosperity could be restored.

In the event such a plan was not feasible, Belmont suggested a drastic reorganization of the nation's military establishment. A conscription system must be instituted calling for the draft of 500,000 men; regiments must no longer be permitted to choose their own commanders (who were to be replaced by West Point-instructed officers); and prospective officers should be dispatched wherever needed and not with reference to their home state. All these changes, Belmont insisted, will create a true "United States Army & will strike a severe blow to that most fatal of heresies—States' rights & States' pride—which lies at the bottom of all our misfortunes." [25]

Two days after penning these observations and admonitions, Belmont received a letter from "one of the wealthiest & most influential planters in Louisiana & Mississippi." The writer, who had been converted to secessionism after Fort Sumter, now gave it up as hopeless and claimed that the administration could terminate the rebellion by "declaring officially for restoration as it was." The banker thought the communication deserved Lincoln's special consideration, particularly in view of his own letter on the possibility of a negotiated settlement, and asked Weed to forward it to the White House as well.[26]

The war-wearied President was besieged with what-must-be-done-immediately-or-else advice and pressed for time besides. Still, the tone of the southerner's words annoyed him to such a degree that he answered Belmont almost immediately. Just what did these ex-secessionists mean when they asked longingly for "the Union as it was?" Weren't they aware that "broken eggs

[24] Belmont viewed this last condition as a way of affording repentant Confederate officers their chance to gain glory for the Union again.

[25] Belmont to Weed, July 20, 1862, Seward Papers.

[26] Belmont to Weed, July 24, 1862, Seward Papers.

cannot be mended?" The Confederacy "has nothing to do now but to take her place in the Union as it was, barring the already broken eggs. The sooner she does so, the smaller will be the amount of that which will be past mending." Then came one of the most caustic and crushing rejoinders ever uttered by the President: "This government cannot much longer play a game in which it stakes all, and its enemies stake nothing. Those enemies must understand that they cannot experiment for ten years trying to destroy the government, and if they fail still come back into the Union unhurt."

Belmont, taken aback by such a personal response and worried lest the President think the southerner's letter mirrored his own feelings, hastily followed up with a conciliatory letter declaring his support for Lincoln's views right down the line. Still, the President must convince the conservative men in the South that "we are fighting *only for the Union*," and that Confederate propaganda about Washington's intentions to "conquer" and "subjugate" are "repugnant to the American ear." Pleading that his good intentions must make up for his lapses in judgment, Belmont enclosed a copy of his previous letter to Weed outlining his twofold plan for a negotiated peace or a military modernization.[27]

Shortly after, Belmont received word from influential people abroad that England was again flirting with the idea of Confederate recognition. He attributed this change of opinion to the "false statements of southern emissaries" and felt the information reliable and important enough for administration ears. Bypassing his usual channels, Seward and Weed, he sent the data directly to Lincoln. In addition, Belmont overstepped the canons of protocol. Not content merely to relay information and give advice on what might be done, he plunged in and criticized what was already being done. He was sure that "the people are ready to bring every sacrifice" for the Union, but "right or wrong they have lost confidence" in Secretary of War

[27] Lincoln to Belmont, July 31, 1862, in Roy P. Basler, ed., *The Collected Works of Abraham Lincoln* (8 vols., New Brunswick, N.J., 1953), V, 350–51; Belmont to Lincoln Aug. 10, 1862, Lincoln Papers.

Edwin M. Stanton and in the general "intermeddling of civilians in military affairs." General Henry W. Halleck should be given the War Department, General George B. McClellan be made Commander-in-Chief of all Union forces east of the Alleghenies, and General Franz Sigel be designated to take charge in the West.[28]

Belmont's criticism of Lincoln's military leadership brought their mutual correspondence to an abrupt end, though the President saw fit to pass on to Stanton that excerpt from the banker's letter which counseled that the War Secretary be replaced.[29] For his part, Belmont did not cease offering military, diplomatic, and political counsel; he simply channeled it through Secretary Seward again. He quoted at length from the letters of Baron Rothschild and other "very influential" people in Great Britain and France on the latest European sentiment toward the Civil War, frequently congratulated Seward for "glorious" and "decisive" victories, and suggested ways of preventing a recurrence of the draft riots which had shocked New Yorkers in the summer of 1863. After July, 1863, the banker's communications to Washington decreased. Northern military victories made foreign intervention unlikely. Moreover, with Democratic preparations for the 1864 presidential campaign under way, quasi-official contacts with men he would try energetically to oust from office were of dubious propriety.[30]

Late in 1863 Belmont's business called him to Paris and London. His departure was so sudden and his contemplated trip so short that he didn't inform Seward until he reached France. He utilized what spare time he had to amass details of Napoleon's and Palmerston's new nonintervention policies, along with ac-

[28] Belmont to Lincoln, Sept. 4, 1862, Lincoln Papers. Only a half year earlier Belmont had applauded Stanton's elevation. "The appointment of Stanton to the War Department gives me some hope that the President appreciates the necessity of such a line of action," that is, bringing conservative Democrats into his administration. Belmont to Barlow, Feb. 10, 1862, Barlow Papers.

[29] Lincoln to Stanton, Sept. 11, 1862, Abraham Lincoln Papers, Collections of The New-York Historical Society.

[30] Belmont to Seward, Nov. 12, 1862, May 18, July 6, 20, 1863, Seward Papers; Seward to Belmont, May 19, 1863, private Belmont collection.

counts of Confederate maneuvers abroad. In Paris Belmont
found the number of rebel agents "legion" and their methods
"unscrupulous." He reported the news of Confederate Vice
President Stephens' pending arrival and the rumor that "he will
make the most liberal offers for recognition & alliance," even
going so far in his desperation as to agree to a gradual emancipation of Negro slaves by Richmond. In England Belmont was
informed by people who are apt to know, that with the exception of
Gladstone & Palmerston the members of the Cabinet are all in favor of
the North. Still we must not shut our eyes to the fact that the taking of
Vicksburg & our successes [particularly Gettysburg] have a good deal
to do with this attitude.

Anglo-American relations still could be improved, particularly
in the area of American press treatment of British behavior.
Such "attacks" as those in the *New York Times* "& other organs of the Republican Party" not only "estrange the good will
of our friends but . . . strengthen the hands of the [British]
opposition." [31]

The American press undoubtedly resented Britain's long vac-
illation, but Belmont's mention of it was motivated more by his
own sensitivity to newspaper criticism than by his sampling of
British opinion. Journalists had found Belmont a ready target in
the past. During the war years they had a field day at his expense. Some Republicans charged him with disloyalty, ranging
from "copperheadism" at home to encouraging Confederate
bond purchases abroad. Democrats-turned-Republicans attacked his "lukewarmness" in supporting the Union. Peace-at-
all-costs Democrats, on the other hand, accused him of treason
to the party. Anti-Semites depicted him as the stereotyped "international Jew banker" who had no roots and loved no country. American Jewish spokesmen defensively denied he was one
of them, pointing to his Protestant marriage and to the fact that
he had never belonged to any American Jewish congregation.[32]

31 Belmont to Mrs. August Belmont, Oct. 19, 23, 1863, Seward to Belmont,
Nov. 25, 1863, private Belmont collection; Belmont to Seward, Nov. 29, Dec.
10, 1863, Seward Papers.
32 Belmont to Seward, May 18, 1863, Seward Papers; Rudolf Glanz, "The
Rothschild Legend in America," *Jewish Social Studies*, XIX (Jan.-April, 1957),

George Templeton Strong, a New York lawyer who kept a
daily diary, exemplified the typical Belmont "baiter." He petu-
lantly interpreted the national chairman's pleas for the victory
of Democratic Congressional and gubernatorial candidates as
proof that Belmont "well deserves hanging as an ally of the rebellion." Strong's passion knew no bounds when he got wind of
Belmont's "two alternatives" letter to Lincoln, particularly that
section suggesting a peace treaty "with dignity," and he vi-
ciously attacked the Democrat as one who "would sing a *Te
Deum* over any pacification, however infamous, and would re-
joice to see Jefferson Davis our next President." [33]

A review of Belmont's wartime activities would refute these
charges. Although in disagreement with certain Administration
policies, he placed his services unreservedly at the command of
Lincoln and his advisers. The information he garnered and
passed on to high government officials testified to his unquestionably sincere desire to be of use. Their answers provided
concrete evidence that they were no less eager to receive his assistance. Being Democratic National Chairman, Belmont had, of
necessity, to participate in anti-administration campaigning during the 1862 and 1864 elections, but he always took care to follow up criticism of Republican policy with praise for the war
effort. Even so, his detractors chose to characterize his utterances as "disunionist subversion." [34]

In retrospect, probably nothing less than Belmont's complete
desertion of his party during the war years could have staved
off the repetitious slanders which gave him so much anguish.
But this he would not, or could not, do. It was not in Belmont,
as it would not be in most people, to surrender leadership and
power before having a chance to exercise them. On the other
hand, for Belmont, an American by choice, not birth, desertion

3–28. Allegations that Belmont would never return to American soil followed
each of his wartime trips to Europe. One of these stories apparently proved so
convincing that his own lawyer offered to buy the magnificently furnished
Fifth Avenue mansion. Belmont to Barlow, Dec. 10, 1861, Barlow Papers.

33 Nevins and Thomas, eds., *Diary of George Templeton Strong*, III, 256, 268.

34 For example, see Belmont's political speeches in the *New York World*,
Sept. 13, 1862, and *New York Times*, Aug. 30, 1864.

of the Union was equally unthinkable. What his critics, even the more enlightened ones, failed to understand was that all the banker's wartime governmental and political activities were prompted by two strong and conflicting principles: loyalty to the idea of an indivisible Union, and loyalty to the party which had caused that Union's rupture. It is doubtful that anyone, no matter what his qualifications, could have assembled a cohesive program out of such disparate components. To have achieved even a coexistence between them, as Belmont did, was an accomplishment worthy of respect.

8

★ ★ ★

Wartime Politics

WHEN BELMONT RETURNED from his first wartime trip to Europe in June, 1862, he found the Democratic organization he was to head in a state of disarray. With party strength sapped by secession, the northern Democrats, instead of aligning themselves in a phalanx against the administration, were squabbling away the remnants of their party patrimony. Faced with these tatters, Belmont was all the more anxious to rectify a situation which he felt had played a large part in the 1860 defeat—Douglas' failure to gain the support of any major New York daily newspaper. Almost as if made to order, the *New York World* presented itself.

The *World* had been established in 1860 by "several Christian gentlemen" who desired to make available to New Yorkers a wholesome, two-cent family newspaper. In 1861 its financial condition forced a merger with another small daily, *The Courier and the Enquirer*, which had also been losing money. The joint enterprise failed, however, to show a profit and was placed on the block. The *World*'s night editor, twenty-seven-year-old Manton Malone Marble, had considerable journalistic experience and believed he could make it a successful paper if funds to reorganize it were found.[1] In April, 1862, Marble got

---

[1] Before his stint on the *World*, Marble had worked for the *Boston Journal*, the *Boston Traveller*, and the *New York Evening Post. New York World*, June 14, 1864; Mary C. Phelan, *Manton Marble of the New York World* (Washington, 1957), 1; Robert S. Harper, *Lincoln and the Press* (New York, 1951), 289.

a six-month mortgage on the *World*'s property, assembled an able, experienced staff, and assumed sole proprietorship.[2] By September Marble realized he would be unable to pay off the note. A Democrat of the Belmont persuasion, he also saw the need for a party voice in the press. He approached a group of prominent Democrats, including Belmont, Barlow, and Tilden, and effected a marriage of mutual convenience by selling them shares in his paper. The *World*'s circulation under its new auspices climbed immediately, so that it soon ranked fifth among the more than twenty metropolitan dailies.[3]

Samuel L. M. Barlow (*Magazine of American History*)

Manton M. Marble (*Harper's Weekly*)

[2] The staff included David G. Croly (father of the better known Herbert), Ivory Chamberlain, James K. Spalding, and Richard G. White.

[3] In 1864 the *World* netted a $40,000 profit. Marble to Belmont, undated (Nov., 1868), Manton Malone Marble Papers, Library of Congress. See also Belmont to Barlow, Aug. 24, Oct. 1, 1862, Barlow Papers.

Until Marble's retirement in 1876, he and Belmont worked closely together and succeeded in making the *World* the leading Democratic organ in the country. The perennial joke among Gotham's newspapermen and politicians—that Belmont, Barlow, and Tilden ran the *World* with a little assistance from Marble—probably contained more truth in it than the banker-politician was willing publicly to concede. Careful scrutiny of the Belmont-Marble correspondence reveals innumerable instances where the national chairman provided Marble with ideas for both editorial policy and operational management. In turn, Marble became a confidant of and sounding board for many of Belmont's fledgling ideas.

Getting newspaper support for the Democratic Party was one thing; convincing voters to cast Democratic ballots in wartime elections was quite another. Many pre-Sumter Democrats now pledged full, unqualified backing to the administration, either as self-styled "War Democrats," as full-fledged Republicans, or as members of the Republican-sponsored "Union Party." Gone from the regular Democratic fold were such enormously popular vote-getters and spokesmen as Sickles, Daniel Dickinson, John Van Buren, and John A. Dix of New York and Benjamin F. Butler of Massachusetts. Because Belmont and other traditional Democrats refused to dissolve what they considered their constitutional function as a loyal opposition, the misapprehension arose that they were "anti-Union" or "non-Union" Democrats. But they saw nothing disloyal in presenting alternatives to military suppression of the South, believing as they did that Republican policies could not lead to the Union's restoration.[4] Whatever the intrinsic merits of this approach, a national temper which equated criticism with disloyalty was bound to affect the election results.

Belmont's immediate concern was the 1862 New York gubernatorial race. When incumbent Republican Edwin D. Morgan declined renomination in order to seek election to the

---

[4] See, for example, Belmont's speech at Newport, Rhode Island, in September, 1862: "Political meddlers and ambitious demagogues step in and arrest our victorious progress." Belmont, *Letters and Speeches of Late Civil War*, 104–07.

United States Senate, Belmont and leading state Democrats saw
an excellent chance to make a comeback. National party committees did not normally "interfere" with the autonomy of state
organizations, but the New York Democratic disaster in 1860
had been so complete, extending right down to the local level,
that Belmont felt it urgent to reconstruct a strong Democratic
base there. In September he attended the state convention in Albany as a delegate, signifying both national interest in the New
York outcome and his personal desire that the convention give
positive support for the war effort. Indeed, he was prepared to
oppose any aspiring nominee who equivocated in declaring his
loyalty to the Union's cause. With confidence and enthusiasm,
the Albany delegates named the still popular former Governor
Seymour who, though somewhat reluctant, consented to run.[5]
He accepted the platform calling for the preservation of the
Union and deploring the machinations of the "disunionists"
who had brought about the war. Belmont left Albany content
that the New York Democrats, chastened by recent experiences, were more united now than he could ever recall.[6]

Soon after Albany, some of Belmont's friends proposed that
he seek the Congressional nomination of his district. The
banker-politician was receptive—the only time he ever seriously
considered running for elective office—and he requested two
close political associates to investigate what had to be done. The
men, Barlow and Isaac Bell, reported that James Brooks, editor
of the *New York Daily Express,* and a local ward politician
named Bradley were busily engaged in rounding up support for
themselves. Belmont, relying on his prominence within the
party, limited his endeavors in the nomination race to writing
friends from his summer home at Newport. The contents of
these letters usually emphasized Belmont's conviction that "my
nomination would give more strength to our [state] ticket than

[5] Seymour wrote to an old friend: "I have reluctantly consented to a nomination this fall. An election will be a misfortune to me." Seymour to Barlow,
Sept. 18, 1862, Barlow Papers.
[6] *New York World,* Sept. 10–12, 1862; Brummer, *Political History of New
York State,* 213–14; Allan Nevins, *The War for the Union* (2 vols., New York,
1959–60), II, 304n.

that of Bradley or Brooks." Barlow warned him that such statements were insufficient, and, as Brooks was the stronger of the
two competitors, Belmont should bargain for Bradley's backing.
Belmont chose to ignore the suggestion. If his reputation as a
loyal, powerful Democrat could not outweigh whatever qualifications Brooks possessed, then "my friends must consider me
not to be a candidate." [7]

Brooks emerged with the designation and won election to
Congress in November, a month which witnessed striking Democratic gains in New York and elsewhere. Seymour won a second Albany term handily, and his party captured seventeen
of New York's thirty-one seats in the House of Representatives.[8]

Belmont was disturbed at English and French newspaper reaction to Democratic electoral gains. He tried to clarify the results in a letter to Lionel de Rothschild by assuring him that the
November results in no way indicated northern eagerness to
end the Civil War at the expense of the Union.[9] These brave
words notwithstanding, Belmont was concerned about the way
the war had bogged down. Early in 1863 he sounded out
Tilden, Marble, and other influential Democrats about the possibility of organizing a "powerful demonstration in our city &
State in order to compel the administration to a change of men
and measures." If nothing were done, he predicted, ruin and national bankruptcy awaited the nation. The suggestion failed to
arouse anything stronger than sympathy. Another Belmont
idea, that of publicizing the "correct" wartime position of loyal,
"conservative" Democrats, led to the formation of the Society
for the Diffusion of Political Knowledge. He hoped it would

[7] Belmont to Barlow, Sept. 27, Oct. 1, 1862, Barlow Papers.

[8] Pennsylvania, Ohio, Indiana, and Illinois, all of which had voted for
Lincoln in 1860, also sent Democratic-dominated delegations to Congress.

[9] Belmont to Lionel de Rothschild, Nov. 25, 1862, in Belmont, *Letters and
Speeches of Late Civil War*, 73–74. Seymour's annual message to the state
legislature, which Belmont assisted in preparing, declared that "under no circumstances can the division of the Union be conceded." Seymour to Belmont,
Nov. 11, 1862, private Belmont collection; *New York Times*, Jan. 8, 1863.

conteract the pro-administration propaganda of Republican clubs, such as the Loyal Publication Society, by opening branches and printing and distributing pamphlets throughout the country.

A small group met at Delmonico's restaurant in New York on February 6, 1863, and launched the society. Belmont, Barlow, Tilden, Seymour, Brooks, Marble, and others in attendance agreed on basic principles. The Union's preservation should not be used by "extremists" as a cloak for emancipation of the slaves and "subjugation" of the Confederate states and civilians. The North must adopt a policy of tolerance and cooperation between moderates of both sections in order to effect a real and lasting peace. The gathering also expressed anger at the administration's "arbitrary arrests" and "interference" with the freedom of the press. News of the meeting was leaked to Republican organs, and the *Evening Post* and the *Times* branded the entire affair a "surreptitious" gathering of disloyal copperheads. Marble's *World* unsurprisingly rushed to the defense of those present and strongly denied opposition allegations of secrecy or intrigue. Even so, the unwanted publicity resulted in the society's stillbirth.[10]

All of this political activity signified nothing more than the preliminary sparring before the main event—the 1864 presidential election. On the Republican side, Lincoln would obviously run for re-election, despite sniping from Greeley, Fremont, and others. To oppose the President, Belmont thought seriously, at one time or another, of Secretary Chase, Governor Seymour, James Guthrie, and Generals Nathaniel P. Banks and George B. McClellan.

Chase, though he held the number two spot in the Lincoln cabinet, made no secret of his differences with the Chief Executive or of his availability for the Democratic designation. But he

10 Belmont to Tilden, Jan. 27, 1863, Tilden Papers; Mitchell, *Seymour*, 266–67; Charles B. Murphy, "Samuel J. Tilden and the Civil War," *South Atlantic Quarterly*, XXXIII (July, 1934), 265–67; Flick, *Tilden*, 140–42; Nevins and Thomas, eds., *Diary of George Templeton Strong*, III, 297.

would consent to become the Democratic candidate only on a frankly emancipationist platform. Belmont, cognizant of copperhead strength among the Democrats of Ohio, Indiana, and Illinois, feared the injection of such a politically divisive issue at the national convention. Seymour's chief asset lay in his governorship of the state with the largest electoral vote; other than this, fellow Democrats had come to regard him as insecure and weak, particularly in view of his equivocal performance during the New York City draft riots of July, 1863. Guthrie's qualifications were threefold: Treasury Secretary under Pierce, a loyal Unionist from the border state of Kentucky, and president of the strategic Louisville & Nashville Railroad. But most people considered Guthrie at the age of seventy too old. Banks, a Democrat-turned-American (Know-Nothing)-turned-Republican and a contender for the 1860 Republican nomination, had previous political experience as a congressman and governor from Massachusetts; in addition, he had been a railroad executive until his appointment as a major-general in the Union Army. But his frequent switching of party allegiance rendered him unacceptable to many Democratic leaders.[11]

General McClellan, whose home base was New Jersey, became Belmont's first choice for the nomination. The "Little Napoleon," as his admirers hailed him, possessed undeniable political assets. He was young—only thirty-seven years old—dashing, a loyal Democrat, and on intimate terms with Barlow, Marble, and Fernando Wood. He had no political experience, but his rank in the Union Army would frustrate Republican attempts to charge the Democrats with "coppery" sympathies. As commander of the Army of the Potomac until his dismissal in November, 1862, he had gained a national reputation as a leader of men. The controversy surrounding his dismissal did

[11] Belmont to Chase, May 29, 1868, Seymour to Belmont, Aug. 12, 1863, private Belmont collection; Belmont to Marble, Dec. 10, 1868, Marble Papers; Isachar Zacharie to Banks, Dec. 28, 1863, in Charles M. Segal, "Isachar Zacharie: Lincoln's Chiropodist," *Publication of the American Jewish Historical Society*, XLIII (Dec., 1953), 71–122.

Horatio Seymour (Library of Congress)

George B. McClellan (Library of Congress)

nothing to diminish his popularity and in fact made him that much more widely known.[12]

Belmont and other Democrats began to work for McClellan's nomination as early as 1862, though the extent to which the general himself participated is arguable. William S. Myers, his principal biographer, maintains that McClellan yielded to party pressure only at the last minute, but the general certainly behaved like a candidate from the moment Lincoln relieved him of his command. Soon after, Belmont sent McClellan copies of letters he had written to Lincoln, Chase, and Seward, urging a revision of administration war policies. In his answer, the general confided his "greatest regret . . . that the administration could not be induced to act in accordance with your views. Some such policy as that you urged must yet be adopted or we

[12] The best account of McClellan's public career is William S. Myers, *General George B. McClellan: A Study in Personality* (New York, 1934).

are lost." Correspondence between Seymour and Barlow, at about the same time, indicated their interest in McClellan as a likely nominee. Barlow headed a movement in late 1862 which raised funds and purchased a four-story house for the McClellan family in Manhattan.

All this made a profound impression on the general and widened the sphere of his social and public activities. Belmont, Barlow, Marble, and other friends found numerous occasions to soothe McClellan's injured feelings and reinforce his sense of injustice received at the hands of the Lincoln regime. Opera and theater patrons frequently saw the general in Belmont's company.[13] The national chairman also presented a masquerade ball in his mansion, at which McClellan was the guest of honor.[14]

All during 1863 Barlow and Marble joshed McClellan about his "presidential candidacy." These party leaders did not fail to notify the general of pro-McClellan demonstrations in the North that followed Union military defeats and hastened to assure him that his popular strength could easily gain him the 1864 nomination and, indeed, the presidency. Marble informed McClellan a year before Election Day that "the people's eyes are turned all one way in their search for the candidate who will win in 1864" and that Seymour echoed this view. The general's endorsement of a Democratic gubernatorial candidate in Pennsylvania in the fall of 1863 also helped link his name with the country's political opposition.[15]

[13] Myers, McClellan, 405–06, 421–22, 438–39; McClellan to Belmont, Dec. 27, 1862, private Belmont collection; Seymour to Barlow, Nov. 15, 1862, Barlow Papers.

[14] One of Belmont's other guests, the thirty-year-old English Marquis of Hartington, engaged the general in conversation while tactlessly displaying a miniature Confederate flag in his buttonhole. McClellan remained impassive in the face of the enemy insignia. When a wounded war veteran present threatened to punch Hartington in the nose, the Englishman apologized. Belmont, taking no chances, escorted the foreigner through a side door leading to the stable, from where Hartington made his escape. Perry Belmont, An American Democrat, 123; Nevins and Thomas, eds., Diary of George Templeton Strong, III, 300–01; Belmont to Barlow, Oct. 12, 1869, Barlow Papers.

[15] Myers, McClellan, 310–11, 429–32; Marble to McClellan, Nov. 16, 1863, George Brinton McClellan Papers, Library of Congress.

On January 12, 1864, Belmont held a national committee meeting at his Fifth Avenue home, the first since the summer of 1860. Most of the twenty-three members attended; only the weather accounted for the absence of some westerners. The chairman opened the discussion by informing his colleagues that Democratic congressmen, meeting at his request, had wired their preference for a May convention to be held in Cincinnati. Some committeemen immediately raised objections to the date, and Belmont joined them. He believed that time could be the party's most efficient ally—time which witnessed added defeats in the field and increased taxes and conscription at home. After additional discussion, the committee chose to forego the obvious advantages of an early campaign organization for the "outs" and fixed July 4, a relatively late (but not insignificant) date for the convention. The group also went against the Congressional recommendation for the convention locale and chose Chicago over Cincinnati, a tribute to the late, revered Douglas. The committee approved a Chicago construction firm's plan to erect a large amphitheater, at an approximate cost of $7,000 to Chicago Democrats and businessmen, to house the 15,000 people expected to attend the convention.

Several members then proposed that the national committee venture beyond its traditional role of merely setting the time and place of the quadrennial meetings. Why not have the committee present to the nation what it regarded as the party's authentic position on vital contemporary issues? Belmont endorsed this innovation, but a majority, reluctant to usurp the national convention's functions, voted it down.[16]

In February Belmont attended the Democratic State Convention to try to mold the New York delegation to Chicago into a solid bloc for McClellan. But four different New York City contingents turned up in Albany's Tweddle Hall and demanded recognition. The convention decided once and for all to put an end to this chronic nuisance and adopted a resolution that state convention delegates from the downstate metropolis should

16 Hugh J. Jewett to Belmont, Jan. 9, 1864, private Belmont collection; *New York World*, Jan. 13, 23, June 17, 1864; *New York Times*, Sept. 1, 1864.

henceforth be elected by State Assembly districts, not by rival groups like Tammany Hall, Mozart Hall, the McKeon Democracy, or the German-American Democratic Organization. The McKeon faction won a majority of the New York seats for the moment. Though Belmont was identified with Tammany, the convention elected him one of the state's four delegates-at-large. Yet the banker's primary purpose in going to Albany went unfulfilled. Belmont and other War Democrats got unit-rule voting for Chicago over the opposition of Peace Democrats, but they failed to get the delegation to commit itself in advance to McClellan.[17]

The weeks preceding the Chicago convention were filled with startling developments in the Republican camp—developments which cheered Belmont and his political cohorts. A few disaffected Republicans met in a Cleveland convention at the end of May and nominated General Fremont, the 1856 candidate, for the presidency. Fremont accepted immediately and delivered a stinging rebuke to Lincoln.[18] A short time later, the President pocket-vetoed the Wade-Davis reconstruction bill, leading its Republican sponsors, Senator Benjamin F. Wade of Ohio and Representative Henry Winter Davis of Maryland, to issue a scathing denunciation of the President whom they had just helped renominate. The last day of June brought another bombshell—Chase's resignation from the cabinet. In addition to these blows on the political front, peace agitation increased after Lincoln's generals suffered a series of military setbacks.

Belmont hastily arranged a top-level party conference midway in June to discuss whether the changing political scene should be matched by a change in Democratic tactics. Governor Seymour and Dean Richmond spoke for a group favoring postponement of the national convention until September in order to overcome existing Democratic dissension on the party platform to be adopted. Decisive changes in the Union's mili-

[17] New York Herald, Feb. 24-26, 1864.
[18] The regular Republicans met at Baltimore the following week, and every state but Missouri came committed to the President's renomination. New York Times, June 9, 1864.

tary situation might swing the mass of the party rank and file decisively over either to a war or a peace platform and thus fix convention policy from the bottom up. Other influential members of the national committee opposed any delay, fearing it could only prevent effective organization.

Belmont, too, was undecided regarding a convention date and asked Barlow to secure McClellan's opinion. The general passed on the word that he had no objection to postponement and, despite the strong objections of the pro-Democratic, antiwar *New York Journal of Commerce* and some midwestern papers, Belmont pushed through an eight-week deferment after a brief meeting with six other national committeemen. Belmont's official pronouncement attributed the changed convention date to the national committee's "deference to the desire of a very large number of the leading members of the conservative Union Democratic Party throughout the country." The chairman then called for a full meeting of the Democratic National Committee on June 30 in Washington so that Congressional Democrats could attend. The purpose of general consultation was the "deliberate consideration of important business" involving seating and procedural arrangements for the convention.[19]

Though Belmont faced the nominating convention anxious to prevent any repetition of Charleston, wishful thinking by itself could not alter certain political realities. A large number of influential midwestern Democrats desired peace and opposed war with other Americans, regardless of political or moral considerations. These "peace" Democrats (like the pro-Confederate "copperheads") stood opposed to a McClellan candidacy. The former commander of the Army of the Potomac, even in semi-retirement, still symbolized to them the Federal Government's unconstitutional attempt to coerce some member states to remain part of the Union against their will. They recalled vividly how McClellan, in 1861, had ordered the "arbitrary arrest" of several Maryland state legislators whom he suspected of favoring that state's secession.

[19] *New York World*, June 13, 14, 17, 23, 24, 1864; Belmont to Barlow, June 14, 1864, Barlow Papers; *New York Journal of Commerce*, June 13, 1864.

Pro-McClellan Representative Samuel S. Cox of Ohio warned that nearly one-half of his state's Chicago-bound delegation were against the general and sought to prejudice his chances in neighboring states. Prominent Indiana Democrats, led by former Senator John Pettit, voiced their aversion to a McClellan nomination and charged him with belonging to a New York City "clique" and being "engineered too much by its bankers." Even Seymour now held back from the general's candidacy, preferring instead seventy-one-year-old Associate Supreme Court Justice Samuel Nelson of New York. In sum, a variety of Democrats opposed to war and to McClellan would have to be accommodated if Belmont and his colleagues expected to lead a united party in the coming presidential campaign.[20]

In the last week of August, Belmont, Seymour, Tilden, and others in the Empire State delegation boarded a train for Buffalo, where they joined Dean Richmond and went on to Chicago. A *New York Times* reporter assigned to cover the convention witnessed their arrival in the Windy City and chose to single Belmont out for special attention. The national chairman, he noted, easily stood out from the run-of-the-mill, office-seeking politician. He belonged to that class of wealthy, liberal contributors which proved invaluable to party organizations. As to motives for such largess, Belmont "no doubt has an eye to some future contingency, for he is not a man whose tastes, associations, or inclinations would otherwise lead him to adopt politics." The journalist supposed that the national chairman, in the event of McClellan's nomination and election, would be duly offered a foreign mission "in compensation of his early and faithful adhesion to 'Little Mac's' cause."[21]

Whatever his future contained, Belmont found much in the present to exasperate him, particularly Seymour's behavior. The governor let it be known that he would refuse renomination to Albany, leaving himself available for other calls to duty. He denied privately any interest in the presidential office, but his

[20] Amasa J. Parker to McClellan, July 24, 1864, Samuel S. Cox to McClellan, Aug. 4, 1864, McClellan Papers; *New York Times*, Aug. 28, 30, 1864.
[21] *New York Times*, Sept. 4, 1864.

friends in the New York and other delegations were declaring their support for him. Belmont discounted Seymour's "announced preference" for Justice Nelson and suspected the governor of harboring "dark horse" aspirations. In a letter to Barlow on the eve of the convention, Belmont described how "Seymour blows hot & cold. . . . He professes not to be a candidate *& will be none if I can help it.*" Belmont's uneasiness was not dispelled when a majority of the Empire State contingent refused even to be polled for its presidential choice as late as the evening before the convention, though he doubted that Seymour's prestige was strong enough to keep New York from giving a first ballot vote to McClellan. Belmont kept the general regularly informed of these developments, both directly and through their mutual friend Barlow.[22]

Belmont, in his capacity as Democratic National Chairman, officially opened the convention at noon, August 29, 1864. His welcoming speech to the assembled delegates was variously described as "easy and convincing" and as "violent." Undoubtedly, both views were partly correct. Belmont sought to unite the conglomeration of Peace Democrats, War Democrats, old-line Whigs, Know-Nothings, so-called Conservatives, States' Rights extremists, and pacifists into an effective force, and simultaneously to hold out some attraction to that sector of the public still uncommitted to a presidential candidate or party. He stressed the urgency of maintaining the Democracy's "devotion to the Union and the Constitution," while castigating "four years of misrule [which] had well-nigh brought the Republic to the verge of ruin." The past and present held sufficient warnings of the disastrous consequences which would befall the country in the event of Lincoln's re-election. Inevitably, the results would be "the utter disintegration of our whole political and social system amid bloodshed and anarchy with the great problems of liberal progress and self-government jeopardized for generations to come." The eyes of the Ameri-

22 Belmont to Barlow, Aug. 26, 28, 1864, Barlow Papers; *New York Times*, Aug. 28, 1864; Mitchell, *Seymour*, 362–66; Barlow to Marble, Aug. 24, 26, 28, 1864, Marble Papers; Barlow to McClellan, Aug. 27, 29, 1864, McClellan Papers.

can people focused on Chicago, where "we meet not as War
Democrats, or as Peace Democrats, but as citizens of a common
country, laboring in a common cause." Belmont, anticipating
the wrangling over the platform, called for "conciliation and
forbearance" to control the convention's deliberations. Finally,
he promised the party that most Americans would rush to the
support of its candidate "provided you will offer to their
suffrage a tried patriot." Many delegates interpreted this remark
to allude to McClellan, and a host of them, notably those in the
eastern state sections, responded with applause.[23]

Opposing factions fought their first important struggle at a
meeting of the Resolutions Committee, charged with drafting
the campaign platform. Belmont foresaw "trouble," for the
Ohio copperhead, former Representative Clement L. Vallandigham, made no secret of his intention to force the "peace
issue." Vallandigham wanted the committee chairmanship, but
an equally determined effort by Tilden and other War Democrats elected Belmont's friend Guthrie, thirteen to eleven. Vallandigham continued his battle, insisting that the committee
favor an immediate armistice: "After four years of failure to restore the Union by the experiment of war," with the Constitution "disregarded in every part, and public liberty and private
right alike trodden down," there should be a cessation of hostilities leading to "an ultimate convention of the states" to restore
peace on the basis of a federal Union. Tilden and Guthrie
(with Belmont and Marble behind the scenes) helped defeat
the proposal in committee. They held that the President alone
should determine the time for such action and that the Confederate states must return to the Union before any permanent
peace could be effected.

The War Democrats' victory, however, was short-lived. Vallandigham's controversial resolution won a majority on the convention floor, inviting the indignant scorn of War Democrats
within the party and Unionists outside. The delegates' ac-

---

[23] Flick, *Tilden*, 148; James G. Blaine, *Twenty Years of Congress: From
Lincoln to Garfield* (2 vols., Norwich, Conn., 1884–86), I, 525–26; *New York
Times*, Aug. 30, 1864.

ceptance of a negotiated peace dismayed Belmont. He tried to spare McClellan by depicting the platform as "less objectionable" than the one the "Western peace men, who are very ultra," actually wanted. But Noah Brooks, a Washington, D.C., journalist, marked the national chairman's "profoundly sad" expression after the delegates had roared approval of the "peace" plank.[24]

Petty annoyances added to Belmont's discomfort. A Maryland delegate, Benjamin G. Harris, threw the auditorium into an uproar by denouncing McClellan as a "ruthless tyrant" for the 1861 arrests. Seymour continued "ogling with the ultra peace men," such as Fernando Wood, evidently with the notion that the convention prize might still be in store for him. George Francis Train, a well-known contemporary "character," amused the crowds in the gallery with uncomplimentary imitations of McClellan, Belmont, and other prominent War Democrats.[25]

Not once during the preliminary proceedings did Belmont doubt McClellan's eventual nomination. The New York delegation finally held an informal ballot the morning of Belmont's opening speech, and the banker joyfully wired Barlow that McClellan received 53 of the 66 half-votes cast. The six New England states also solidly backed the general, as did many delegates from other geographical sections. On the evening before the formal balloting, the optimistic Belmont sent Barlow a brief telegram which, for the first time in five days, did not utilize

[24] Mitchell, *Seymour*, 366–67; Flick, *Tilden*, 148–49; Noah Brooks, *Washington in Lincoln's Time* (New York, 1958), 168; Belmont to McClellan, Sept. 3, 1864, McClellan Papers. Republican newspapers later reprinted a letter from Confederate journals in which Vice President Stephens praised the Democratic peace plank, much to the annoyance of Belmont, McClellan, and the War Democrats. The Vallandigham plank, Stephens wrote, "presents a ray of light which, under Providence, may prove the dawn of the day to this long and cheerless night, the first ray of light I have seen from the North since the War began. It cheers the heart . . . and quickens the hope." *New York Times*, Oct. 16, 1864.

[25] *Official Proceedings of the Democratic National Convention Held in Chicago* (Chicago, 1864), 39; William F. Zornow, *Lincoln & the Party Divided* (Norman, Okla., 1954), 131; *New York Times*, Sept. 2, 1864.

their privately arranged cipher: "All going well. Success sure."
The balloting began Wednesday morning, August 31, and at
the end of the first tally McClellan had twelve votes over the
necessary two-thirds figure. Most of the anti-McClellan delegations now switched votes to the candidate, though holdouts for
former Governor Thomas H. Seymour of Connecticut, a
cousin of Horatio, prevented a unanimous nomination.[26]

Belmont, still smarting privately from the "Vallandigham
plank," moved tirelessly behind the scenes to round out the
ticket with another War Democrat. His leading choice, James
Guthrie, would complement McClellan, and his nomination
would help counter Lincoln's shrewd choice of Tennessee's
Military Governor Andrew Johnson, also a War Democrat, for
the Republican vice presidential place. But Belmont's proposed
balance of a northern War Democrat with a southern War
Democrat conflicted with the will of the convention majority,
which favored an eastern War Democrat balanced with a western Peace Democrat. Their choice was Representative George
H. Pendleton of Ohio, a pacifist.

On the first ballot, Guthrie led Pendleton, 65½ to 54½, but
these totals fell far short of the necessary 151 votes, the rest
being split among six other men. Belmont hoped Guthrie would
now gather support from the delegates backing these minor
candidates. Instead, more and more delegates came to feel that
Pendleton's nomination would be a better contribution to party
unity by mollifying the anti-McClellan men. In a repudiation of
Belmont's express preference, his own state, New York, led the
way by switching from Guthrie to Pendleton on the second
ballot. Pennsylvania followed New York, and a Pendleton
stampede ensued.

Belmont was aghast at the prospect of the Union's former
military chief coupled with the Democrats' most outspoken
"peace" man. No public official had labored harder or longer to
obstruct and discourage the Union war effort. Pendleton had
consistently maintained that coercing seceded states was uncon-

[26] Belmont to Barlow, Aug. 30, 1864, Barlow Papers; Belmont to McClellan,
Sept. 3, 1864, McClellan Papers; New York Times, Aug. 30, Sept. 1, 1864.

stitutional and regularly voted against measures intended to
raise government revenue and increase Union Army enlist-
ments. Only a few months earlier, he had opposed a Congressional resolution "that it is the political, civil, moral, and sacred
duty of the people to meet the rebellion, fight it, crush it, and
forever destroy it." Yet like it or not, the McClellan-Pendleton
ticket was not just a Belmont nightmare but a fact.[27]

One more item remained on the convention agenda—the selection of a new national committee. Belmont had had his fill of
the leadership post long before these convention reverses. On
the opening day he had written Barlow that "I have a most hor-
rid time here, & I don't think you'll catch me again on a National Committee." But the victory of McClellan and the defeat
of Guthrie caused Belmont to reconsider. He had worked
strenuously for McClellan's successful nomination and still believed the general would defeat Lincoln. Would he not be in a
stronger position for a government post in his present party capacity than in none at all? Belmont had also to consider the possibility that the party machinery might fall into the hands of
the "peace" men. With them in control, many loyal Americans
would be alienated from the Democratic Party for the war's
duration and probably long after. Personal ambitions and political exigencies combined to overcome Belmont's earlier reluctance. Dean Richmond, still New York's Democratic chieftain,
renamed Belmont to the state's seat on the national committee,
and the banker's reputation secured him another term as chairman.[28]

The end of the convention hardly heralded the end of tick-
lish party situations. Belmont knew that for the sake of unity
McClellan's formal letter of acceptance must appear to repudiate the spirit of the Vallandigham plank without seriously an-
tagonizing the "peace" men and copperheads. The day following his return from Chicago, the chairman wrote McClellan a
long letter in which advice was thinly disguised as suggestion:

27 *New York Times*, Sept. 1, 4, 23, 1864; Brummer, *Political History of New
York State*, 405–06.
28 Belmont to Barlow, Aug. 29, 1864, Barlow Papers; *New York World*,
Sept. 2, 1864.

I congratulate you with all my heart to your glorious nomination, which with God's help we mean to make in November a glorious election. . . . It is absolutely necessary that in your reply of acceptance you place yourself squarely & unequivocally on the ground that you will never surrender one foot of soil & that peace can only be based upon the reconstruction of the Union. In other words, cessation of hostilities or an armistice can only be agreed upon after we have sufficient guarantee from the South that they are ready for a peace under the Union. . . . You know best how to express all this. . . . [Your letter is of such] importance that I deemed it my duty to write to you about it.[29]

Other Democratic leaders sent their opinions. Barlow stressed caution: "Our wisest friends hope that the alternative of *war* by name may be excluded from your letter by use of other terms equally forcible. . . . If this can be done . . . it seems to me better." From the other side, Vallandigham, suspecting that McClellan would be pressured to assume a more vigorous prowar stance than that contained in the platform, wrote him a "strictly private" letter. He begged the nominee to "hear the words of one who has nothing so much at heart as your success. Do not listen to any of your Eastern friends who in an evil hour may advise you to *insinuate* even a little war into your letter of acceptance." Vallandigham warned McClellan that any words suggesting the necessity of further war upon the South would cause two hundred thousand men in the West to withhold their support. "Accept the word on this subject of one who knows." [30]

McClellan's letter of acceptance, issued September 9, demonstrated that his "Eastern friends" were the paramount influence. Nowhere did he refer to the controversial Vallandigham plank, though he did attempt to modify the party's official stand on the arrangements by which the Union could be restored. The national convention had proclaimed, through acclamation of the "peace" plank, its desire for the cessation of hostilities *before* entering into negotiations toward restoring the Union. McClellan, in effect, now reversed the order. In line

[29] Belmont to McClellan, Sept. 3, 1864, McClellan Papers.
[30] Barlow to McClellan, Sept. 3, 1864, Vallandigham to McClellan, Sept. 4, 1864, McClellan Papers.

with Belmont's advice, he insisted that the old Union be re-established before pacification could prevail. Thus, where the convention said "Peace first and Union afterward (if it can be had)," McClellan replied, "Union first and then peace," for no peace could be permanent without the Union.[31]

As was expected, McClellan's statement met with extreme disfavor in "peace" Democratic circles. Barlow learned of Charles O'Conor's intention to write an open letter attacking the nominee's acceptance statement, but he assured McClellan that two Philadelphia lawyers, "Reed & Rundle," had promised to assist in dissuading the recalcitrant O'Conor. Fernando Wood's *Daily News* accused McClellan of having reneged on his approval of the Vallandigham plank, "both in its letter and in its spirit." Wood called for a new Democratic National Convention, "either to remodel the platform to suit the nominee, or nominate a candidate to suit the platform." Small gatherings of "peace" Democrats throughout northern cities denounced McClellan and urged another nominee upon the party. Vallandigham was so incensed after reading McClellan's letter that he authorized the withdrawal of his name from party campaigns in his home state.[32]

Belmont tried to ignore this chorus of disapproval. He wrote Marble of the "universal admiration" for the general's statement. "Indeed, if we carry the election at all it will be owing *entirely* to the stand which the General has taken." He even told Republican friends it would surely secure McClellan the White House. Yet, underneath this surface confidence, Belmont worried about Pendleton. The national chairman and his cohorts deluged the Ohioan with telegrams requesting him to "understand" McClellan's position.[33] Pendleton's answer was to inform Belmont that he preferred to forego the ceremony of

31 *New York Times*, Sept. 9, 10, 1864.

32 Barlow to McClellan, Sept. 12, 1864, McClellan Papers; *New York Times*, Sept. 12, 15, 1864; Edward C. Kirkland, *The Peacemakers of 1864* (New York, 1927), 136–37.

33 Belmont to Marble, Sept. 13, 1864, Marble Papers; Amos Kendall to McClellan, Sept. 10, 1864, McClellan Papers; Nevins and Thomas, eds., *Diary of George Templeton Strong*, III, 482; *New York Times*, Oct. 16, 1864.

notification usually tendered major party nominees and that he
would rather not campaign "on the stump." His Congressional
speeches constituted the record he would stand on, and besides,
he could not see how, in all propriety, he could ask people to
vote for himself.[34]

Under the circumstances Belmont wanted to avoid any repetition of the fund-raising problems that occurred during the
Douglas campaign. He was convinced that thousands of Americans would contribute toward the party's expenses if they were
certain that their money would be legitimately and advanta-
geously used. One way Belmont hoped to remedy this was by
soliciting contributions through regular editorials and advertise-
ments in every loyal Democratic newspaper.

In another approach he established a Central Executive Campaign Committee, sponsored by respectable Democrats such as
lawyers Tilden and O'Conor, banker William B. Duncan,
journalists Marble and William C. Prime, and seasoned politicians John Kelly, John T. Hoffman, and William Marcy
Tweed. Besides the financial duties, Belmont charged the committee with the publication and distribution of documents and
pamphlets designed to bring about an electoral triumph. Within
a week after McClellan's acceptance letter, the committee,
through the offices of Marble's *World*, prepared twenty-seven
campaign documents. They ranged from former New York
University Professor Samuel F. B. Morse's *Ethical Position of
Slavery in the Social System*, which attacked Lincoln's Emancipation Proclamation, to Union General Franz Sigel's *Why I
Won't Stump for Old Abe*, a critical appraisal of administration
policies designed ostensibly for German-American voters.[35]

[34] Pendleton to Belmont, Sept. 27, 1864, McClellan Papers. Most of the
"peace" newspapers eventually emulated Pendleton's attitude by ignoring Mc-
Clellan's letter and concentrating their fire on the Republican administration
and the war. The quasi-official *New York World* supported McClellan's right
to his own views and maintained that the general "of course" accepted the
Chicago platform "when he accepted the nomination." *New York World*,
Sept. 17, 1864; *New York Times*, Sept. 18, 1864.

[35] McClellan to Barlow, Sept. 4, 1864, Seymour to McClellan, Sept. 5, 1864,
Frederick O. Prince to McClellan, Sept. 17, 1864, McClellan Papers; Belmont
to Marble, Sept. 24, 1864, Duncan to Marble, Sept. (?), 1864, Marble Papers;
New York World, Oct. 7, 11, 1864.

If the administrative machinery was functioning smoothly, the same could not be said of the campaign itself. McClellan had not expanded on his postnomination statement or spelled out the ways in which he would implement it. His acceptance letter was his first and final stand on any issue of consequence for the balance of the campaign. Whatever the cause of his inertia, McClellan's idea of an "active" campaign meant remaining at his New Jersey home so as to be available to greet any and all peregrinating Democrats. This contrasted sharply with Douglas' 1860 methods and techniques and threw an additional burden upon the national committee.[36]

The active support of highly optimistic McClellan enthusiasts lightened Belmont's load somewhat in the early weeks of the campaign, but as time progressed it fell more and more to Belmont to promote the candidate whom he was in large measure responsible for the party's having picked. He organized McClellan ratification meetings, bonfires, and other celebrations then deemed essential to stimulate party spirit and attract the average voter. Belmont frequently spoke at these events, hammering home his convention theme "to restore the Union as it was" and criticizing the administration's erosion of states' rights. He warned listeners to beware of the Republican-sponsored National Union Party with which the administration planned to "confuse" Union-loving Democrats into supporting a war "waged for us by Abolition." [37]

Belmont was instrumental in persuading an unwilling Governor Seymour to become a candidate for reelection. His convincing argument, seconded by Marble, Tilden, and Richmond, centered on Seymour's earlier opposition to McClellan's candi-

[36] Myers, *McClellan*, 458–59.

[37] Belmont, *Letters and Speeches of Late Civil War*, 113–20; Zornow, *Lincoln & The Party Divided*, 45; Nevins and Thomas, eds., *Diary of George Templeton Strong*, III, 488–89; *New York Times*, Sept. 15, Oct. 22, 1864; *New York World*, Sept. 19, 1864. This ad hoc "Union" ticket was especially worrisome, as the number and quality of War Democrats endorsing the Lincoln-Johnson ticket continued to grow all during the campaign. Former New York Democratic officeholders and contributors who publicly announced for Lincoln included Francis B. Cutting, Moses Taylor, Edwards Pierrepont, John A. Dix, Alexander Hamilton, Jr., Peter Cooper, Robert B. Roosevelt, Alexander T. Stewart, and Henry G. Stebbins.

dacy. The fact of this opposition, coupled with the governor's refusal to run, could be regarded by voters as evidence that Seymour had no confidence in the general's ability to carry the country in November. Seymour yielded to party pressure.[38]

Experience had taught Belmont the importance of a strong showing in state elections. Sensing a good opportunity for McClellan in New Hampshire, he contracted with a Boston printing firm to circulate a number of pamphlets to each household in the state. One Boston newspaper editor asserted that Belmont personally paid the entire printing and distribution cost of $15,000, an item which horrified the Boston patrician, Edward Everett: "What a scandal that an election might be carried by the money of a German Jew . . . , the agent of the Rothschilds!" [39]

Belmont's twenty-two years of summer residence in Newport, where his friends included Rhode Island's political, social, and religious leaders, gave him a particularly strong interest in that tiny state's political destiny. Thanks to the questionable leadership of William Beach Lawrence and his son, Isaac, who were "enough to kill any political party," the Democrats there did not enjoy "good repute." The national chairman consulted Thomas M. Clark, the influential Episcopal Bishop of Rhode Island, who advised him to "secure" some of the state's more moderate newspapers, as no good Democratic organ existed there. The clergyman also promised to write an anti-Lincoln political pamphlet. Unfortunately for the Democratic cause, the pamphlet caused an uproar among pro-administration Episcopalians. When the commotion was followed by a decrease in dinner invitations, Clark withdrew his work from circulation, and by the end of October was reported to be delivering "vigorous" war sermons. Belmont even tried to attract the support of the anti-Lincoln Republican Senator William

[38] Mitchell, *Seymour*, 372–73; *New York Times*, Aug. 18, 1879.

[39] *New York Times*, Sept. 18, 1864; Paul R. Frothingham, *Edward Everett: Orator and Statesman* (Boston, 1925), 463–64. The figure of $15,000 was undoubtedly exaggerated, for at this same time "lack of means" was rendering it "absolutely impossible" to furnish hard-up Maryland Democrats with anything but speakers. Belmont to Marble, Oct. 24, 25, 1864, Marble Papers.

Sprague, not knowing that Sprague hated McClellan even more than the President and that the senator's father-in-law, Salmon Chase, had persuaded him not to engage in any overt anti-Lincoln acts.[40]

In October, key elections were due in the swing states of Pennsylvania, Ohio, and Indiana, and Belmont looked forward to these tests of strength. He asked McClellan to get some of his wealthy New York friends to "exert themselves a little" by sending money and providing speakers for the Democratic ticket in Pennsylvania. He got Marble to mail a printed circular requesting contributions to over 400 prominent Democrats "of different cliques." The result was an enthusiastic (if rare) display of party generosity. Cognizant of the crucial German-American vote in the Keystone State, Belmont, with the aid of Oswald Ottendorfer, publisher of the *New-Yorker Staats-Zeitung*, succeeded in dispatching a number of "good German speakers" to Pennsylvania in the closing weeks of the canvass. The chairman even considered, at one time, inviting Pendleton to stump Pennsylvania for the state ticket, for though he feared the vice presidential nominee's "peace proclivities," the Ohioan's "silence does us as much harm as anything he would be likely to say."

Optimistic reports from Pennsylvania Democrats led Belmont to hold back on Pendleton's services. Indeed, the assurances were so persuasive that Belmont, in advance of the event, publicly called on all loyal New York City Democratic clubs to illumine their respective headquarters on October 17, signifying Gotham's congratulations "to our brothers in Pennsylvania on their hard-earned and triumphant success." When the returns came in, Pennsylvania went solidly Republican, and Democratic celebrations were hastily canceled, much to the amusement of administration papers.[41]

Belmont's sources in Ohio were more accurate in their pre-

40 Belmont to Marble, Sept. 13, 1864, Marble Papers; Nevins and Thomas, eds., *Diary of George Templeton Strong*, III, 498.
41 Barlow to McClellan, Sept. 23, 1864, Belmont to McClellan, Oct. 1, 1864, McClellan to Barlow, Oct. 21, 1864, McClellan Papers; Belmont to Marble, Sept. 24, Oct. 25, 1864, Marble Papers; *New York Times*, Oct. 17, 20, 28, 1864.

election pulsetaking than the ones in Pennsylvania. The prognosis was a Democratic defeat, the only thing open to question being the size of that defeat. John A. Green, Jr., estimated that thousands of Ohio Republicans preferred McClellan over Lincoln, but would vote with their party in the October contests.[42] Rufus P. Ranny, Ohio's national committeeman, reported from Cleveland that he saw little chance of carrying the governorship, the state legislature, or a majority of the Congressional seats. Congressman Cox complained that the Republican state legislature had gerrymandered his district in an effort to defeat him and asked for all possible assistance from national committee headquarters. Belmont promised Cox a sizeable batch of campaign documents "as soon as issued" and, owing to the low state of available funds, sent him a personal contribution of $500. Campaign propaganda and financial donations availed the Ohio Democrats and Cox nothing in October. An already pessimistic Belmont was dazed by a Republican victory of such magnitude that a 15–4 Democratic edge in Ohio's delegation to the House of Representatives turned into a 16–3 Republican one.[43]

The situation in Indiana was just another variation on the same theme. Guthrie, a candidate in neighboring Kentucky for a United States Senate seat, believed southern Indiana "safe," but expected "little good" from the central and northern sections. National committeeman William E. Niblack of Vincennes, a former congressman running for re-election, reported on the "unbeatable amount of Republican expenditures and propaganda" blanketing the Hoosier State. Former Congressman John G. Davis predicted that opposition "fraud" would overcome the antiwar proclivities of most Indianans. Other correspondents pleaded for funds and pamphlets for use in the

[42] Green to Belmont, Oct. 3, 1864, Marble Papers. Green was a friend of *Cincinnati Enquirer* publisher Washington McLean, whom Belmont knew from Douglas days.
[43] Ranny to Belmont, Oct. 5, 1864, Cox to Belmont, Sept. 15, 1864, private Belmont collection; Belmont to Cox, Sept. 23, 1864, Samuel Sullivan Cox Papers, Brown University. Cox, following his defeat, moved to New York City and served irregularly in its Congressional corps from 1869 to 1889.

state canvass, for, as one of them put it, "the Oct. elections will decide that of Novr." The results bore out the pessimism of Belmont's correspondents, and Indiana went the way of Ohio.[44]

The unhappy results of the October elections forced Belmont to importune McClellan and Pendleton to participate more actively on the campaign trail. He got the general to take a political trip to Pennsylvania and arranged for Pendleton to leave his home state at last. The national chairman placed only one condition on the nominees' politicking—that under no circumstances should they appear together on the same platform. If Republican newspapers persisted in ridiculing the Democrats for wearing two faces, for having a platform susceptible of double construction, and for shouting war cries in one place and peace in another, that couldn't be helped. But there was no point in emphasizing the Chicago convention's folly by presenting its choices on one dais.[45]

Belmont, in his capacity as chief executive officer of the Democratic Party, felt it his duty to intervene in the debate surrounding military suffrage. Voting in the field constituted a novelty for the era. Every state's constitution and election laws referred to electors casting ballots within their state boundaries and in their defined election districts. Republican spokesmen on state and national levels now conceived the idea that states, either by legislative enactment or constitutional provision, could authorize their citizens to vote while outside state boundaries.

Democrats uniformly and persistently opposed military suffrage because they believed a fair and free election in the field impossible. They feared that individual soldiers would be influenced by their superiors to vote the Republican ticket or even that entire regiments would vote "as the colonel said." No state with a Democratic majority passed a soldiers' voting bill, while those with Republican or "Unionist" forces in legislative

---

[44] Barlow to McClellan, Sept. 23, 1864, Belmont to McClellan, Oct. 1, 1864, McClellan Papers; Barlow to Belmont, Sept. 30, 1864, Davis to Belmont, Oct. 2, 1864, private Belmont collection; William P. Davis to John G. Davis, Oct. 24, 1864, John Givan Davis Papers, Indiana Historical Society.

[45] McClellan to Barlow, Oct. 21, 1864, McClellan Papers; Belmont to Marble, Oct. 25, 1864, Marble Papers; New York Times, Oct. 28, 1864.

leadership did. The latter generally attempted to meet Democratic fears by inserting very stringent provisions in the laws,
designed to secure soldiers from undue influence, while capital-
izing on those fears by disseminating political pamphlets to
citizen-soldiers citing chapter and verse of Democratic opposition to military suffrage.[46]

Belmont did not share the general Democratic suspicion of
soldier voting and viewed it as a key factor in determining the
outcome of the presidential race. In an optimistic vein, he felt
that McClellan's popularity among the troops would more than
outweigh that percentage of soldiers which identified its patriotic endeavors with the Lincoln administration. Still, he realized
that arranging with a Republican regime in Washington for fair
elections behind military lines posed a major problem. In a letter to Secretary of War Stanton, a former Democrat, Belmont
urged that "all qualified voters in the military service of the
Government [be permitted to exercise] . . . their rights of
suffrage, when on actual duty, wherever they happen to be, on
the day of election." Would the War Department authorize the
admission of persons, designated by Belmont, to enter within
the military lines and issue Democratic voting tickets? "Our
soldiers should have the . . . same freedom of choice they
would have at home. Their faithful services in the cause of their
country entitle them to this privilege."

Stanton's reply, sent through Assistant Adjutant General Edward D. Townsend, assured Belmont that the War Department
would make available "proper and equal facilities" under a general regulation for the distribution of voting tickets. In fact, the
matter had already been referred to the Union commander,
Lieutenant General Ulysses S. Grant, for his opinion on wording the regulation. Belmont hastily dispatched a Colonel Lan-
sing to interview Grant and secure his authority to circulate the
Democratic ballots. At the same time, the national chairman
wrote to the heads of each Democratic state committee, asking
them to set up machinery with which to supervise voting in

[46] Josiah H. Benton, *Voting in the Field: A Forgotten Chapter of the Civil
War* (Boston, 1915), 306–13, 320.

those regiments and divisions containing their eligible voters.[47]

Belmont's concern about fraudulent military suffrage put him on guard against the possible employment of illegal or unfair methods in the civilian canvass. Using the friendly pages of Marble's *World* to publicize the national committee's complaints, Belmont castigated Andrew Johnson's imposition, purportedly in his role as Tennessee's military governor, of a test oath which sought to exclude from the polls "every man who opposes the policy of Lincoln and his party." Belmont also criticized the silencing of Baltimore's only Democratic newspaper. The national chairman could not even relax his vigilance at home. Party workers in his own Fourth Congressional District, for which Belmont had been chosen presidential elector, discovered a flood of ostensibly Democratic voting tickets containing glaring inaccuracies. Many of them, for example, contained the name of Abram J. Dittenhoffer, the Republican elector for the district, in Belmont's rightful place.[48]

Belmont had become accustomed to the fact that his foreign background, Jewish upbringing, and occupation as an international banker had been a lodestone for Republican slanders during campaigns, but he had always felt that his assets to the Democratic Party outweighed this liability. However, war has a tendency to transform everything it touches, and Belmont's vulnerable position proved no exception. Within the course of the 1864 campaign he was subjected to Democratic as well as Republican injury, running the gamut from sly innuendo to outright libel.

The first attack upon Belmont's integrity predated even the national convention. In a series of letters to McClellan, Colonel Max Langenschwartz, an old and close army friend, warned of "Jew-President Belmont's machinations." The German-born

[47] Belmont to Stanton, Sept. 21, 1864, Seward Papers; Townsend to Belmont, Sept. 23, 1864, Barlow Papers; Belmont to McClellan, Oct. 1, 11, 1864, McClellan to Barlow, Oct. 13, 1864, McClellan Papers; McClellan to Belmont, Oct. 13, 1864, private Belmont collection; Myers, *McClellan*, 463. Benton, *Voting in the Field*, 313, concludes that the soldier vote for President had no significant effect on the outcome.

[48] *New York World*, Oct. 11, 31, Nov. 8, 1864.

Langenschwartz blamed Belmont "and other strong worshippers of Vallandigham" for postponing the national convention
in order to defeat McClellan. After the Chicago convention, he
changed the story to fit the facts, though the mood remained
the same. "The jew A.B." had manipulated the general's nomination in order to transform him into "a wooden instrument."
After the election, Belmont's "true" policies—Confederate independence, French conquest of Mexico, and the obliteration of
America's greatness—would be promulgated. McClellan merci-
fully spared Belmont the contents of these letters. He might as
well not have bothered, because the worst was yet to come and
in such a public manner that it could not possibly escape Belmont's notice.[49]

In Ohio, the peace-at-all-costs *Columbus Crisis*, a nominally
Democratic paper, rejected the traditional journalistic custom
of carrying the party nominee's name on its masthead. Its
reason—McClellan's nomination constituted a "sellout to Wall
Street and the Rothschild interests." The *Chicago Tribune*, the
most powerful Republican paper in the Midwest, editorialized
on what it called the "key question before the country" in the
1864 election: "Will we have a dishonorable peace, in order to
enrich Belmont, the Rothschilds, and the whole tribe of Jews,
who have been buying up Confederate bonds, or an honorable
peace won by Grant and Sherman at the cannon's mouth?" [50]

Writing in the *New York Times* under a nom de plume, "A
Veteran Observer" also expressed concern over the "Jewish"
leadership of, and Rothschild influence within, the minority
party:

Let us look at a few undeniable facts. The notorious undenied leader of
the Democratic Party at Chicago was the agent of the Rothschilds. Yes,
the great Democratic party has fallen so low that it has to seek a leader
in the agent of foreign Jew bankers. Tell it not in Gath, nor in the
streets of Askelon.

[49] Langenschwartz to McClellan, June 27, Sept. 12, 1864, McClellan Papers.
[50] Wood Gray, *The Hidden Civil War: The Story of the Copperheads*
(New York, 1942), 201; *The Israelite*, XI (Sept. 23, 1864), 99.

"How art thou fallen!
Oh! Lucifer, son of the morning!" [51]

As Belmont well knew, newspapers were not the only instruments of propaganda. James Worrall of Pennsylvania used one of Belmont's favorite tools, the rally, against him. Speaking at Cooper Union to a gathering of "true" Democrats supporting Lincoln, Worrall lamented the captivity of the old Jacksonian Democratic Party by the moneyed aristocracy of Europe and Wall Street.

The agent of the Rothschilds is the chief manager of the Democratic Party! (Cries of 'that's so' and cheers). . . . What a first rate Secretary of the treasury he would make, if Mr. McClellan happened to be elected! (Laughter) There is not a people or government in Christendom in which the paws, or fangs, or claws of the Rothschilds are not plunged to the very heart of the treasury . . . , and they would like to do the same here. . . . We [Americans] did not want to borrow [from the Rothschilds], and the Jews have got mad, and have been mad ever since. (Cheers) But they and Jeff Davis and the devil are not going to conquer us. (Prolonged applause)

The emotional climate of American society at this time also explains why Allan Pinkerton, the legendary private detective, could swallow the fantastic rumor that Belmont and other McClellan partisans were plotting the murder of Lincoln in the event of his re-election! [52]

Belmont refused to dignify such slurs by personal refutation, though the American Jewish press was concerned enough to attempt to discredit them. *The Israelite* and *The Jewish Messenger* of New York defied Belmont's slanderers to prove that the Democratic National Chairman was anything more than the American "correspondent" of the Rothschilds and that the latter ever "assisted the rebel treasury to the extent of a dollar." Furthermore, Belmont had done nothing in the past quarter

[51] *New York Times*, Oct. 9, 1864. In his daily diary George Templeton Strong referred to Belmont as a "mere successful cosmopolite adventurer and alien," who exploited Americans for "foreign capitalists" and had "no affinity with our country or people." Nevins and Thomas, eds., *Diary of George Templeton Strong*, III, 508–09.

[52] *New York Times*, Nov. 2, 1864; Myers, *McClellan*, 460–62.

century to confirm or assert his Judaism, and the fact of his
marriage "in a church to a Christian lady" had led to his "universal repudiation" by the American Jewish community. The
allegation that "all the funds in the Democratic treasury are
supplied by 'Rothschild's agent' " was ridiculed by *The Jewish
Messenger* as nothing short of "romance." [53]

Only one slander moved Belmont to public retaliation—when
he was insinuated to be an illegitimate Rothschild. His fury was
aroused when a *New York Evening Post* editorial stated that
"Prominent among the intriguers who sought to shape the policy of the [Chicago] convention was Mr. August Belmont . . . ,
a reputed son and accredited agent of the Rothschilds." He immediately instituted a civil suit for libel, involving the words "a
reputed son." Former New York County District Attorney A.
Oakey Hall and other close friends seconded it with criminal
libel charges. The paper's proprietors apologized for "un-
founded" remarks made during the heat of the political campaign, and the libel cases never came to trial.[54]

Against this background of invective and abuse Belmont,
outwardly as calm and optimistic as ever, presided over a final
pre-election meeting of War Democrats. Speaking at Cooper
Union, the chairman delivered what he deemed to be a sum-
mary of party policy:

This, gentlemen, is the only way in which we can ever hope to restore
the Union and bring peace and prosperity to our common country.
Give to the South the choice of an honorable peace under the Union
and the Constitution, or a fruitless struggle against the irresistible power
of a united North, and you will see State after State leave the Confederacy of Jefferson Davis and return to their allegiance under the Union.
But who can doubt that the South will fight to the last extremity if the
fatal policy of confiscation and forcible emancipation is to be persisted

[53] Glanz, "Rothschild Legend in America," 21; *The Jewish Messenger*, XVI
(Nov. 4, 1864), 132; *New York Times*, Nov. 6, 1864.
[54] *New York Evening Post*, Oct. 6, 11, 1864; Bowen, *Elegant Oakey*, 47–48.
Belmont always remembered Hall's open letter to the *Evening Post*, five days
after the unfortunate editorial, demanding justice for the injured banker. Such
support explained Belmont's stubborn defense of Hall at the end of the decade,
when "respectable" Democrats demanded Hall's ouster from "gentlemen's
clubs," following exposures of the notorious Tweed ring.

in, and that is the policy to which Mr. Lincoln and his party are pledged, should they be able to keep themselves in power.[55]

Election Day neared, and the more Belmont's ears rang with the applause and shouting of pro-McClellan crowds at political rallies, the more his partisanship distorted his sense of political realism. He became so convinced of electoral victory that he bet $4,000 with a fellow Wall Street banker, N. E. Thalmann, on the outcome of the presidential race. In the same vein, he made use of the *New York Times* letters columns to challenge Lincoln partisans to put up their money under such terms as to place the administration in an unfavorable posture. In one such letter Belmont wrote:

A correspondent in your paper seems anxious to have a bet on the coming Presidential election. I offer the following: I will bet the sum of $10,000, the money to be deposited in the New York Trust Company, that if Mr. Lincoln should be elected, we will be in a state of war during the term of his administration, or will be forced into a disgraceful peace, with separation; and the same amount, to be similarly deposited, that if Gen. McClellan is elected, the Union will be restored within his term of office.

Needless to say, no one volunteered to accept such ambiguous terms. The national chairman even attempted political wagers during social occasions. Bystanders chatting in the lobby of the Academy of Music between opera acts reported overhearing Belmont state publicly "that he would bet a thousand dollars" on a McClellan victory, along with an additional thousand that the price of gold would rise to 300 by Election Day. No one covered these later bets either.[56]

Public knowledge of Belmont's sporting proclivities caused him to undergo a humiliating experience. The chairman rose early on November 8 and went to the polls before breakfast. He was about to cast his ballot when an elections inspector challenged his right to vote and charged him with violating a state law prohibiting betting on elections to public office. The

---

[55] *New York World*, Nov. 3, 1864.

[56] Belmont to Marble, Dec. 10, 1868, Marble Papers; *New York Times*, Oct. 26, 31, Nov. 3, 7, 1864; *New York World*, Nov. 2, 5, 7, 8, 1864; Robert S. Holzman, *Stormy Ben Butler* (New York, 1954), 141.

official rejected Belmont's argument that as the wager only applied to the principal race he be allowed to vote for state and local offices. The chairman's rising discomfiture only added to the glee of pro-Lincoln onlookers, until at length he gave up the protest.[57]

Belmont's vote could not have averted the disastrous election outcome. McClellan lost to Lincoln in the Electoral College, 212 to 21; Seymour lost the New York governorship to Republican Congressman Reuben E. Fenton; and Belmont lost his $4,000 to Thalmann. The general thanked Belmont—through Barlow—for services rendered. Seymour, tired after a respectable number of years in public office, said farewell to political campaigns and retired to his Utica farm.

Belmont, unfortunately, possessed no past glories which might aid posterity to gloss over the last two presidential contests and did not relish retiring from the political ring with failure as his epitaph. The memory of the time and money he had fruitlessly expended to unseat Republicans did not rankle half as much as the bitter knowledge that he had failed to impress his carefully considered ideas about party candidates and policies upon other Democratic leaders. For them to attribute McClellan's defeat to Republican frauds at the polls and to clever manipulation of the soldiers' vote seemed too simple to Belmont. He believed that the irreparable damage had been committed by Democrats themselves. As he grumbled to Marble, "If only the convention at Chicago had listened to my advice to place Guthrie instead of Pendleton in nomination for Vice President and declare in favor of the Union and a vigorous prosecution of the war, *as I advocated so earnestly in our delegation,*" the Democratic Party's postelection status would now be totally different. Instead, "different men & principles were saddled upon our ticket." [58]

[57] Benjamin F. Butler, *Butler's Book: Autobiography and Personal Reminiscences of Major-General Benjamin F. Butler* (Boston, 1892), 761, 770; Belmont to Marble, Dec. 10, 1868, Marble Papers; *New York Times*, May 3, 1865; Nevins and Thomas, eds., *Diary of George Templeton Strong*, III, 510.

[58] McClellan to Barlow, Nov. 10, 1864, McClellan Papers; Belmont to Marble, Nov. 30, 1864, private Belmont collection.

Belmont's election post-mortem overlooked the fact that his own campaign performance had been less than forthright, either because he tried to accommodate all shades of opinion within his party or because he had not yet come to terms with the nation's changing realities. Time and again he demanded restoration of the "Union as it was," without acknowledging that this could only be effected by maintaining national authority and crushing illegal resistance to it. The administration party grasped this essential truth and won the election. Belmont and his fellow Democrats, using the rhetoric of the antebellum era, did not—and lost.

9

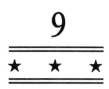

The Party Reunited

BELMONT, as national chairman of a defeated party, devoted little attention to partisan politics in the months immediately following the election. Recent dramatic Union military successes obviated Democratic criticism of governmental war policies. For the moment, any public statements could be left to the titular leader, General McClellan, to be backed up by Democratic officeholders. If the effect of Belmont's own inaction were to render him less conspicuous to criticism, ridicule, and slander, so much the better.[1] On occasion, individual national committeemen tried to draw Belmont back into public debate. Cyrus H. McCormick, the reaping machine inventor and Illinois committeeman, proposed that Belmont summon a postelection convention of Democrats the nation over, that such a body should "make an effort . . . , with the sanction of the Administration, at a successful negotiation with the South for the restoration of the Union, under the Constitution." Belmont, familiar with Republican policies and goals and painfully aware of his previous attempts to advise the government, completely ignored McCormick's suggestion.[2]

The events of early 1865 ended the national chairman's furlough. In January McClellan, rejecting pleas from Democratic

[1] Even as November's results faded into history, the personal scars remained. More than three months after Election Day, Belmont complained bitterly to Secretary Seward: "I have been made the object of the most severe, unjust & absurd attacks by the Administration press, & I have reason to know that *even the President* has to a certain extent given credence to the calumnies which have been published against me." Belmont to Seward, Feb. 21, 1865, Seward Papers.

[2] *New York World,* Nov. 22, 1864.

friends and politicians that he lead the party until the next presidential election, announced his intention to go to Europe. Belmont was shocked and wrote Barlow to dissuade McClellan
from leaving the country "so soon after the election." He
warned that the general, notwithstanding his recent retirement
from the army, "cannot well absent himself from the country
on a mere tour of pleasure," with a Civil War still being fought
on a huge scale, "without incurring for himself & the Democratic Party censure & misrepresentations of all kinds." The
thirty-nine-year-old McClellan, nursing his election wounds, refused to pick up the gauntlet of duty and left on his scheduled
trip. For Belmont, the general's departure recalled Stephen
Douglas' death four years earlier. The Democratic Party would
again lack the postelection services of the man it had just se-

George H. Pendleton (Library of
Congress)

Andrew Johnson (Library of Congress)

lected as titular leader, and party leadership and policymaking decisions would once more have to rest upon the national chairman's shoulders.[3]

Even had McClellan remained in the United States to guide the Democrats, Belmont would surely not have been content on the sidelines after the watershed of April, 1865. Within a two-week span the war ended, Lincoln was assassinated, and Andrew Johnson became the nation's seventeenth President. Differences over southern reconstruction soon arose between Johnson and the Republican Congressional leadership. The new Chief Executive's immediate amnesty grants to former Confederate leaders and his plans for the speedy readmission of the seceded states provoked dissenting murmurs from many Republicans.

These cracks in the Republican facade were welcome to the ailing Democratic Party. Their prewar Congressional strength had atrophied to less than one-third of each house's membership. Every Democratic leader, from Belmont down, recognized the necessity of renewed southern representation in Washington. The South had not only traditionally furnished the party with effective (not to mention destructive) leaders in the past, but had supplied it with sufficient voting strength to maintain a powerful position on the national scene. Any hope of future Democratic hegemony depended upon the defeated South's free, uninhibited exercise of prewar rights. Less than three months after Appomattox, Belmont drafted "An Address of the National Committee to the Democracy of the United States," which stressed the party's potential support in the South and asked the North to forgive, forget, and facilitate the efforts of "the erring members of our political family . . . to resume their wonted places in the social circle. Let them be welcomed as was the prodigal son in the parable and received back with all their rights and privileges unabridged." [4]

Clearly President Johnson favored the same ends. Belmont

[3] Belmont to Barlow, Dec. 21, 1864, Barlow Papers; Myers, *McClellan*, 463–66; McClellan to Belmont, March 19, 1865, private Belmont collection.

[4] *New York World*, July 11, 1865; Eric L. McKitrick, *Andrew Johnson and Reconstruction* (Chicago, 1960), 68–69.

and his colleagues, delighted with Johnson's "enlightened" view
of southern restoration and with the number of "conservative"
Republicans favoring his course, attempted to persuade the
President, a lifelong Democrat, to lead the party of Jefferson
and Jackson. The summer and autumn of 1865 witnessed a constant flow of suitors between New York and the White House.
Tilden, Richmond, Barlow, and others returned home smitten
with Johnson's views. Rumors even circulated that the President prayed for Democratic successes at the polls in the state
elections that fall. Manton Marble, after a long interview at the
White House, claimed that Johnson "persistently avowed himself a Democrat—as much today as ever." The New York State
Democratic Convention, which opened in Albany on September
6 and had as its intended purpose the drafting of a campaign
platform for Democratic candidates, wound up claiming Johnson "as one of our own" and endorsing presidential reconstruction. The national chairman expressed his "complete satisfaction" with the convention's actions.[5]

Along other political lines, the 1864 election campaign demonstrated to Belmont and other New York party leaders the
importance of auxiliary party agencies similar in nature to the
Republican Union League clubs. These clubs, functioning in
major cities, enlisted cultured, polished gentlemen, known primarily for their civic and professional activities, in behalf of the
Lincoln ticket. Belmont believed that a Democratic counterpart
of the Union League could serve a number of purposes: as a
forum for party spokesmen and their public views, as a valuable
fund-raising conduit during election campaigns, and as a reputa-
ble alternative within the New York party to Tammany Hall.
After lengthy discussions, Belmont and a handful of "silk-
stocking" Democrats founded and incorporated the Manhattan
Club, at Fifth Avenue and Fifteenth Street, in October, 1865.[6]

[5] *New York Times*, May 10, 30, June 7, 1865; Belmont to Barlow, July 11,
1865, Barlow Papers; Barlow to Tilden, Aug. 31, 1865, Tilden Papers; *New
York World*, Sept. 7-9, Oct. 3, 1865.
[6] Henry Watterson, *History of the Manhattan Club: A Narrative of the
Activities of Half a Century* (New York, 1915), 49, 143; Matthew P. Breen,
Thirty Years of New York Politics: Up-to-Date (New York, 1899), 201-02;

The Thirty-Ninth Congress, with its strong Republican majority, convened in December, 1865. The first tangible evidence
of the presidential-Congressional breach came when the Republican caucus refused to recognize the "Johnson" regimes already
established in all but one state of the old Confederacy. Congress
followed up this negative step with positive ones. It created a
Joint Committee of Fifteen to which all bills and resolutions
pertaining to reconstruction were to be referred, thereby indicating Congressional intention to dominate reconstruction
policy. In April, 1866, the Civil Rights Act was passed over
Johnson's veto, followed two months later by the Fourteenth
Amendment. In July both houses again overrode a presidential
veto and established a reorganized, enlarged Freedmen's Bureau
designed to protect the constitutional privileges of southern
Negroes. These actions, along with basic disagreement between
the administration and Congressional leaders over the causes of
bloody racial outbreaks in Memphis and New Orleans, exacerbated Republican division and instilled new hope in the hearts
of the Democratic minority.

Out of this inter- and intraparty turmoil came a major effort
to establish a new political party composed of pro-Johnson Republicans and of Democrats favoring the general tenor of the
President's program. This new movement, the National Union,
called for a "truly national" convention (that is, one which
would include "patriots" from all sections), to meet in the
"City of Brotherly Love," Philadelphia, on August 14. It advocated the election of sufficient followers to Congress to sustain
any additional Johnson vetoes of "Radical" legislation. Prominent New York Democrats, including Tilden, Fernando Wood,

Nevins and Thomas, eds., *Diary of George Templeton Strong,* III, 581; Belmont to Marble, Feb. 1, 1868, Marble Papers; *New York World,* Nov. 25,
1890; *New York Tribune,* Nov. 25, 1890. Of the $55,000 needed to purchase
the club's headquarters Belmont subscribed $10,000 and Tilden $5,000. The
money was returned within a year as 300 members, each paying $200 as
initiation dues, deposited into the club treasury more than the purchase price.
Other incorporators were Marble, Barlow, Richmond, John Van Buren, Edward Cooper, Andrew H. Green, and John T. Hoffman. The club, still in
existence, though politically dormant, recently celebrated its centennial.

former Congressman Francis Kernan, Sanford E. Church, a former lieutenant governor and now Chief Justice of the State Court of Appeals, and Dean Richmond, still Democratic State Chairman, supported the movement and announced their intention to attend the Philadelphia meeting.[7]

Important Democrats around the nation also rallied to the pro-Johnson movement, claiming that the country stood on the verge of a major development in American party politics—a realignment of the major parties.[8] Their enthusiasm confronted Belmont with a crucial problem. Could the Democratic goals be achieved more readily by going outside the party to form a new organization free from prior connotations or by keeping within the old party lines while reaching for some kind of entente with their opposite numbers on the Republican side? Personally, the chairman agreed with the President's approach to southern reconstruction and had expressed as far back as March "sincere admiration for the patriotic & statesmanlike course which you have pursued as Chief Magistrate." [9] Yet Belmont felt that with readmission of the South to full electoral participation only a handful of northern states would be necessary to restore a Democrat to White House occupancy under the existing political division and without such a drastic change. Belmont also hesitated because he felt that a Democratic organizational alliance with the Johnson wing of the Republican Party might carry with it a commitment to support the President should he seek re-election.

Considering the groundswell of pro-Johnson sentiment within Democratic ranks, Belmont, as national chairman, was compelled to act. He could fill all national committee vacancies, summon all committeemen to meet at an early day, and have them all put their names to a public address affirming unquali-

[7] McKitrick, *Andrew Johnson and Reconstruction*, 181; Lawanda and John H. Cox, *Politics, Principle, and Prejudice, 1865–1866: Dilemma of Reconstruction America* (Glencoe, Ill., 1963), 64–66.

[8] Senator Reverdy Johnson of Maryland and Senator-elect Alexander H. Stephens of Georgia offered their services to the new political force.

[9] Belmont to Johnson, March 24, 1866, Andrew Johnson Papers, Library of Congress.

fied approbation of the National Union convention, thereby
hoping to scotch wholesale defections; or he could announce
the dismantling of the national Democratic Party so that its adherents could go over in a body to the National Union, thereby
trading party identity for political reward.[10] Without disclosing
his own preference, the expression of which might discourage
full and open consultation, Belmont asked Barlow to get in
touch with Tilden, Marble, and Frederick O. Prince of Massachusetts and forward their ideas on the subject to him. Above
all, he assured Barlow, "I want only to do what is best for the
Country & what will most effectively kill the Radicals in & out
of Congress & really restore the Union." [11]

For their part, Belmont's colleagues generally approved of
Andrew Johnson and his policies, but wanted him to come over
to the Democratic Party—not the party to him. A number of
northern and southern Democrats attended and applauded the
National Union Convention. Tilden, for example, helped draft
the August convention's "Address to the People" and accompanied a Committee of One Hundred to the capital to offer the
President full support in the contest with his opponents. But
when the New York State Democratic Convention met at Albany on September 11 to nominate a state ticket the most it did
for Johnson was to deliver a ringing endorsement of the National Union's "principles" in its own campaign platform.[12]

Johnson, encouraged by the convention's encomiums, embarked on a speaking trip around the country to defend his
"moderate" policies and attack his Radical Republican antago-
nists. This "swing around the circle" took him on an eighteen-
day tour of larger cities. His New York supporters included
leading merchants, financiers, and Democrats—all interested

[10] In fact, Montgomery Blair, one of the new group's organizers, sent an
emissary to New York to urge Belmont's assistance at the Philadelphia convention. William E. Smith, *The Francis Preston Blair Family in Politics* (2
vols., New York, 1933), II, 366.

[11] Prince was the Massachusetts national committeeman who served for a
long time as the committee's secretary. Belmont to Barlow, June 26, 1866,
Barlow Papers.

[12] Eugene Casserly to Tilden, Sept. 9, 1866, Tilden Papers; *New York World*,
Sept. 12, 13, 1866.

in reopening traditional economic and political channels between Gotham and the South and all viewing Johnson's program as the most expeditious way to achieve them. On the evening of August 29, some of these distinguished New Yorkers, including such prominent Democrats as Belmont, Tilden, Augustus Schell, and Abram S. Hewitt, wined and dined the President at a gala banquet at Delmonico's restaurant. Virtually the identical group graced the platform at a huge National Union rally, three weeks later, designed to show Johnson's strength in the nation's number one city. Though Belmont chose not to speak at this meeting, his name was on the program as a member of the reception committee.[13]

Historians still argue over the factors behind American voting behavior in 1866, though there is little disagreement that the results constituted a major blow to the Chief Executive. Anti-Johnson Republicans emerged victorious in every northern state featuring a gubernatorial race. This defeat destroyed the National Union, and Belmont and other Democratic leaders concentrated once again on rebuilding their own party.

In December, 1866, national chairman Belmont summoned to his Fifth Avenue home the five other members of his executive committee—Prince of Massachusetts, William A. Galbraith of Pennsylvania, Rufus Ranny of Ohio, Lewis V. Bogy of Missouri, and George H. Paul of Wisconsin. They agreed that the pending readmission of the southern states into the Union made it imperative to fill southern vacancies on the national committee. In addition, the leaders placed themselves on record as favoring representation at the 1868 national convention of all southern states.[14]

Belmont moved quickly to implement the committee's decision and designated Representative Niblack, the Indiana mem-

13 *New York Times*, Aug. 30, 1866; Stanley Coben, "Northeastern Business and Radical Reconstruction: A Re-examination," *Mississippi Valley Historical Review*, XLVI (June, 1959), 88; George R. Woolfolk, *The Cotton Regency: The Northern Merchants and Reconstruction, 1865-1880* (New York, 1959), 41-43.
14 William A. Galbraith to Belmont, Jan. 25, 1867, Gideon Bradford to Belmont, Feb. 18, 1867, private Belmont collection.

ber, to assist him.[15] The two wrote letters to southern state
Democratic committees, and though not making it explicit they
implied a preference for candidates who had "Unionist" reputa-
tions before Sumter. The task proved easier to outline than to
accomplish. State Democratic organizations had been disrupted
during the war and were now dominated by former Confederate politicians. In Georgia, serious objections to Belmont's first
choice, Herschel Johnson (Douglas' 1860 running mate and a
Confederate senator for three years), caused the chairman to
look for a less controversial man. The seat went instead to Ab-
salom H. Chappell, a sixty-six-year-old former Whig congressman now affiliated with the Democrats, who had been too old
for wartime conscription and was reputed to have remained a
staunch Unionist during the Confederate era.[16] Belmont's first
choice for the Virginia vacancy, John S. Millson of Norfolk, a
six-term congressman before the war, curtly declined his appointment "for a variety of considerations." In Florida, a Judge
Marvin had to be replaced when his "Radical leanings" were
discovered. In Texas, John Hancock, a state legislator expelled
from office in 1861 for refusing to take an oath of allegiance to
the Confederacy, not only refused to sit on the national committee but advised Belmont to dissolve the party. Not until his
fourth choice did Belmont find a Texan who agreed to serve.
By 1868 Belmont succeeded in filling every committee vacancy
except that of North Carolina. There, his initial preference,
William E. Pell, publisher of the influential *Raleigh Sentinel*,
was suspected of working for the Republicans, and his next
man, Lewis Hanes, editor of the *Saulsbury Old North State*,
declined for the reason that "the war has reduced me to pov-

[15] This was a departure from the usual practice whereby state organizations
chose their national committeemen.

[16] Niblack to Belmont, March 23, 28, 1867, Chappell to Belmont, May 16,
1867, Feb. 1, 1868, private Belmont collection. Chappell declined the appointment at first, being highly active in Georgia's Conservative Party. By February,
1868, when it was clear that the southern Conservatives had much in common
with northern Democrats, Chappell withdrew his declination and took his
place on the national committee.

erty & I would be unable to attend the meetings of the Committee if I could accept." [17]

Other Belmont correspondents evinced a greater desire to help steer the party. Former California Congressman Joseph W. McCorkle, now a resident of Virginia City, Nevada, responded vigorously to the news that he would represent his new state on the committee:

With great pleasure, I stand ready to aid and assist you in any movement you may consider advisable to reorganize and put in fighting trim the Democratic Party. . . . We must not remain idle if we intend to make a fight. . . . Our campaign should be an offensive one and a continuous charge from now until the day of the presidential election.

John A. Nicholson of Delaware, Josiah Minot of New Hampshire, and Isaac E. Eaton of Kansas all promised Belmont to use every means in their power to minimize party dissension in the coming years and to turn over to the 1868 presidential nominee a unified, harmonious national organization.[18]

Following some modest Democratic gains in northern state elections during autumn, 1867, Belmont sent out a call for a full meeting of the national committee to consider plans for the 1868 convention.[19] Well aware of the potential significance of such a gathering of former enemies, the chairman intentionally selected February 22 in the nation's capital as the time and place,

[17] Millson to Belmont, April 15, 1867, Niblack to Belmont, March 28, 1867, Hancock to Belmont, May 17, 1867, Hanes to Belmont, April 16, 1867, James H. Clanton to Belmont, Feb. 16, 1868, Alfred J. Lancy to Niblack, Feb. 18, 1868, R. Ould to John Morrissey, Feb. 22, 1868, private Belmont collection.

[18] McCorkle to Belmont, July 21, 1867, Niblack to Belmont, Dec. 15, 1867, private Belmont collection.

[19] A previous committee meeting at Belmont's residence on March 12, 1867, consisting of the northern members, had been arranged to take up a suggestion that a national convention be summoned in the summer of 1867. The purpose of the convention would be to acquaint party leaders from the new states, Nevada (1864) and Nebraska (1867), and the South with the regularly established organizations in the North. The proposal was rejected as "inexpedient." William A. Galbraith to Belmont, Jan. 25, 1867, Gideon Bradford to Belmont, Feb. 18, March 11, 1867, William N. Converse to Belmont, March 18, 1867, Frederick A. Aiken to Belmont, April 4, 1867, private Belmont collection; New York World, March 13, 1867.

hoping that the double use of the Washington symbol would be inspirational.[20] Belmont also arranged for the committee to attend local Washington's Birthday ceremonies as a group to publicize renewed Democratic unity in the country.

Twenty-nine of the thirty-seven committeemen, plus the Democratic congressmen then attending regular sessions at the Capitol, met at the Metropolitan Hotel on the designated day. All Washington was buzzing with the news that President Johnson had just dismissed Secretary of War Stanton in defiance of the Radical-sponsored Tenure of Office Act, setting in motion Congressional impeachment plans. With such crowning proof of opposition wrangling, the assembled Democrats enthusiastically echoed Lawrence S. Trimble, Kentucky's national committeeman, in resolving to rise "above all local or petty jealousies in the [presidential] contest." Belmont tried to exemplify this spirit by making no distinction between committee members from the North and those from states still bereft of Congressional representation.

The main item of business concerned the location and date of the nominating convention. Belmont submitted a bid for a July 4th convention in New York, noting that the eastern city had never entertained a national convention. Lewis Bogy of Missouri presented St. Louis' request to serve as the host city. Bogy, a commissioner in the Bureau of Indian Affairs, reported to the committee that Missouri Democrats constituted a numerical majority of voters there. Yet "we have been and are yet governed by a [Republican] faction who have got possession of the state government" and through a system of "fraudulent" registration "excluded" Democrats from the polls. Any large gathering of Democrats in St. Louis would "have the tendency

[20] Charles Mason, representing the District of Columbia, suggested an earlier date because of the "great necessity of taking some immediate steps to meet the great demand for aid in the shape of documents, speakers, etc. The public mind is to some degree now in a plastic state. The voters . . . now have leisure to read, which may not be the case a few months hence." Mason preferred a January meeting, but Belmont overruled him. Mason to Belmont, Jan. 7, 1868, private Belmont collection.

to give our friends courage and backbone." Belmont's choice of time and place prevailed, notwithstanding Bogy's plea.[21]

The formal meeting adjourned, but Belmont had a surprise in store for the visiting national committeemen—a state dinner at the White House. The national chairman had brought off a magnificent political coup, and the public recognized it as such. Just two days later the House overwhelmingly approved a resolution to try the President before the Senate on charges of "high crimes and misdemeanors," giving credence to Democratic assertions that the whole impeachment affair was politically inspired. The White House dinner also led to a number of rumors. Some Republican newspapers solemnly averred that Belmont's committee had sworn to support Johnson at their national convention. Others circulated a contradictory report that the Democratic National Chairman had openly rebuked the President at his own table for introducing politics into the conversation! Given Belmont's sense of political and social propriety, the reports must be treated as pure fiction.[22]

Administrative duties occupied Belmont on the heels of the successful Washington meeting. He activated the Democratic Congressional Campaign Committee and persuaded Wisconsin Senator James R. Doolittle, a Democrat-turned-Republican-turned-Democrat, to serve as cochairman, along with the ever-helpful Congressman Niblack. Next, he established a new group, a Democratic National Resident Subcommittee in Washington, which he hoped would assume responsibility for mailing out copies of relevant government documents and Congres-

21 Trimble to Belmont, Jan. 11, 1868, Bogy to Belmont, Jan. 22, 1868, Frederick O. Prince to Belmont, Jan. 22, 1868, Joseph W. McCorkle to Belmont, Jan. 28, 1868, L. R. Tweed to John T. Hoffman, Feb. 4, 1868, private Belmont collection; *New York World*, Feb. 23, 1868. In line with previous Democratic convention procedure, each state was awarded as many delegate votes as it had electoral votes. In modern practice, convention representation also takes into account additional factors, such as each state's number of United States Senators and the support given by each state to the previous presidential ticket.

22 *New York Times*, Feb. 29, 1868; Nevins and Thomas, eds., *Diary of George Templeton Strong*, IV, 191.

sional debates as the need to do so arose during the coming presidential contest. Finally, before plunging into the thick of the preconvention nomination struggle, Belmont issued a public letter to all Democratic state chairmen, in which he beseeched them to bend every effort to attract "Johnson Conservatives" (that is, Republicans), to the Democratic banner.[23]

[23] Belmont to Marble, Feb. 1, 1868, Marble Papers; Niblack to Belmont, March 1, 1868, private Belmont collection; Belmont to Tilden, March 2, 1868, Tilden Papers; Charles H. Coleman, *The Election of 1868: The Democratic Effort to Regain Control* (New York, 1933), 56.

10

★ ★ ★

Seymour and a Fumbling Campaign

WHILE REPUBLICAN LEADERS clearly favored General Ulysses S. Grant for their party's 1868 presidential nomination, the Democrats could boast no such unanimity. Not since 1852 had there been a preconvention period so devoid of a heavy favorite for the party's chief prize. President Johnson commanded general respect among Democrats, and his name frequently came up for consideration. But Belmont, despite his arrangement of the Washington's Birthday dinner, never contemplated the Chief Executive as the Democratic standard-bearer, and any movement for his nomination faded noticeably after the Senate failed to follow up presidential impeachment with conviction. David R. Locke, a contemporary Republican-leaning humorist who wrote under the pseudonym Petroleum V. Nasby, applied his devastating wit to this sudden Democratic disenchantment:

The President wuz a readin telegrams and letters, and they wuz not uv a carikter to pleeze him. The first wuz from Belmont, and read thus:

"I hev, ez yoo know, the highest possible regard for yoor Eggslency, and shel regret exceedinly to see yoo deprived uv yoor high offis; but reely, yoo kin scarcely eggspect the Democracy to embarass themselves by espousin yoor coz. The fact iz, no party hevin a fucher before it kin tie itself to a ded past. The teemster draws a sigh over a ded mule, but ez a ded mule can't draw his cart, he natcherly turns his eyes onto them still possess uv vitality. I hope yoo see the pint without my explainin it. Eggscuse me for comparing yoo to a ded mule, but the simile wuz the first that segested itself to me.

"With profound respect, I am, etc.

"P.S. Should biznis call me to Tennessee, I shel do myself the honor to call on yoo in yoor dignified retirement."

The President wiped an avalanche uv teers wich follered the reedin uv this unfeelin letter.[1]

If Belmont was unenthusiastic about a Johnson candidacy, he was adamantly against the aspirations of former vice presidential nominee Pendleton, now a senator. Republicans made no secret of their determination to use Grant's military record as a campaign issue, and Belmont remembered only too well "Peace" Democrat Pendleton's willingness to compromise with secession. Even more controversial was Pendleton's sponsorship of the "Ohio Idea" in which he advocated a program of currency expansion. He not only proposed that the large federal war bond issues known as the "five-twenties" be redeemed in paper money—greenbacks—but that national bank notes in circulation also be gradually replaced by greenbacks, a heretical idea in view of the party's half-century-old "hard-money" attitudes. Furthermore, he criticized the Treasury practice of paying interest on all its bond issues in gold, even though some did not legally require it. Pendleton echoed a widespread view when he said that these debt payments in specie gave federal bondholders enormous windfalls. He demanded the same money "for the bondholder and the plowholder." [2]

Belmont, along with many bankers, lawyers, and public officials, labeled Pendleton's plan "repudiation." He recalled the promises of Treasury Secretaries Chase and Hugh McCulloch and insisted that the Federal Government bore a moral commitment to redeem the war bonds in specie. The chairman's political and financial inclinations clearly put him in the forefront of

[1] David R. Locke, *The Struggles (Social, Financial and Political) of Petroleum V. Nasby* (Boston, 1893), 509–10. This quotation was written on March 8, 1868.

[2] Robert P. Sharkey, *Money, Class, and Party: An Economic Study of Civil War and Reconstruction* (Baltimore, 1959), 100–01; Irwin Unger, *The Greenback Era: A Social and Political History of American Finance, 1865–1879* (Princeton, N.J., 1964), chapter I.

any stop-Pendleton drive, and the charge leveled against him, that he was subtly sabotaging Pendleton's candidacy, undoubtedly contained more than a kernel of truth.[3]

Belmont's involvement, early in 1868, in a nasty exchange with a "repudiationist" state treasurer of Pennsylvania increased his animosity to those who followed Pendleton's financial heresy. Republican Governor John W. Geary of Pennsylvania had fulfilled a campaign pledge to expand the money supply by promptly refunding the state's outstanding debt in greenbacks. The London Rothschilds, who on Belmont's recommendation had paid gold for a half-million dollars' worth of Pennsylvania state bonds for themselves and for their customers, asked their New York correspondent to protest the state's repayment in "a depreciated currency" and to inquire if Pennsylvania would permit the Rothschilds to hold on to the bonds pending a negotiated settlement. State Treasurer William H. Kemble's reply to Belmont exacerbated the situation. Not content with branding the banker's "complaint about the injustice of our not paying you in gold" as "ridiculous," his closing line, borrowed from Shakespeare, bore an unmistakably anti-Semitic tone: "We are willing to give you the pound of flesh, but not one drop of Christian blood."

Kemble's coarse and impertinent tone led Belmont to deliver a stinging, though ineffective, reply. He characterized the Pennsylvania bonds "the most disastrous security ever negotiated" by his London correspondents and severely rebuked Kemble for having shown himself "too much of a blackguard to be capable of the instincts of a gentleman." The banker vainly waited a week for a second response from Harrisburg and then had the entire exchange of correspondence published in the *World*, the *Times*, and the *Herald*. Letters poured in to

---

[3] Chester M. Destler, *American Radicalism, 1865–1901: Essays and Documents* (New London, Conn., 1946), 46–49. *The New York Times* predicted in May that Belmont's opposition posed the main obstacle to Pendleton's nomination, for "pockets are often more potent than friendships, and to the former Mr. Belmont holds the key." *New York Times*, May 6, 1868.

Belmont's office praising his strong censure of the advocates of repudiation, but he never forgot this ugly episode.[4]

One such laudatory message came from Charles Francis Adams of Massachusetts who, having returned after seven years of distinguished service as Minister to Great Britain, was looked on as a possible presidential candidate. A *New York Times* editorial in late February praised Adams' diplomatic career and then bodly proclaimed that "no fitter candidate could be named [to the presidency] in the whole country." His precise political affiliation at the moment remained an unanswered question, and within this context any letter from him had special significance for Belmont. Adams confessed having "not often had the satisfaction of agreeing with you politically" but admitted his "lively satisfaction at your . . . neat flooring of a very stupid swindler." He went on to stress that "past political differences weigh very little with me," a remark which Belmont, in his fever for a nominee, interpreted as bearing on the 1868 campaign. The party chairman sounded the Bostonian out on the possibility of accepting the Democratic presidential nomination should it be offered him. Instead of responding forthrightly, Adams hesitated. He would not refuse a draft but could not now commit himself. Adams pointed out that his two chief liabilities—lack of a political base and the antagonism of Irish-Americans toward him—would prove hard to overcome. These practical difficulties, plus his indecision, removed his name from further Democratic consideration.[5]

As the Pendleton boom gathered momentum and the July 4th convention drew closer, Belmont intensified his search to

[4] David Montgomery, "Radical Republicanism in Pennsylvania, 1866–1873," *Pennsylvania Magazine of History and Biography*, LXXXV (Oct., 1961), 448; Belmont to Messrs. N. M. Rothschild & Sons, Feb. 4, 1868, Belmont to Kemble, Jan. 28, Feb. 4, 1868, Kemble to Belmont, Jan. 30, 1868, private Belmont collection; Belmont to Marble, Feb. 9, 1868, Marble Papers.

[5] Adams to Belmont, Feb. 27, 1868, private Belmont collection; Martin B. Duberman, *Charles Francis Adams, 1807–1886* (Boston, 1961), 335; *New York Times*, Feb. 24, 1868. Belmont's seventeen-year-old son, Perry, a Harvard undergraduate, approved his father's veto of Adams: "[He] is a newcomer in the Party, with whom the whole Party will not be satisfied, especially the Democrats in the West." Perry Belmont, *An American Democrat*, 134–35.

find a suitable candidate. In an effort to determine whether Mc-Clellan's name still aroused enthusiasm among Democrats, Belmont leaked the news to newspaper reporters that the general ranked high on the list of contenders. He capped this by spreading the word that party members still talked of the old ticket, McClellan and Pendleton, knowing that the latter would never consent to another second place designation. Finally, he persuaded the *World* to note the "strong desire" for McClellan "among the Democrats of the Northwest and of New York City." Biting ridicule in midwestern Democratic journals deflated this trial balloon almost as soon as it became airborne. A Cincinnati newspaper delivered the most telling blow by predicting that a McClellan renomination would "ensure Republican success by running the man who didn't take Richmond against the man who did." Democrats periodically suggested additional presidential candidates to their national chairman, such as Civil War heroes Admiral David G. Farragut and General William T. Sherman. If anything, such feeble gestures only proved the confusion and lack of purpose within the party's upper echelons.[6]

The more Belmont surveyed the 1868 scene, assessing General Grant's strength and the impact of the Civil War and reconstruction on American voters, the more he was convinced that sixty-year-old Salmon Chase, now Chief Justice of the United States Supreme Court, would make the most attractive Democratic candidate. On the one hand, Chase's close association with the martyred Lincoln could be counted on to gain support from "Johnson" Republicans and from all those Democrats who had defected since Sumter. On the other, his deliberate neutrality as presiding officer at the Johnson impeachment trial virtually severed his already tenuous link with Republican leaders and would make his candidacy palatable to the Democrats. Many other prominent New Yorkers also favored Chase, among them Democratic State Chairman Tilden, Marble, Sey-

6 *New York Herald*, March 18, 29, May 18, 1868; *New York World*, May 19, June 1, 1868; Coleman, *Election of 1868*, 175.

mour, Barlow, William Cullen Bryant, Charles O'Conor, William Marcy Tweed, and James Gordon Bennett.

With Grant's nomination in late May underscoring the need for an immediate and attractive Democratic prospect, Belmont wrote directly and confidentially to the Chief Justice.[7] The chairman's opening remarks alluded to Chase's continuous "sympathies with the broad principles of the Democratic party on the questions of finance, free trade & states rights" and to his "firm, impartial & Noble stand during the President's trial." Then, putting aside generalities, he stated his main purpose clearly and candidly:

Among many of the leading men of the Democratic party your name has been suggested as the most powerful one to be put into nomination as our Candidate for the Presidency. I concur fully in this view & shall most cheerfully use all my efforts & influence to bring about your nomination & work arduously for your election, provided you will consent to become our Candidate.

Belmont attempted to gloss over any possible disagreement by Chase with the Democratic platform to be adopted at the national convention:

In regard to the Negro suffrage I take for granted that you would rather be in favor of allowing the States to vote on that question . . . , than to subscribe to allowing the unfair proposition of the [Republican] Chicago platform, by which the Southern States, even after their readmission to the Union, are to remain under the Dictation of Congress.

In conclusion, the national chairman reminded Chase that the entire communication "is made in the strictest confidence . . . , without the knowledge of anybody, but after being fully convinced that most of the leading Democrats in our State are for you."[8]

Chase's reply, while not discouraging, indicated that trouble lay ahead for his Democratic supporters. "I still think that upon questions of finance, commerce and administration generally the old Democratic principles afford the best guidance." But, he

[7] Flick, *Tilden*, 172–75. Belmont had arranged an earlier conference between Chase and Tilden, but it never materialized.

[8] Belmont to Chase, May 29, 1868, in Jacob W. Schuckers, *The Life and Public Services of Salmon Portland Chase* (New York, 1874), 584–85.

cautioned Belmont, "I united, as a member of the [Lincoln] Administration, in the pledge it made to maintain the freedom of the enfranchised people." The Thirteenth and Fourteenth Amendments only "partly redeemed" the pledge. Its "perfect fulfillment requires, in my judgment, the assurance of the right of suffrage to those whom the Constitution has made freemen and citizens." To make absolutely certain that there be no mistaking by his Democratic sponsors of his stand on Negro voting rights, Chase spelled it out: "I have been and am in favor of so much of the reconstruction policy of Congress as bases the reorganization of State governments in the South upon universal suffrage." With that on the record the Chief Justice offered the usual disclaimer about not desiring the presidency but willing to accede to his countrymen's wishes if they chose him.[9]

Belmont's hopes for a Chase nomination dimmed considerably in the light of the Chief Justice's unequivocal response. Personally he didn't care whether universal suffrage were voted up or down. The only *sine qua non* in a Democratic candidate involved "soundness" on the greenback issue; Radical Reconstruction he regarded as a lesser evil. But as a party leader, he considered white southern support in 1868 absolutely essential if the party were to make a comeback. Chase's resolution on such a key and controversial issue was hardly calculated to effect this result. Southern voices already spoke out against a Chase boom, insisting that a Democratic standard-bearer must "promise deliverance" from Negro suffrage.[10] Yet, the convention would meet in a month, and none of the other possibilities had much chance of besting the Republicans and their popular war hero.

Meanwhile, editorials in the *World*, whose publisher, Marble, did not know of the Belmont-Chase correspondence, pondered the advantages of the Chief Justice's candidacy and concluded

[9] Chase to Belmont, May 30, 1868, private Belmont collection.

[10] William M. Browne to Howell Cobb, May 12, 1868, Gazaway B. Lamar to Howell Cobb, May 15, 1868, L. Q. Washington to Howell Cobb, May 31, 1868, in *Annual Report of the American Historical Association for the Year 1911* (2 vols., Washington, 1913), II, 695–98.

that he was the best man the party could choose. After all, the United States Senate would still remain in Republican control regardless of the 1868 elections, and neither Pendleton nor Mc-Clellan could secure that body's cooperation. If elected President, Chase would certainly attract the support "of the ablest of the Republican Senators" and bring an end to "Jacobin rule." The *World*'s stream of pro-Chase material continued apace, and with the convention less than a month away, Belmont was forced to tell Marble of his exchange with Chase. The *World* immediately reversed itself. If it were true, Marble declared in a mid-June editorial, that the Chief Justice stood fully committed to Negro suffrage, then the *World*, though maintaining its respect for his ability, must withdraw his name from further serious consideration.[11]

Rejecting Chase proved easier than replacing him with an attractive alternate. On the weekend preceding the convention, the *World* had not yet come up with a name strong enough to challenge Chase's rumored strength in the East or Pendleton's acknowledged power among midwestern Democrats. Chase's nomination would associate the party with federal protection for Negro voters—which Marble thought a bad thing—while a Pendleton designation would mean the end of the Democrats as the "hard-money party"—which looked even worse. A convention victory for either man would only prolong intraparty dissension and guarantee Grant's success. Ultimately, the party would have to find a *tertium quid*, a Democrat considered "right" on Negro suffrage as well as on currency.

Horatio Seymour, New York's wartime governor, had gradually emerged as the most likely compromise candidate. His name regularly appeared on lists of potential nominees despite his repeated denials of any interest in the nomination and his repudiation of preconvention efforts in his behalf. In March, when Seymour addressed the New York State Democratic Convention at Albany, he discouraged the use of his name as a favorite son. As late as June 25, he delivered a speech in New

[11] *New York World*, June 1, 4, 9, 15, 1868; Nevins and Thomas, eds., *Diary of George Templeton Strong*, IV, 217.

York City declaring Chase to be the only candidate capable of beating Grant. His sincerity, however, has been questioned by contemporaries and later historians who charged him with hypocrisy during the preconvention campaign—"refusing the crown to make certain of getting it." One journalist noted that the former governor presented excellent reasons against his own nomination and still better ones against anyone else's.[12]

Rumor named Belmont among Seymour's supporters, a situation which made Seymour's disclaimers all the more suspect. Back in February, the pro-Pendleton, anti-Wall Street *Cincinnati West and South*, disgruntled at the national chairman's choice of New York over Cincinnati for the convention site, declared Seymour's nomination "a foregone conclusion," for "was not August Belmont our master, as well as master of the situation?" That Belmont never favored Seymour's selection but instead plotted strategy with Chase's daughter, "Kate" Chase Sprague, up to the eve of the convention indicated that he was certainly no Seymour backer and could hardly be considered "master of the situation." [13]

Belmont's worry over a candidate was almost submerged in administrative and executive chores as convention time neared. Requests for tickets flooded his office and created an annoying situation. He possessed neither the time nor the clerical staff to process each application. Belmont also realized that for every person fortunate enough to receive a convention pass one hundred would accuse him of favoritism, corruption, or packing the public galleries. The national chairman finally disposed of the problem by arranging for ticket distribution through state delegations and by having Democratic newspapers around the country advise readers of the new procedure. To insure against fraudulent tickets, Belmont also had the press report that new, differently colored tickets would be issued on the morning of

12 *New York Herald*, March 12, 13, June 26, 1868; *New York Evening Post*, July 6, 1868; Alexander, *Political History of the State of New York*, III, 202–03.

13 Coleman, *Election of 1868*, 181, 220; James C. Kennedy to Salmon P. Chase, July 3, 1868, Chase Papers.

each convention day at the national committee headquarters and that only a delegation chairman or an authorized deputy would be permitted to pick up his state's allotment.[14]

On Saturday, July 4, Belmont left his seat on the platform in Tammany Hall, strode to the rostrum, and officially welcomed over 800 delegates to the tenth Democratic National Convention. The newly decorated hall was as garish as the assemblage was motley. Huge bronze statues of Roman soldiers flanked the platform, while the walls surrounding the delegates were emblazoned with the official crest and flag of each state. The crowd burst into applause at the sight of Belmont, a tribute less to his popularity than to his having headed the party's executive organization at a time when no one else would run the political risk or take on the corresponding expense. Carried away by his reception, Belmont hailed the architectural monstrosity as a "magnificent temple erected to the Goddess of Liberty by her staunchest defenders and most fervent worshippers," the "time-honored Society of Tammany."

Heterogeneity had always characterized the Democratic Party, and this convention was no exception. Here was its national chairman, a German-Jewish international Wall Street banker, addressing, on the one hand, xenophobic and inflationist midwesterners who hated and feared what Belmont represented (and who had entered the convention hall with imitation five-dollar bills pinned to their lapels), and, on the other, former Confederate military officers, administrators, and politicians whose late cause Belmont had so often denounced. These differences notwithstanding, Belmont urged his "fellow Democrats" to rally around "the Union, the Constitution, and the laws."

The "most vehement and continued cheering" constantly interrupted his speech as he castigated the "evils" of Radical Reconstruction, insisted that the former Confederate states be restored to full membership in the Union, and protested against the test oaths being administered to former Confederates as "revolting to justice and civilization." In a gibe at the Republicans,

14 *New York World*, June 20, July 2, 4, 1868.

he expressed Democratic gratitude to Johnson and to Chase for resisting Congress' usurpation of executive authority. Anticipating a convention debate over greenbacks, Belmont scorned soft-money ideology and referred scathingly to a "vicious, irredeemable, and depreciated [paper] currency." [15] A Democratic observer noted how Belmont, at the conclusion of his address, seemed "much moved" at the ensuing display of "oldtime heartiness and Democratic confidence." But to a contemporary Republican, Belmont's "lurid speeches had become the accepted signal-guns of national Democratic conventions, and he did not disappoint expectation." [16]

On July 7 the convention adopted a platform, much of which echoed Belmont's address. Resolutions demanded that the former Confederate states be returned to their presecession status, arraigned the Republicans for fraudulently placing the South under a Negro supremacy sustained by military despotism, denounced each Reconstruction act, and assailed the Radical attempt to strip the Chief Executive of his constitutional powers. But Pendleton's, not Belmont's, views formed the basis of the currency planks which advocated public debt payments in "lawful money" and called for "one currency for the government and the people, the laborer and the officeholder . . . , the producer and the bondholder." [17]

Belmont's anger at the convention's easy passage of the Pendleton plank and his continued inflexibility on this issue prevented his playing an effective role in the subsequent maneuvers over a candidate. He could not back a man who would favor

[15] At one point Belmont criticized the Republicans for nominating a military man to the highest civilian office in the land. Imagine his embarrassment several days later when General Winfield Scott Hancock surged into the lead for the Democratic presidential nomination on the sixteenth ballot. But a number of Democrats felt the party could do no better than fight one Union general with another. Mitchell, *Seymour*, 411.

[16] *Official Proceedings of the National Democratic Convention of 1868* (New York, 1868), 3–5; *New York World*, July 5, 1868; Blaine, *Twenty Years of Congress*, II, 397–98. There is a detailed account of the 1868 convention in Homer A. Stebbins, *A Political History of the State of New York, 1865–1869* (New York, 1913), 325–50.

[17] *Official Proceedings of the National Democratic Convention*, 37–60.

the soft money plank; yet he realized the handicap (*vide* Mc-Clellan and the 1864 peace issue) any nominee would have running on a platform he could not endorse. The only solution was a candidate strong enough to repudiate the offensive plank or hypnotic enough to get the voters to ignore the discrepancy. In the chairman's mind, Chase alone could accomplish this, but even the New York delegation had other ideas. The Empire State, voting under the unit rule, backed "favorite son" Sanford Church for seven ballots and Indiana Senator Thomas A. Hendricks for the next fourteen.

The total convention picture showed Pendleton setting the pace for the first fifteen ballots, but he could not achieve the necessary two-thirds vote and withdrew. General Winfield Scott Hancock of Pennsylvania then moved into the commanding position until the twenty-second ballot, when Hendricks caught up with him and appeared about to stampede the convention. At this crucial juncture, one of those vagaries occurred from which even best-laid strategy is not exempt. Personal factors overcame ironclad principles. The Ohio supporters of Pendleton, who had been feuding with the Hendricks managers, threw their votes to presiding officer Horatio Seymour, despite his well-known views favoring "hard-money."

Seymour, protesting at this sudden turn, left the platform to discuss the situation with his home delegates. Meanwhile, state after state proceeded to switch to him until his total passed the two-thirds mark, making this the first time a major party chose its presidential nominee against his wishes. For Vice President, the convention overwhelmingly picked former General Francis P. Blair, a Democrat-turned-Free-Soiler-turned-Republican-turned-Democrat, whose family had been prominent in American politics since the 1820s.[18]

With the platform and candidates decided, the only important item remaining was the national party organization. Belmont had no intention of staying on as national chairman, but even if he had, the events of the past few days would have

[18] *Ibid.*, 74–161. For a discussion of Seymour's attitude before and during the convention see Mitchell, *Seymour*, 433–41.

given him pause.[19] In 1864 his enthusiasm to win with McClellan had overcome his antipathy to the "peace" plank. Now, both candidate and platform were unpalatable. When the state delegations met to choose their national committeemen for the next four years, New York took a day longer than the rest to reach its decision, increasing speculation about the identity of Belmont's successor. Yet the completed list contained Belmont's name again, and as soon as the new committee met it reelected Belmont to the chairmanship.[20]

There is no record whether an appeal to vanity or to duty changed Belmont's mind. Quite likely Seymour's supporters used the same argument on Belmont that Belmont had used on Seymour in getting him to accept renomination to Albany in 1864. It would look bad and cause Democratic voters to lose confidence if the national chairman stepped down just when another New Yorker became the presidential nominee, particularly as it was known Belmont never wanted Seymour for the office. Belmont's presence at the helm again would also reassure eastern hard-money men and perhaps persuade them that the greenback plank had been adopted only to pacify other sections of the party.

Belmont, assessing the campaign problems with which he would have to deal, saw little cause for optimism. The currency plank had become an emotional, almost traumatic, issue for western Democrats. It was sure to cause trouble in the next several years, when most of the federal refunding program would be carried out. The nomination of the anti-greenback Seymour worried him, too, for he simply could not believe Seymour capable of the shrewdness needed to handle such an explosive issue. The former governor appeared neither temperamentally nor intellectually suited to the presidency and would be lucky to attract half the votes Chase would have received. To the

19 Even the *World* had assumed that Belmont's opening address to the convention signified a closing chapter in his political career. Furthermore, western and southern greenbackers had expressed uneasiness that a Wall Street capitalist, known to have strongly opposed the Pendleton plank, controlled the Democratic National Committee. *New York World*, July 5, 1868.

20 *New York World*, July 8-12, 1868.

chairman there was no mistaking that the party had blundered badly.[21]

Belmont, always a loyal party man, plunged into the welter of campaign duties. He arranged for the publication of a complete work on Seymour's political and public life and, for the convenience of Democratic politicians and newspaper editors, even got it indexed. He pressed George Wakeman, a *World* correspondent who served as "official reporter" for the national convention, to write up the proceedings "as soon as possible," that they might be distributed nationally. Besides the funds necessary to print the proceedings, the national committee also incurred expenses for additional campaign literature, publicity, and speakers. Bills for advertising and office expenses poured into committee headquarters.[22] To meet these and other costs, Belmont persuaded seven wealthy Democrats to join him in contributing $10,000 each to a special fund, from which "sums shall be expended in such manner as the national Democratic committee shall determine." Augustus Schell, a prominent local Democrat for over two decades, took charge of this fund.[23]

Word of this political largess resulting at least in part from party desperation to get back in power must have spread. This may explain why R. W. Latham, a Washington, D.C., Democrat, promised that $3,000 a month would "secure" the capital's thirty newspaper correspondents, "who make the views and give the tone to every important newspaper in the country. . . . There are no such men in this country for energy and

[21] A Seymour letter to Barlow soon after the convention amply illustrates Belmont's apprehension: "I dread putting on the harness again. I feel like a gelded & jaded horse that is forced to take to the road. . . . I shrink from victory more than I do from defeat." Seymour to Barlow, July 23, 1868, Barlow Papers.

[22] Thomas M. Cook and Thomas W. Knox, eds., *Public Record of Horatio Seymour . . . 1856 to 1868* (New York, 1868); Frederick O. Prince to Belmont, Aug. 14, 1868, private Belmont collection; Belmont to Marble, Aug. 14, 1868, Marble Papers; Mitchell, *Seymour*, 463.

[23] The seven were Tilden, Augustus and Richard Schell, George I. Magee, Charles O'Conor, Thomas C. Durant, and Cyrus H. McCormick. John Bigelow, ed., *Letters and Literary Memorials of Samuel J. Tilden* (2 vols., New York, 1908), I, 245.

smartness as the reporters stationed here." Frederick P. Stanton, a five-term Tennessee congressman in the 1840s and 1850s, would be delighted, added Latham, "to take charge of the money and disburse it." Belmont rejected Latham's scheme.[24]

Democratic discrepancies on the currency issue necessitated some political legerdemain on the subject of greenbacks. Spokesmen in the West pointed to the platform as evidence of Democratic sympathy with soft-money sentiment, while in the East Belmont's postconvention counsel to Marble set the tone: "Dwell as little as you can upon the financial issue, but pitch into Negro suffrage [and] reconstruction outrages." This kind of rhetorical contortion might have lulled the average voter who wanted to hear that all was well, but it could hardly be expected to survive the gauntlet of the opposition press unscathed. Republican editors relished the chance to capitalize on any discontent remaining from the convention battle. They reminded readers how Belmont, in his address, had attacked the "vicious, irredeemable and depreciated [greenback] currency." One paper stated that Belmont's reelection as the party head for another four years "surely was rubbing it in to the western Democrats." After all, did he not work for the Rothschilds, those large federal bondholders and advocates of specie repayment?[25]

Pro-Grant papers singled out other aspects of Belmont's convention speech as well. The *Herald* wrote that the Democrats, judging by Belmont's address, "obviously have not heard of any great changes [taking place]. . . . They twaddle on in their arrogant self-sufficiency and artful blindness as if the nation had not four years ago repudiated them absolutely for these very vices." John W. Forney, now a leading Republican journalist, assaulted the chairman's talk for dwelling on war and postwar issues, while "not a line of denunciation of the horrible crime of the rebellion" appeared in it.[26]

24 Flick, *Tilden*, 182; Coleman, *Election of 1868*, 299; Bigelow, ed., *Letters and Literary Memorials of Tilden*, I, 240.
25 Unger, *Greenback Era*, 90–92; Belmont to Marble, July 11, 1868, Marble Papers; Coleman, *Election of 1868*, 294.
26 *New York Herald*, July 6, 1868; *New York World*, July 14, 1868.

Belmont had grown less sensitive by now to Republican charges, but constant Democratic carping at his activities vexed him. The *Cincinnati West and South* carried a series of editorials accusing Belmont of treason to the party and claiming that in his resentment against western Democrats over the currency plank he deliberately engineered Seymour's nomination in order to drag the party down to defeat. Belmont found even more galling the fact that J. R. Reed, author of the vituperative columns, advertised himself as the "leading writer" of the *Cincinnati Enquirer*. He immediately wrote Washington McLean, publisher of the *Enquirer*, with whom he maintained close ties since the days they both supported Douglas, and asked for an explanation.

McLean's apologetic reply denied knowledge of Reed's connection with the *West and South*, which he described as "a small reservoir of malice and spleen," and announced Reed's immediate discharge from the *Enquirer*. The publisher assured Belmont that "I very cheerfully bear testimony that you acted in perfect candor and consistency with all parties at the convention, and that you were activated by . . . a sincere desire for the success of the Democratic Party." This was not the end of Belmont's trouble with the Ohio press. Another soft-money Democratic paper, the *Cincinnati Commercial*, spread a report that New York ward politicians were accusing Belmont of "lukewarmness" in the campaign and of refusal to contribute toward its expenses.[27]

More subtle but important criticism of the national chairman emanated from his own political back yard. Seymour notified Tilden late in July that the national committee could not be counted on to organize the party canvass. "We have been a long time out of power and are apt to call upon those who *used to be* efficient without making allowance for the change made by time." What the nominee had in mind was something along the lines of the so-called "Jackson" clubs recently organized in New Jersey and Connecticut. There, aggressive, young Demo-

[27] McLean to Belmont, July 30, 1868, private Belmont collection; Coleman, *Election of 1868*, 294.

crats had formed secret organizations outside official party channels and elected themselves to newly created positions. Seymour favored wider use of such tactics, because their secrecy gave them "the charm of novelty," while "they hold out a motive to active young men by giving them power at once in their localities." After a few conferences with Democrats in other states, Tilden organized the "Order of the Union Democracy," placing himself at the head and Augustus Schell as "Vice Chief." But for all Seymour's lack of faith in the national committee, the clubs set up by the Order were far from successful and promptly disappeared after Election Day.[28]

In view of Seymour's admitted reluctance to act like a leader, his slur on Belmont's leadership was ungracious. Still, a scrutiny of Belmont's activities in the months after Seymour's nomination shows that the chairman's work did lack the energy and inventiveness that had characterized his efforts in the previous two campaigns. He went through the necessary motions but omitted the extras that had become hallmarks of his campaign style. Whether the ill health he complained of crimped his efforts for Seymour, or whether the futility of a Seymour candidacy caused his ill health, he sponsored fewer rallies, delivered fewer speeches, and wrote no open letters as he had before.[29] The first group of fall state elections, which had called forth such a flurry of activity in 1860 and 1864, did not stir Belmont to go beyond administrative and financial tasks of the deskbound variety. When his pessimism about the results proved accurate, this, too, failed to rouse him.[30]

Even intimations that some fellow Democrats sought a change in the national ticket stimulated no response from Belmont. Through August and September other party leaders pri-

28 Seymour to Tilden, July 20, 1868, Tilden Papers; Flick, *Tilden*, 183; *New York World*, Dec. 3, 1868.

29 In a letter to Colonel John Dash Van Buren, a Seymour friend, Belmont confided that his poor health would restrict campaign activities on his part to a minimum. Van Buren to Seymour, Sept. 23, 1868, Horatio Seymour Papers, Collections of The New-York Historical Society.

30 Reports in August from optimistic New England national committeemen proved faulty, as Maine and Rhode Island went Republican the next month. Frederick O. Prince to Belmont, Aug. 14, 1868, private Belmont collection.

vately bemoaned the unfortunate situation at the convention which produced a Seymour-Blair ticket while rejecting Chase, Johnson, Hancock, and Hendricks. Seymour's candidacy aroused little popular excitement, and Blair's proved a distinct embarrassment to the party. Blair had written a preconvention letter to James O. Broadhead, a Missouri lawyer, declaring that the "real and only issue in this contest was the overthrow of reconstruction, as the radical Republicans had forced it on the South," and that the man inaugurated as President in March, 1869, should "trample into dust the usurpations of Congress." Using his own words against him, Republican organs asserted repeatedly that Blair, if elected, would persuade the vacillating Seymour to overthrow the new southern state governments by force and engulf the entire region in flames once again.[31]

Yet, this lackluster campaign might have run a normal course had not the October Democratic defeats in Pennsylvania, Ohio, and Indiana caused party discontent to smolder. Strangely enough, the spark that ignited it came not from an anti-Belmont source but from his friend Marble in an October 15 *World* editorial. The mouthpiece which Belmont had acquired in 1862 had decided to speak with its own tongue. Annoyed with Seymour's lethargy and Blair's blundering, Marble made the incredible demand that the Democratic National Committee select a new national ticket. While most of the editorial centered upon Blair, its wording could easily have applied to Seymour as well.

We have still nearly three weeks for action. . . . If mistakes have been made, it is better that they should be corrected now, than that the country should be dragged through four more weary years of strife.

Seymour told friends that any alteration must include his own withdrawal and that, indeed, he would be relieved if another were substituted in his place. Blair averred his willingness to resign if the party requested him to do so.[32]

Democrats bombarded Belmont with demands for clarification of the *World*'s statement. Jonah D. Hoover of Washing-

[31] *New York World*, July 3, 1868; Smith, *Blair Family in Politics*, II, 413–17.
[32] *New York World*, Oct. 15, 1868; Mitchell, *Seymour*, 468–69; Smith, *Blair Family in Politics*, II, 424–25.

ton, D.C., chairman of the Democratic Resident Committee, wired the same day:

Does World article receive approval of friends of Governor Seymour? President [Johnson] and Cabinet unanimously for change of ticket to Chase. . . . Public favor here strongly favors movement. . . . Meeting for consultation at nine this evening. Telegraph immediately views of yourself and friends so I can act intelligently.

Wilbur F. Storey, publisher of the *Chicago Times* and a former national committeeman, telegraphed succinctly: "What does World mean?"

Belmont, faced with a threat of mutiny, repressed his personal misgivings about Seymour and for compelling political reasons became the champion of a man who, ironically, no longer had faith in him. He consulted Tilden and Schell, the latter having just returned from an interview with Seymour at his Utica home. The three leaders agreed that a better ticket could be easily devised—say Chase and Hendricks, or even Hancock and Hendricks. But they also realized that the choice of Seymour and Blair had been made by a duly authorized national convention, thousands of dollars had already been spent, and October was really too late to consider a change. Over their three signatures, they put forth the position of the national committee in a telegram to Hoover:

No authority or possibility to change front. All our friends consider it totally impracticable and equivalent to disbanding our forces. We in New York are not panic-stricken.

The reply to Storey read even more forcefully. Belmont labeled "absurd" the "suggestion" to change the ticket. Such talk was "wholly unauthorized & unknown" to the national committee and "is received by our masses with astonishment, derision, and indignation." Belmont then offered his own analysis of the October results. Considering the losing margin in the three states "we came nearer to our expectations than Republicans to theirs." Whether the national chairman realized that his statement could be taken two ways was not clear.[33]

[33] Hoover to Belmont, Oct. 15, 1868, private Belmont collection; Belmont, Tilden, and Schell to Hoover, Oct. 15, 1868, in *New York World*, Oct. 17,

The unrelenting opposition of Belmont and Tilden doomed the *World*'s time-for-a-change proposal. For a while Marble pleaded with Blair to undertake the "chivalrous" deed of withdrawing voluntarily. When Blair demurred, the *World* concentrated on goading Seymour into more aggressive activities. An October 17 editorial begged the presidential nominee to lead an offensive against the attacking Republicans. "An army without leadership is a helpless mob. . . . It is the business of leaders to lead." Seymour acquiesced and on October 20 issued an itinerary for a speaking tour of Buffalo, Cleveland, Chicago, Detroit, Indianapolis, Columbus, Pittsburgh, and Philadelphia. The *World* praised Seymour's new political posture as much as it had damned the old one.[34]

Belmont did his best to convey the impression that harmony once again prevailed in high Democratic echelons with a strongly worded "Address to the Conservatives of the United States." Issued in his official capacity and printed in every Democratic journal, the address contained no reference to recent intraparty disputes and at last pitched into the opposition. Belmont denied Republican accusations that a Democratic victory would bring on revolution and defiance of the established order. Angrily denouncing the Republican slogan, "the late Democratic Civil War of Rebellion," and the Republican pamphlet, "The Public Debt: A Democratic Legacy," he assured fellow Democrats they fought for "a good and righteous cause." Belmont extolled Seymour as "that tried statesman, a patriot who stood by the Union in its darkest hour . . . , a man equally beloved for the purity of his private character and honored for his public virtues." He promised the electorate that a Democratic administration would achieve economy in government, equitable taxation, beneficial development of natural resources, placement of federal finances on a solid, stable footing,

---

1868; Belmont, Tilden, and Schell to Storey, Oct. 17, 1868, in Bigelow, ed., *Letters and Literary Memorials of Tilden*, I, 250–51.

[34] *New York World*, Oct. 16–23, 1868; Mitchell, *Seymour*, 472. Seymour's trip was not as taxing as it appeared. He delivered the same speech at every stop.

and a "gradual and safe return" to specie payment. Back in his old form, he concluded with a clarion call to the party's adherents. Never mind Republican gloating over recent state elections. For the patriotic, loyal, conservative Democratic Party, "One victory is enough. Our ranks are unbroken. Our courage is unabated. Once more to the breach and this time—victory!" [35]

Other Democratic newspapers which had joined the *World's* dump-the-ticket drive were not ready to yield to the exigencies of party unity. The *Baltimore Sun* and the *Washington National Intelligencer* insisted that Belmont summon the full national committee to consider Marble's October 15 proposal. Even the national chairman's well-intentioned address of October 20, contended the *National Intelligencer*, could not satisfy those who still demanded Seymour's replacement by Chase, Hendricks, Hancock, or even President Johnson.[36]

Paradoxically, Belmont's reappearance in the public spotlight, designed to bolster the ticket, only succeeded in refocusing unwanted attention on himself. Criticism of the chairman's leadership replaced criticism of Seymour and Blair. Some Democrats felt that he had managed the entire canvass ineffectively and that public airing of an intraparty fracas violated a cardinal political tenet by giving comfort to the opposition during a campaign. Democratic politicians were heard "abusing Belmont soundly for his alleged ineptness" and for having "sold out to the enemy."

Even loyal Seymour papers, though satisfied with Belmont's defense of the ticket, criticized his general conduct. Why did the national chairman allow thirty days to elapse after the nomination before consulting the "governor?" asked one editor who presumably kept track of Belmont's every move in the period between July 9 and August 8. When Belmont finally contacted Seymour, the same critic went on, "it was done with a demand that Mr. Seymour should promise to permit Wall Street to name the Secretary of Treasury in case of his election." Seymour, the account continued, "promptly and forcibly repelled"

---

35 *New York World*, Oct. 20, 1868.
36 Coleman, *Election of 1868*, 354–56.

this "impertinent and disgraceful demand," with the result that Belmont, his "lackey" Marble, and Wall Street plotted for the nominee's defeat. An item appearing in the weekly *Round Table* echoed the same idea and laid Seymour's pending loss squarely in the lap of "those who have pulled wires, handled pursestrings, and concocted ideas for the national committee." [37]

With two weeks remaining in the campaign, rumors circulated that Belmont intended to depart for Europe. The stories originated with the *Philadelphia Press*, a Republican newspaper, which referred to the national chairman's October 20 address as a "farewell speech," probably meaning that it was his final formal address of the campaign. The pro-Grant *New York Sun*, on the lookout for further evidence of Democratic surrender to futility, picked up the "farewell speech" reference and reported Belmont's "plan" to leave the country immediately. His ostensible excuse for departing, the *Sun* warned its readers, would emphasize his health, though those "in the know" understood his actual reason to be extreme anxiety to escape a forthcoming political Waterloo. Belmont never left the country during 1868, but, as with so many other journalistic insinuations against him, he never denied or rebutted these rumors, refusing to be drawn into endless rounds of charge and countercharge with seasoned publicists.[38]

Even Belmont's well-known sporting instinct was muted by his doubts of the standard-bearer. By Election Day he had wagers with five Republicans on various races, but none on the outcome of the national contest. The only bet involving Seymour which Belmont was confident enough to make was that the former governor would carry his home state. Fortunately

[37] *New York Herald*, Oct. 19, 27, 1868; *Washington National Intelligencer*, Oct. 22, 1868.

[38] *New York Sun*, Oct. 22, 1868. Two historians have accepted the *Sun*'s "scoop." See Stebbins, *Political History of New York, 1865–1869*, 384–85; and Coleman, *Election of 1868*, 294. A thorough search of Belmont's letters in the Marble Papers indicates that his letters came either from New York or Newport during October, November, and December, 1868. See, for example, Belmont to Marble, Oct. 31, Nov. 12, Dec. 10, 1868, Marble Papers.

for Belmont's pocketbook, New York constituted one of the few items salvaged by the Democrats, as Seymour bested Grant there on Election Day by nearly 10,000 votes. Unfortunately for Belmont's reputation, however, the general easily overpowered Seymour in the electoral vote, 214–60. Like McClellan before him, Seymour left the political scene, refusing to acknowledge that his duty to the party did not end with his defeat by the electorate.[39]

After the Democratic losses of 1860 and 1864, bygones were bygones, and if there were recriminations in Democratic quarters, they were aired in private and confined to a relatively brief period. With the 1868 failure, however, irate Democrats were in no mood to desert the battlefield for the rest home. Starved for power, patronage, and prestige (and with the horizon empty of a sign of salvation), they looked around for a likely victim on whom to vent their spleen. With Douglas dead, McClellan gone, and the retired Seymour too insubstantial to nourish their anger, only one target remained—Belmont. His "approval" of the draft-Seymour movement, his "tepid" activity in the subsequent contest, and his stubborn refusal to alter the ticket in October—when to adhere to the status quo could only spell disaster—had all contributed to the shoddy state of the Democracy. Not since Buchanan's 1856 victory had a Democrat won election to the White House, and the three succeeding candidates—losers all—had been the national chairman's "choices." [40] The pro-Republican *New York Times*, gleefully editorializing on the postelection rupture in Democratic ranks, told of "moderates" hurling insults at the "Belmont Committee" and being joined by "extremists" who leveled aspersions of "faithlessness, duplicity, and corruption" at the "venal element" represented by Belmont and "his" *World*.[41]

Belmont had never dignified pre-election brickbats by replying to them, but now he bristled at the postelection assaults on

39 Belmont to Marble, Oct. 31, Dec. 10, 1868, Marble Papers.

40 In all fairness, Belmont's critics might have acknowledged that Buchanan had also been one of his "choices."

41 *New York Times*, Nov. 5, 1868.

his organizational leadership. He asked Marble to controvert them on the *World*'s editorial page, simplifying the publisher's task by providing the substance for such a rebuttal. Regarding attacks on his lack of enthusiasm for party goals, Belmont reminded Marble that "I have spent in these three [presidential] elections over $80,000 out of my own pocket," not to count perennial contributions to Democratic candidates for Congressional, state, and municipal offices. To accusations that his tenure was studded with defeats, Belmont turned the tables and charged his accusers with that responsibility. Southern Democrats should not have bolted the Douglas ticket in 1860. "Peace" Democrat Pendleton should never have been accepted as McClellan's running mate in 1864. And if the party had really heeded him in the last convention it would have opposed the "impracticable" greenback policy and would have selected Chase to carry its campaign banner. In sum, "if the Democrats West and South had followed my example [in 1860, 1864, and 1868] . . . , the political status of the party would be very different from what it is now." Marble not only devoted two editorial columns to a defense of the national chairman but went further. He rebuked "impecunious" westerners for failing to contribute one dollar to the national committee during the campaign, leaving all expenses to be borne by "twenty Democrats in New York City and a half-dozen others in New York State." [42]

Personal family correspondence suggests that Belmont intended to retire from the chairmanship of the Democratic National Committee after Election Day, 1868.[43] But the fulminations by frustrated Democrats, designed to force his departure, achieved the opposite effect. He changed his plans and settled into office again, stubbornly determined to leave only on his own terms and in more favorable circumstances. He believed

---

[42] Belmont to Marble, Dec. 10, 1868, Marble Papers; *New York World*, Dec. 15, 1868. Marble retaliated with a calumny of his own when he concluded that "not all the god-forsaken idiots in the country" worked on Greeley's *Tribune*, after all.

[43] Perry Belmont, *An American Democrat*, 135.

that most national committee members appreciated his resource-fulness and would back him against ouster moves.

Nevertheless, early in 1869 Belmont felt it prudent to strengthen his position by undertaking two projects. One was meant to offset Democratic charges of "disloyalty" to the party in the recent election campaign and the other to overcome pe-rennial Republican intimations of "disloyalty" to the Union during the Civil War. For the first, he sought Tilden's help. Tilden had had ample opportunity to observe the national chairman in action since the time they had helped found the Democratic Vigilant Association ten years earlier, and as re-cently as October, 1868, they had acted jointly to halt the dump-Seymour movement. Belmont wrote an "open letter to the Democratic rank-and-file," praising his own work in 1868, and asked Marble to secure Tilden's signature before publishing it in the *World*. Tilden stalled, offered excuses, and then flatly refused, claiming unwillingness to stir further intraparty fric-tion. Belmont, shocked and angry, withdrew the letter and began nursing a grudge toward Tilden for his "more than un-gentlemanly conduct." [44]

As for his Civil War attitude, Belmont contemplated publica-tion of a volume of selected correspondence which would speak for itself and bequeath to posterity an honest record of his pro-Union sentiments and deeds before and during the struggle. Though he had considered this undertaking for some time, the impetus was furnished by a February, 1869, letter which, four years after Appomattox, still mixed fact and fancy when discuss-ing Belmont's wartime activities. The banker had mailed a $1,000 check to a testimonial affair honoring Civil War hero General William T. Sherman. In appreciation, one of the orga-nizers wrote Belmont: "I sincerely regret that many people ei-ther through ignorance or malice should choose to class you among those who lacked sympathy with our country in its hour of trial."

Belmont discussed the project with Marble and Barlow and

[44] Belmont to Marble, March 30, 1869, March 1, 1870, Marble Papers.

scouted his files for favorable items. Letters to Douglas and to southern unionists would divulge his stand during Buchanan's lame duck months; his correspondence with Seward, Chase, Lincoln, Weed, and the Rothschilds would demonstrate even to the most prejudiced minds the lengths to which he advocated and aided Union victory and Confederate defeat. Meanwhile, the attacks on Belmont subsided, and in late spring, easier in mind and spirit, he sailed with his family on a European trip, hopefully leaving politics behind.[45]

Politics, however, did not forget about Belmont in his absence. The summer of 1869 saw a new all-out offensive, led by State Senator William M. ("Boss") Tweed, head of Tammany Hall, to drive Belmont from his party post. At the August, 1869, State Democratic Convention Tweed had sought to remove Tilden from the state chairmanship. Thwarted in that attempt, he went after something even bigger—New York's seat on the national committee. He persuaded two small Gotham dailies under Tammany's thumb, the *Citizen* and the *Atlas*, to accuse Belmont of "deliberate treachery" to the Democratic Party and demand his immediate ouster as national chairman.

The journals' venom equaled anything Greeley's *Tribune* had spewed forth in the 1850s. First of all, Belmont represented the Rothschilds who "are for the bondholders" and not the Democratic Party whose 1868 platform pledged equal treatment to bondholders and taxpayers. Therefore, he really worked to defeat the party by subverting its main campaign issue. In the second place, the London and Paris Rothschilds controlled the Democratic Party as long as their figurehead, Belmont, remained at the helm. Though Belmont may have become a naturalized American, "he has in no way renounced his attachment, his allegiance, and his bias toward European and aristocratic institutions. He is not only not a Democrat—he is not even, practically, an American citizen." Thus, the foreign-

[45] John Butterfield to Belmont, Feb. 13, 1869, private Belmont collection; Belmont to Marble, March 30, 1869, Marble Papers; Belmont to Seward, April 19, 1869, Seward Papers; *New York Herald*, Nov. 25, 1890; Belmont to Barlow, April 30, 1869, Barlow Papers.

born banker's removal was essential if "Americans" were to run their own party.[46] Finally, Belmont had neglected the "executive business of the campaign." Therefore, the party really stood to lose nothing by his dismissal.

Republican newspapers, particularly the *Times*, took notice of the avalanche of criticism. The *Times* rebuked its journalistic brethren for casting aspersions on Belmont's origin, reminding them that the "so-called Democracy" of the city would be nothing "without its foreign influence." It upheld Belmont's version of his 1868 role and approved it, noting that he had originally opposed both the nominees and the "repudiation" platform. *Harper's Weekly* published a pertinent and sympathetic cartoon by the relatively unknown, twenty-nine-year-old Thomas Nast entitled, "The Democratic Scapegoat." It depicted a downcast Belmont with horns and the body of a goat. The "scapegoat" bore on his back five heavy bags, with the labels "Sins of the Democrats," "Defeat in 1864," "McClellan," "Defeat in 1868," and "Seymour and Blair." Tammany toughs were kicking Belmont and hurling garbage at him. Tweed stood off to one side near a sign reading: "Tweed Association—A. Belmont is an Inefficient, Undevoted, Unsuccessful and Unpopular Chairman—Furthermore that his Dearth of Capacity, Lack of Purpose, Indifference as to Results and Want of Acceptability were the Chief Cause of our Defeats." A chair on a dais read "Reserved for Mr. Tweed—Democratic National Committee." [47]

From Paris, Belmont reacted bitterly to the "terrible war Tweed is waging against me." He suspected Augustus Schell's brother, Richard, of being behind Tweed. "If Schell only knew how much I care about [the chairmanship]. . . . Tweed or he or any other damned scoundrel is welcome to it." Belmont's friend, Barlow, wrote and asked the banker if he might do any-

[46] "Remember," the *Citizen* warned, "how the immortal Washington begged his countrymen to beware of foreign influences." Quoted in *New York Times*, Sept. 21, 1869.

[47] *New York Times*, Sept. 14, 15, 17, 20, 21, 1869; *Harper's Weekly*, XIII (Sept. 11, 1869), 592.

thing in New York for him. The affirmative reply requested Barlow to "Enlist some of our prominent friends to counter Tammany's blows [and] you would render me a real & essential service. . . . But pray be discreet." The national chairman refused to have it known that he felt Tweed's stings.[48]

Belmont arrived back in the United States in November, 1869. In view of the political sabotage attempted in his absence, he was especially eager to hurry along the final stages of his Civil War correspondence. Originally intended to absolve him of guilt in Republican eyes, it could now be used to good ad-

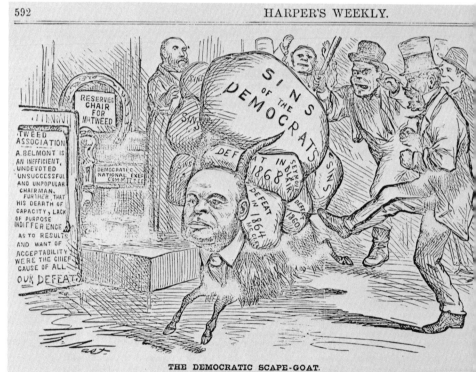

592   HARPER'S WEEKLY.

THE DEMOCRATIC SCAPE-GOAT.

"The Twentieth Ward Jackson Club, presided over by Mr. THOMAS COSTIGAN, adopted the following Resolution, on motion of Mr. JOHN DELANY, at their meeting last evening: *Resolved*, That the farther continuance of Mr. AUGUST BELMONT in the chair of the National Democratic Executive Committee is fraught with great peril to the existence and Salutary Influence of the party; that, inasmuch as he is lethargic in the performance of his official duties, wavering in his political faith, and distasteful to THE IRISH SECTION OF THE DEMOCRACY, that he be forthwith requested to vacate his position."

Thomas Nast cartoon from *Harper's Weekly*, September 11, 1869.

[48] Belmont to Barlow, Sept. 30, Oct. 12, 1869, Barlow Papers.

August Belmont, circa 1869.
(Courtesy of Mr. August
Belmont)

vantage on Democrats as well, reminding them that though Republicans in the highest places solicited his advice he had never deserted the party as so many others had. Belmont persuaded Seward, then in retirement at Auburn, New York, to lend him several original wartime letters, copies of which he had misplaced. Marble used the *World*'s presses to run off the edition, and by summer, 1870, Belmont began distributing *A Few Letters and Speeches of the Late Civil War* to scores of friends, active and retired politicians, and other high public officials of both parties. A brief preface indicated that the contents would serve as a vindication of his wartime patriotism and, in a broader sense, as a defense of Democratic leadership in the 1860s.[49]

49 Belmont to Seward, March 15, 1870, Seward Papers; Belmont to Marble, March 1, 1870, Marble Papers.

Incoming compliments gave Belmont immense satisfaction and made the finished product well worth the effort and expense. Robert C. Winthrop of Massachusetts, a Whig Speaker of the House of Representatives in the late 1840s, pronounced the volume "an ample refutation of that wholesale charge of disloyalty, so often & so recklessly brought against the Democratic Party." His old friend Daniel Sickles, who had joined the Republican Party and been made a Union general, "confessed" that the book "reveals to me much—very much—more than I had known. . . . I have taken the liberty to read some passages to friends of mine—Republicans whose impressions had done you great injustice." [50] Even the minister of the Belmont family's church, the Reverend John Cotton Smith, admitted he had earlier doubts about Belmont's "views in regard to our national difficulties" and only now realized the national chairman's "admirable record, not only of loyalty to the Government, but of valuable service in its behalf." [51]

The move to oust Belmont as national chairman never regained force after 1870. Tweed, faced with a strong challenge to his Tammany leadership, scarcely had time to continue pursuing any national ambitions. In July, 1871, the *New York Times* began reprinting documents which showed evidence of Tweed's corrupt practices, and the following year he was arrested and convicted of having plundered the municipal treasury of at least 75 million dollars. Belmont joined anti-Tweed reformers and was later elected a "sachem," or governor, of a

---

[50] Winthrop to Belmont, Oct. 10, 1870, Sickles to Belmont, undated, private Belmont collection. That not all Republicans shared Sickles' change of heart is evident from an 1874 *New York Tribune* editorial, motivated by public discussion of Rothschild sympathies during the American Civil War: "We are glad, however, to accept Mr. Belmont's assurance that he himself never faltered in his conviction that the war for the Union was sure to succeed, and shall be even better pleased when he explains how he reconciled that faith with his attitude in the darkest hour of the struggle as chairman of the National Committee of his party . . . [whose 1864 campaign] platform solemnly declared the war for the Union a failure." *New York Tribune*, Aug. 3, 1874.

[51] Thomas A. Hendricks to Belmont, Oct. 4, 1870, Stewart Brown to Belmont, Dec. 8, 1870, Rev. John Cotton Smith to Belmont, March 10, 1871, private Belmont collection.

temporarily cleansed Tammany. The other attackers realized Belmont was an elusive target. Not being an elected official he could not be voted out of public office. There was no way to force Belmont out if he would not step down and if his fellow national committeemen would not act. Neither event occurred, and other issues and other elections arose to divert attention from the party's unprofitable past.

11

★ ★ ★

Greeley's Incredible Nomination

By 1871 BELMONT REALIZED that though he had withstood the move to oust him from his party post, there was no sign of the more favorable circumstances under which he had hoped to resign. His 1870 book had gained him respect, but this respect had not made the fractious members of his party any readier to adopt the positions he recommended. The Ohio Democrats whose policies and leaders had caused him so much anguish seemed mindlessly bent on repeating themselves. Belmont believed, for instance, that the 1868 platform incorporating Pendleton's "greenback" plank had cost the party the presidency; yet in May, 1871, an Ohio State Democratic Convention nominated General George W. McCook for governor on a platform which restated the Pendleton "folly."

Belmont, extremely provoked, confided his worries to Marble. The Ohio Democrats must be persuaded to underplay the greenback issue; otherwise, Republicans would capture the 1871 election and the state's valuable twenty-two electoral votes the following year. What made the Ohio platform look even more foolish and suicidal was its deliberate flaunting of a federal statute. For while the Pendleton plank of 1868 "was bad enough . . . there was some law for it, as the Bonds don't say anything about the principal being payable in Gold & the holders had only the assurances of [Treasury Secretaries] Chase and McCulloch." But in March, 1869, Congress had passed the Public Credit Act, making the interest and principal "alike payable in Gold on all the Bonds." To the Wall Street banker, "the Ohio Resolution [was] therefore actually *repudiation*." [1]

Belmont also wrote a lengthy letter to McCook, castigating the "Bourbon" spirit which now reared its ugly head by "rehashing the pernicious greenback doctrine & the cant about Bondholders." The banker based his own position on political, not financial, expediency (though his views as an international banker were not necessarily incompatible). "I have not the interest of one dollar at stake. I am not a 'bloated Bondholder,' & have [no] . . . federal obligation among my worldy goods. All I care for is the success of the Democratic Party." The Republican leaders and press knew full well that "charging us with disloyalty and copperheadism" no longer worked with the public,

so they charge us now with revolutionary & disorganizing intentions. This is our great stumbling block & unless we can prove to the American people that we intend to accept the Government as it will be handed to us, without disturbing the political & financial situation, otherwise than by placing them on a sounder basis . . . , we can never hope for their votes.

By all means, Belmont urged McCook, "exert your influence to keep the unfortunate plank in the background . . . , as it is made of paper, & d—d bad paper too, & we are sure to break through if we try to stand on it." Disregarding Belmont's advice, McCook followed Pendleton's attitude and geared his campaign to the currency issue. When Belmont heard this, he predicted, sadly but correctly, that Republican Edward F. Noyes would defeat McCook.[2]

Democratic disagreement over greenbacks, however, did not begin to compare with the upheavals occurring in Republican ranks over a variety of issues. Republican disagreements dating from the Johnson administration disappeared only momentarily under President Grant. By 1870 a dissident movement was already under way in Missouri, where a large number of citizens who had fought in the Confederate Army and had been dis-

---

[1] *New York Times*, June 16, 1870; Belmont to Marble, June 4, 7, 1871, Marble Papers.

[2] Belmont to McCook, June 5, 1871, Marble Papers.

franchised by an amendment to the state constitution now demanded the right to vote. Republicans in the legislature divided
on the question, and a group, guided by United States Senator
Carl Schurz and former Senator Benjamin Gratz Brown, combined with the Democrats to remove the disqualifications. The
same coalition also placed Brown in the governor's mansion.[3]

Gradually the movement spread throughout the country. Its
program broadened to include the immediate granting of "full
citizenship" to all former Confederates, the reestablishment of
civilian government in all southern states, civil service reform, a
return to specie payments, tariff revisions, and the limitation of
Presidents to a single term. Powerful newspaper editors—in a
day when dailies outranked all other communications me-
dia—rallied behind the new movement.[4] By 1872 the Republican breach attained such formidable proportions that a substantial minority bolted the regular party, set up its own political
organization, and prepared to nominate a separate presidential
ticket.[5]

Belmont quickly grasped the significance of Republican fac-
tionalism and sought to turn the situation to Democratic advantage. Should he delay calling together his committee—charged
with selecting a time and place for the national nominating convention—as long as practicable? Such a tactic would allow
Democrats more opportunity to evaluate the new movement's
nominees and program.

Other Democrats approved Belmont's tactic. Congressman
Niblack reported from Washington that "our leading friends
here . . . favor postponing" a "call" to national committee

[3] In Washington, Senator Charles Sumner's vehement opposition to Grant's
Santo Domingo Treaty of 1870, which cost the Massachusetts Republican his
chairmanship of the Committee on Foreign Relations, also contributed to
growing party disaffections.

[4] The more noteworthy included Horace Greeley, Samuel Bowles of the
Springfield (Massachusetts) Republican, Henry Watterson of the Louisville
Courier-Journal, Murat Halstead of the Cincinnati Commercial, Horace White
of the Chicago Tribune, William Cullen Bryant of the New York Evening
Post, and Edwin L. Godkin of the weekly Nation.

[5] A dated but still superior work on the Liberal Republicans is Earle D.
Ross, The Liberal Republican Movement (New York, 1919).

members "for a considerable time yet." The Liberal Republican actions at their May convention "will very much assist us in determining what we ought to do." C. M. Woolley, an Ohio Democrat who kept Belmont regularly informed on current midwestern events, advised against calling the national committee together until after the regular Republicans renominated Grant in June. By then, Woolley contended, it might not even be necessary to hold a Democratic convention at all, especially if the Liberal Republicans put up a strong ticket, "say, [Senator Lyman] Trumbull [an Illinois Democrat-turned-Free-Soiler-turned-Republican-turned-Liberal Republican] at the head and, say, Horace Greeley at the foot." Of course, Woolley went on, Democrats will disagree on the wisdom of canceling the convention, but the party's "despondent condition" would enable Belmont to lead it down whichever road he himself chose.[6]

After consulting Congressional Democrats in Washington, Belmont undertook an experiment in Democratic-Liberal Republican fusion. Using Connecticut as a test case, he made an agreement whereby Liberal Republicans would endorse the Democratic ticket in the spring, 1872, state elections, and the Democrats in turn would support Senator Orris S. Ferry's reelection bid as an "independent" Republican. In May the Democrats carried a majority of seats in the legislature and later made good their promise to Ferry.[7]

Even more significant for his party's future were the confidential negotiations Belmont initiated with Schurz, the foremost Liberal Republican. Following a series of meetings and letters, the two *landsmenner* arrived at a mutually acceptable arrangement regarding the best time to summon the Democratic National Committee and the convention. Belmont would not issue the "call" to his committee until the first week in April; the committee meeting would not take place until after the May

---

[6] Niblack to Belmont, Jan. 17, 25, 1872, Woolley to Belmont, Jan. 25, Feb. 10, 1872, private Belmont collection.

[7] Belmont to James R. Doolittle, March 19, 1872, Belmont Papers, LC; *New York Tribune*, May 16, 1872; *Biographical Directory of the American Congress: 1774–1949* (Washington, 1950), 1153.

convention of Liberal Republicans chose its candidates; and the
national convention would not be held until the second or third
week after Grant's renomination in June. In a spirit of interparty amity, Belmont volunteered to help secure names of
prominent New York Republicans for a public declaration of
support in behalf of the coming Liberal Republican convention
at Cincinnati.

The most crucial matter discussed by Belmont and Schurz
concerned the candidate the Liberal Republicans would choose
as Grant's opponent; this, even more than the convention platform, would determine the extent of Democratic endorsement.
To both men, Charles Francis Adams stood out from the group
of presidential aspirants. The reasons which militated against his
candidacy as a Democrat in 1868 would not matter now if he
were first nominated by the Liberal Republicans. The chairman
considered the Massachusetts independent "by far the strongest
& least vulnerable candidate" available, and he could not impress enough upon Schurz "the importance of selecting him at
the head of your ticket." With Senator Trumbull or Governor
Brown in second place the combined slate would possess "immense strength." Any other pair of nominees, he warned,
would be doubtful of victory. In April Belmont traveled
through the Midwest and sounded out "prominent men in both
parties." The trip strengthened his convictions, and to a Cincinnati newspaper reporter he openly and officially favored the
New Englander for President. Marble's editorials seconded Belmont and repeatedly referred to Adams as a "more able, up-
right, independent, safe and patriotic President" than any qualified American.

By the last week of April, Belmont could outline the conditions for an unbeatable Liberal Republican-Democratic campaign: Adams for President, on a platform denouncing the
"abuses & corruption" of the Grant administration, "military
despotism" in the South, and "centralization of power," and
boldly advocating "general amnesty & a Revenue tariff." If
Schurz could effect all this, "every Democrat throughout the
land [stands] ready to vote for your candidates."[8]

[8] Belmont to Schurz, April 1, 23, 1872, Carl Schurz Papers, Library of Con-

The Liberal Republican convention assembled on May 1 at Cincinnati's Exposition Hall. Debate over a platform only momentarily diverted attention from a nomination battle made even more intense by the general belief that the victor would also receive Democratic endorsement. Adams' chances looked favorable; he had the backing of Schurz and a plurality of the voting delegates. Besides, many supporters of the other contenders—Greeley, Trumbull, Governor Brown of Missouri, Associate Supreme Court Justice David Davis of Illinois, and former Governor Andrew G. Curtin of Pennsylvania—indicated Adams as their most likely second choice. On the first balloting, Adams' 205 votes (out of a necessary 358) led a field of six, though not a few people were stunned to see Greeley place second with 147, almost fifty votes ahead of Trumbull, Brown, and Davis, all of whom received equal opening support.

Then, an incredible event occurred. Brown, anxious to stop the frontrunning Adams, strode to the rostrum and handed Schurz a note requesting permission to speak. Though the convention had determined earlier to dispense with nominating speeches, Schurz inexplicably granted Brown's request. The latter proceeded to withdraw his own name from contention and asked the delegates to nominate Greeley. The assembly responded with mingled cheers and hisses. Gradually, the other candidates withdrew, and the race narrowed down to an Adams-Greeley competition. On the sixth ballot, the convention stampeded toward Greeley. To no one's surprise, "Warwick" Brown easily captured second place on the ticket.[9]

The nomination caused consternation among several Liberal Republican leaders. Schurz believed the delegates had made a "slaughter-house of the most splendid opportunity of our time," with Brown and Democratic Senator Blair, Seymour's 1868 running mate, deserving the greatest blame. Trumbull, though refusing to renege on an earlier promise to support the Cincinnati choices, spoke of "the outburst of mirth the [Greeley] nomination will call forth." Byrant's *New York Evening*

gress; *New York Tribune*, April 1, 1872; *New York Times*, April 15, 23, 1872; *New York World*, April 24, 30, 1872; Duberman, *Charles Francis Adams*, 357.
    [9] *New York Times*, May 1-4, 1872.

Post and Edwin L. Godkin's weekly, *The Nation*, repudiated the slate. Prior enthusiasts of Liberal Republicanism, citing the movement's original purpose "to decompose and recompose political affinities," claimed that Greeley's victory resulted from chicanery, intrigue, bargaining, and compromise and left many a fervent reformer dampened in spirit.[10]

If Greeley's nomination at Cincinnati worried many Liberal Republicans, it caused an explosion in Democratic ranks. So much interparty harmony might have been achieved by nominating any candidate except Greeley. Adams, Trumbull, Davis, or any one of a half dozen "dark horses" suggested at Cincinnati could have been accepted—if not with exhilaration, at any rate without embarrassment or humiliation. But Greeley's national reputation rested on his systematic, relentless, and often vituperative assaults on Democrats and their party. Since the 1840s he had constantly lumped them all together, labeled them "slaveholders," "slave-whippers," "traitors," and "Copperheads," and frequently accused them of thievery, debauchery, corruption, and every known form of vulgarity and sin. "Greeley as the Democratic nominee?" wailed the incredulous Marble, whose paper had long waged bitter journalistic and political warfare with Greeley and the *Tribune*. "Why, the honest, thinking mass of Democrats could no more vote [for him] than a Jew be persuaded to eat pork!" [11]

Belmont, about to meet with the national committee to formulate plans for the Democratic National Convention, was caught in a nightmarish predicament. While the party in general had been Greeley's target, Belmont had been the bull's eye since 1852 when the *Tribune* editor set the tone for the years to come with his exaggeration and distortion of Belmont's con-

---

[10] Horace White to Schurz, June 15, 1872, Schurz to Edwin L. Godkin, June 23, 1872, Schurz to W. M. Grosvenor, Dec. 25, 1872, in Frederic Bancroft, ed., *Speeches, Correspondence and Political Papers of Carl Schurz* (6 vols., New York, 1913), II, 382–85, 448–50; Bryant to Trumbull, May 8, 1872, quoted in Horace White, *The Life of Lyman Trumbull* (Boston, 1913), 384–91; Mark M. Krug, *Lyman Trumbull: Conservative Radical* (New York, 1965), 334; *New York World*, May 4, 1872.

[11] *New York World*, May 6, 7, 18, 20, 29, 1872.

sul generalship and warnings against "Jew bankers." Even had
Belmont's personal emotions not been involved, the survival of
the Democratic Party was again at stake. The national chairman
had labored diligently to keep it alive as a political institution,
despite the inroads made on its membership during the Civil
War period and despite the blandishments of the National
Union movement in 1866. Wouldn't Democratic endorsement
of Greeley lead to a dissolution of the national organization?
Yet, what feasible alternative remained? A separate Democratic
presidential candidate would hurt the Liberal Republicans more
than the regulars behind Grant and would only reinforce the
opposition's grip on the Federal Government.

The drama of the situation tantalized the press. A correspondent for the *New York Daily News*, waiting outside 109 Fifth
Avenue for the national chairman to take his Saturday afternoon stroll, caught Belmont's attention long enough to ask a
few questions. What did he think of the Cincinnati candidates?
Smiling, Belmont quoted a proverb: "Speech is silvern, but silence is golden." When pressed for something more concrete,
he recited yet another maxim: "If we cannot have what we
love, let us love what we have." The insistent reporter, not easily brushed aside, followed Belmont and inquired whether his
remarks anticipated an eventual Democratic acceptance of the
Greeley candidacy.

I cannot tell. . . . We must wait until we see its effect upon the press,
the people, and, in fact, on many things. It must develop. I go further. It
may be policy to adopt the ticket. Mr. Greeley, in my opinion, will run
well in the Southern States. But it is too soon to judge yet. I will do
most anything to beat this Administration. . . . The Philadelphia [regu-
lar Republican] convention must meet yet. In the meantime I judge it
better for the party to say or do nothing. That is better. What we might
say now would probably be perverted or turned against us when the
nominations are made.[12]

Friends and political acquaintances sought further elaboration
of Belmont's views, especially as they appeared to disagree with
"his" paper, the *World*. Most of the queries centered around

12 Quoted in *New York Tribune*, May 6, 1872.

the unavoidable question: who could be worse for the country and the party, Grant or Greeley? Whatever mental reservations Belmont had, his public comments were as judicious as the one he gave the *News* reporter. "So much am I impressed with the fatal consequences in store for our common country by the re-election of Grant," he wrote an Ohio Democrat, "that I would willingly vote for my deadliest enemy in order to prevent such a catastrophe." Belmont granted that Greeley's nomination at Cincinnati was "one of those stupendous mistakes which it is difficult even to comprehend," but the Democrats would have to deal with it realistically. To the possibility that Greeley's nomination might alienate too many Democrats, the chairman countered with the assertion that if a Democratic convention could endorse the *Tribune* editor "with anything like unanimity" the large body of rank-and-file will accept his "conversion" and vote for him. In the same vein, Belmont urged James Lyons, a Virginia state legislator and former Confederate officer, that he abide by the national convention's decision and "like a good soldier follow the given command." The cards had been cut, the Democratic Party had been dealt a Greeley, and they must play it to the best advantage or lose the whole game.[13]

On May 8 the national committee met in the Belmont residence to decide if, when, and where to hold the next national convention. A motion to defer all decisions until after the Republican convention in June met overwhelming defeat. Former Confederate General William B. Bate of Tennessee fared no better when he proposed that the committee abandon all plans for a convention and simply and unequivocally endorse Greeley and Brown. Isaac E. Eaton of Kansas precipitated a two-hour discussion by moving that the convention be summoned as soon as possible, but this also failed to gain majority support. Throughout the session, Belmont parried these suggestions because he had made a confidential promise to Schurz to hold the Democratic meeting after the regular Republican one. When all

[13] Belmont to Woolley, May 21, June 1, 1872, quoted in *New York World*, June 8, 1872; Belmont to Lyons, June 3, 1872, Barlow Papers.

members had had their say Belmont mustered enough votes to designate July 9 for the convention date and Baltimore—supposedly "free from all undue outside influence"—as its site. Just before adjourning the committee debated whether to insert pro-Greeley compliments within the "call" for the national convention. Surprisingly, a number of southern committeemen supported the idea, but a majority disapproved of setting such a precedent, lest it be misconstrued as an attempted interference with the "independence" of the convention.[14]

Assured of an 1872 convention, Democrats launched a full-scale debate over Greeley's prospective nomination. Many found it difficult to accept him. Marble kept up a steady criticism in the *World*, concentrating on Democratic "exaggeration" of Greeley's strength among Republicans and insisting on a "Straight-Out" Democratic nominee. Representative Daniel W. Voorhees, serving a fifth term in Congress and considered Indiana's chief spokesman, attacked Greeley on the House floor as "the most odious man to the Democratic Party. . . . Could I look the Democrats of my district in the face and support a man who is in favor of every villainy for which I ever denounced the Radical party?" Alexander Stephens, the old war horse of Georgia politics, was aghast at the "political mania" sweeping southern Democrats. "Who could have believed that men who could not vote for Douglas in 1860 would be huzzahing for Greeley now? Did the world ever witness such a spectacle?"[15]

Despite these vocal opponents, a formidable pro-Greeley bloc took shape, especially in the South. Southerners were pleased at Greeley's attitude, as exemplified by his payment of Jefferson Davis' bail in 1867 and his readiness to readmit former Confederates to public life. In addition, they hoped their endorsement of a famous Republican Unionist might finally rid them of the albatross of treason. John Forsyth of Alabama spoke of over-

14 *New York Tribune*, May 9, 27, 1872; *New York World*, May 9, 14, 1872.
15 David G. Croly to Marble, May 10, 1872, Marble Papers; *New York World*, May 14, 15, 17, 1872; *Congressional Globe*, 42 Cong., 2 Sess., May 13, 1872, 3379–80; Stephens to J. Barrett Cohen, July 2, 1872, in *Annual Report of AHA for 1911*, II, 717.

whelming support for Greeley in his region. John M. Harrell, Arkansas' national committeeman, believed that Greeley's influence over hundreds of thousands of Republicans who read the *Tribune* regularly would attract most of these voters from the Grant banner. "Marse" Henry Watterson, editor of the *Louisville Courier-Journal,* praised Greeley's talents and took issue with those Democrats who carped on the candidate's party "irregularities." Greeley's gain would be a Democratic gain, and besides, the party had nothing to lose. "Put Greeley in the White House; make Carl Schurz Secretary of State; and what more do you want?"

The *Missouri Republican,* despite its name the most powerful Democratic newspaper in the state, compiled a survey of over one hundred Democratic journals throughout the nation and came up with these statistics: 65 percent already advocated Greeley's nomination; 25 percent contained editorials favorable to Greeley though preferring to await the Baltimore results before openly endorsing him; and 10 percent demanded a "Straight-Out" Democrat as the 1872 standard-bearer.[16]

The New York State Democratic Convention at Rochester in May illustrated the strength of the Liberal Republican movement. The meeting's main purpose was to select delegates to Baltimore, but the representatives of the Empire State Democracy went further and wholeheartedly endorsed the entire Liberal Republican platform. Though the convention tabled a motion to pledge the Baltimore delegation to Greeley, the action fooled no one; the group was stuffed with acknowledged Greeley men and bound by the unit rule.

Belmont, not in attendance, expected to be named a delegate-at-large as in the past, but the leaders at Rochester dumped him in favor of Augustus Schell. The national chairman attributed this humiliation to the belief that he secretly controlled the *World* and another influential New York paper, the German-language *Staats-Zeitung,* both of which remained outspokenly

16 *New York World,* June 4, 8, 1872; Arthur Krock, ed., *The Editorials of Henry Watterson* (Louisville, 1923), 33–39; statistics cited in *New York Tribune,* May 11, 1872.

hostile to Greeley. Perhaps Belmont overlooked a simpler explanation. With the party in a state of confusion, the New York leaders hoped to avoid giving the westerners their usual opportunity to trot out the charges of "Wall Street" dictation that the banker's presence in the delegation invariably stimulated.[17]

The unanimous renomination of Grant at the Republican convention in June took the steam out of any meaningful stop-Greeley movement. One by one the wayward Democrats stepped back into the cheerless comfort of the Greeley express. Voorhees withdrew his opposition. Another Hoosier, Hendricks, once considered a leading candidate by the "Straight-Outers," accepted a gubernatorial nomination and pledged to work closely with Liberal Republicans in the state. Governor Theodore F. Randolph of New Jersey, whom the *World* earlier called "the most active and zealous opponent" of a Democratic-Liberal Republican coalition, yielded to "political realities," as did Senator Pendleton. In New York, Seymour and Tilden publicly announced for Greeley. Democratic newspapers such as the *Boston Post*, the *Hartford Times*, and the *Washington Patriot*, which had belonged to the anti-Greeley section, succumbed to the inevitable. Even the *New York World* groped its way back into the Democratic fold as the date for the national convention neared. A lead editorial on July 3 predicted Greeley's nomination at Baltimore on the first ballot a certainty and deplored alleged attempts by dissident Democrats to run a separate ticket in defiance of the convention's express will.

Pre-Baltimore polls of delegates indicated that Greeley would indeed have more than the necessary two-thirds support. Some enthusiastic Democrats, too impatient to await the convention, were already stumping for Greeley and Brown. More than a week before the Baltimore meeting, former Confederate Governor Zebulon B. Vance of North Carolina exhorted an audience in his home state to overcome earlier anti-Greeley prejudice and line up solidly behind him. "We have been singing Democratic

[17] *New York Tribune*, May 16, 17, 1872; *New York World*, May 16, 17, June 8, 1872.

hymns for forty years down here, and we have never recognized Greeley as a Democrat before. But if the Baltimore Convention puts him in our hymn-book, we'll sing him through if it kills us." [18]

Belmont arrived in Baltimore the day before the convention. With the Greeley-Brown ticket a foregone conclusion, speculative delegates mulled over the national chairmanship. A *New York Herald* correspondent heard talk of "a determined effort" to oust Belmont from his post, assuring his readers that "the fight on this matter . . . is one of the condiments which will give 'spice' to the convention." To all queries touching on his position Belmont had a pat answer: "No comment." But when the subject of Greeley's nomination came up, he claimed to be as "earnest" for the *Tribune* editor "as any man" in Baltimore.[19]

The Democrats formally assembled on a blistering hot July 9 in Ford's Opera House, and after some preliminary business they heard Belmont deliver what was to be his valedictory as chairman. It was, for the most part, an uninspiring performance, replete with partisan generalizations: Grant's 1868 election had resulted in executive and Congressional "usurpation" of all governmental functions; a "military despotism," "enforced by bayonets," overrode civil authority in most southern states; and "Caesarism and centralization" threatened to sweep away all remaining constitutional bulwarks erected by the Founding Fathers. Such phrases, far from bringing the crowd to its feet, barely managed to evoke any kind of audience reaction down on the "hotter than hell" convention floor.[20]

Belmont was attempting to move to the business at hand

[18] *New York World*, July 1, 3, 8, 1872; *New York Tribune*, July 8, 9, 1872; *New York Times*, June 22, 1872; Mitchell, *Seymour*, 503; Flick, *Tilden*, 241.

[19] *New York Herald*, July 6, 9, 1872.

[20] New York newspaper reaction to this section of Belmont's address was predictable. The *World* and the *Tribune* hailed the utterances, the latter labeling them "excellent and earnest." The pro-Grant *Times* thought it revealed Belmont's hypocrisy. The neutral *Herald* pronounced the speech to be "in admirable taste" and lauded its "entire absence of that personal abuse that has unfortunately already manifested itself in some of the party organs." All of July 10, 1872.

when a singular scene took place. No sooner had he mentioned Greeley by name than a large, bald-headed man, carrying a huge fan in his hands, stood up in the center of the hall and started yelling "Hurrah for Greeley" at the top of his lungs, all the while waving the fan over his head with great energy. Few of the listless, sweating spectators responded to such stimulation, but Belmont accommodatingly stopped talking, so as to allow the "claqueur" the spotlight. Soon, his continued yelling and waving grew contagious, and the delegates slowly rose and joined in the cheering for Greeley, leading one critical observer to call the episode "altogether the weakest specimen of manufactured enthusiasm ever seen." [21]

Regaining the crowd's attention, Belmont mentioned Greeley again, virtually apologizing for the untasty dish the party was being asked to swallow. He recalled the "violent attacks against myself, individually, which from time to time appeared in his journal." Certainly, the chairman told the throng, Greeley "is not entitled to sympathy or preference at my hands." Still, from that moment back in 1860 when Stephen Douglas had designated him Democratic National Chairman, Belmont had worked unstintingly for party unity. Now, a bewildering variety of circumstances swung most Democrats behind the Liberal Republican movement. Should the Baltimore delegates, in all their wisdom, "decide to pronounce in favor of the Cincinnati candidates, I for one shall bury all past differences and vote and labor for their election."

Belmont's declaration represented the wishes of the majority of the delegates. They, in their turn, knew such a declaration represented a sacrifice on Belmont's part, and they gave him warm applause. Before yielding the floor, Belmont sadly, but not unexpectedly, announced his resignation from the post he'd held for a dozen years. Several western delegates cried "Good, good," but, ignoring them, he delivered a parting slap at his perennial critics and staunchly defended his tenure as a party leader.

21 *New York Times*, July 10, 1872.

While I was grieved and deeply mortified to see at various times my motives and actions misconstrued by several Democratic papers, and that some even descended to the fabrication of the most absurd falsehoods concerning my social and political conduct, I have had the proud and consoling satisfaction that my colleagues on the National Committee and all those who knew me did justice to the integrity and purity of my intentions in all the trying situations in which my official position has placed me.[22]

Prolonged applause came from every corner of the hall as Belmont returned to his seat. Minutes later, Congressman Henry D. McHenry of Kentucky moved a resolution which was adopted unanimously:

Resolved, that this Convention, in receiving the announcement of the Honorable August Belmont . . . , desire to express their sense of his long, able, and efficient service in a most responsible and difficult position, and while submitting to his desire to be relieved from its labors and duties, confidently rely upon his wise counsel and cordial aid for the future as in the past.[23]

Belmont was now just another rank-and-file Democrat, and to him the remainder of the convention could only be anticlimactic. He boarded a train for New York the same afternoon, though the balloting for candidates was not scheduled until the following day. His early departure also robbed him of a chance to witness the selection of a new national chairman. Belmont must have been wryly amused when he learned that after all the chronic complaints about wealthy easterners controlling the party the national committee chose Augustus Schell, another New York millionaire.

Belmont never kept his convention promise to "vote and labor" for Greeley and Brown. He sat out the campaign and in November cast his ballot for an old friend, Charles O'Conor, candidate on a dissident "Straight Democratic" ticket for the

[22] *Official Proceedings of the National Democratic Convention Held at Baltimore, July 9, 1872* (Boston, 1872), 3–5.

[23] *Ibid.*, 7. The *World* expectedly echoed the resolution's sentiments in its lead editorial the following day. The *Times* unappreciatively called Belmont's twelve years in office "the most disgraceful period" in the Democratic Party's history. Both of July 10, 1872.

presidency.[24] He was pleased to see that Grant's electoral vote margin over Greeley exceeded the 1868 one over Seymour, but he thought more than 29,489 Democrats should have supported O'Conor. With his futile partisanship in behalf of such an unimportant splinter candidate, Belmont seemed to be signaling the end of his service to the Democratic Party.

[24] Perry Belmont, *An American Democrat*, 192.

12

★ ★ ★

The Electoral Crisis of 1876-1877

BELMONT'S WITHDRAWAL from active party politics in 1872, followed by plans for a ten-month European vacation, gave rise to rumor and curiosity. *Golden Age*, a weekly magazine, notified readers that the fifty-nine-year-old banker, "a wealthy foreigner of Jewish extraction," proposed to quit his adopted country, return to his European "employers," the Rothschilds, and "assist them in making money." The *New York Times*, which missed one of its favorite whipping boys during the 1873 campaign for minor municipal and state offices, asked in an editorial: "What has become of the great Mr. Belmont? . . . Is he dead . . . politically, or is he only sleeping, as they say on the tombstone? . . . Mr. Belmont may not be a Jefferson, but he is pretty much all the Democrats have left." [1]

Even if Belmont had felt inclined to reappear on the political scene, personal misfortunes would have hampered him. The Panic of 1873 broke in September, following the collapse of the once-powerful Philadelphia investment banking firm of Jay Cooke and Company. August Belmont and Company, like many American and European businesses, reverberated from the effects of the crisis. Thirteen months later Belmont still felt "much harassed by the unfavorable result of all my business operations." Chronic headaches and dyspepsia plagued him, and his young daughter, Jeannie, was incurably ill. [2] No wonder

---

[1] *Golden Age*, II (Nov. 29, 1872), 9; *New York Times*, Nov. 1, 1873.
[2] Belmont to Marble, undated [Oct., 1874], Marble Papers; Jeannie P. Belmont to Belmont, Aug. 7, 1875, Mrs. Elizabeth Belmont Feist to Belmont, Dec. 2, 1875, private Belmont collection; interview with Mrs. Eleanor Robson Belmont,

August Belmont, circa 1876. (Courtesy of Mr. August Belmont)

that Belmont scarcely appeared at public, much less political, functions in 1873.

The following year, a combination of factors—continuing economic disaster, dimming Civil War emotionalism, disenchantment with administration policy on banking, currency, tariffs, subsidies, and the national debt, and the perennial opposition cry for political reform—led to sizeable Democratic victories in Congressional and state elections. Democrats won ten Senate and seventy-seven House seats; the House gains gave them a

Dec. 4, 1963. Jeannie had suffered since her childhood from a stomach disorder, and her doctors administered increasing doses of morphine to ease her pains.

169-109 margin over the Republicans and their first opportunity to organize that chamber since 1857. The new political tide buoyed the New York Democrats. A pre-election ratio of twenty-six Republicans to nine Democrats in the Congressional delegation became eighteen to seventeen; Francis Kernan of Utica was slated to become the first Empire State Democrat sent to the United States Senate since 1845; and Tilden won the governorship with a handsome 50,000-vote majority.

Such harbingers of party success for the 1876 presidential campaign rekindled Belmont's dormant political spirit. "The political revolution," he wrote his son, August, Jr., "is a great one & I trust the conservative spirit of the best leaders of the Democratic party will prevail, so that we make no mistake in '76, but offer a good man & a good platform to the American people." He declined an invitation from the Brooklyn Constitutional Club, a Democratic group, to address their "jollification" celebration, but sent a message to be read at the meeting. Belmont warned his fellow party workers that 1874 constituted a Republican "Waterloo" which "we must follow up with a Sedan if we mean to wrest power from their hands." When the Manhattan Club arranged a pre-inauguration reception for Governor-elect Tilden late in December, Belmont, newly installed as club president, presided over the fete to which he had invited leading Democrats from other states. Newspaper reporters noted the former chairman's relaxed disposition and humorous introductory remarks.[3]

As Belmont knew, incumbent governors of New York were automatically in the national limelight as leading contenders for presidential nominations. Tilden, already identified in the public mind with political and administrative reform, naturally became a strong favorite for 1876. The governor's prominence displeased Belmont, despite the fact that they had much in common. Tilden's chairmanship of the Democratic State Committee

[3] Belmont to August Belmont, Jr., Nov. 11, 1874, Michael C. Kerr to Belmont, Dec. 27, 1874, private Belmont collection; Belmont, *Letters, Speeches and Addresses*, 194–95; *New York Times*, Dec. 30, 1874.

from Dean Richmond's death in 1866 until 1874 had coincided in part with Belmont's national chairmanship. Both men had initially supported Douglas, McClellan, and Chase for presidential nominations and had reluctantly endorsed Greeley in 1872. Both kept close political and social company with such influential state Democrats as Marble, O'Conor, Barlow, Seymour, Kernan, and "Honest John" Kelly, leader of a reformed Tammany Hall. But to Belmont, these similarities could not cancel out his grudge against Tilden for refusing to be drawn into the Belmont-Tweed conflict of 1869. Not only had Belmont then scored Tilden's "ungentlemanly conduct," but he had also given his pledge to Marble that "If Mr. Tilden were President tomorrow & offered me the first mission or any office coveted by me as the aim of all my ambition, I would spurn it, coming

Samuel J. Tilden (Courtesy of Dodd,   Carl Schurz (Library of Congress)
Mead & Company)

from him." [4] When the expected presidential boom for Tilden began in 1874, Belmont rose to challenge it.

Belmont simultaneously developed a strong personal and political attachment to Delaware Senator Thomas F. Bayard, whom he had met at the 1872 convention. Bayard, scion of an important political dynasty, was a lawyer serving his second term in the Senate.[5] There, he established a reputation second to none in his constant denunciation of "vindictive" Radical Reconstruction, demonstrating little change in the views he held during his pro-Breckinridge days of 1860.[6] He was one of the few major politicians at Baltimore to speak out against Greeley's nomination. Afterward, he graciously announced his acquiescence in the party's choice and then immediately left for a long European vacation, "due to reasons of health." [7]

On first appraisal, Bayard and Belmont appeared to share few characteristics. Bayard was a patrician to the manner born; Belmont had to struggle for entry into society's charmed circles. Bayard was haughty and aloof, his letters and orations coldly legalistic; Belmont was by nature gregarious, his correspondence florid. Bayard stubbornly refused to acknowledge the evolving nature of a post-Appomattox, industrial America, while Belmont's long career in politics had taught him the virtues of practicality. Perhaps Belmont wistfully perceived in Bayard a prototype of what he himself might have become had birth and

---

[4] Belmont to Marble, March 1, 1870, Marble Papers.

[5] His grandfather and father, James A. Bayard, Sr., and Jr., respectively, and an uncle, Richard A. Bayard, had already served in the United States Senate. *Biographical Directory of Congress, 1774–1949*, 826.

[6] There is no adequate biography or political study of Bayard, but see Charles C. Tansill, *The Congressional Career of Thomas Francis Bayard, 1869–1885* (Washington, 1946). Benjamin H. Brewster, a Republican lawyer who exposed the Star Route scandals while Attorney General under President Arthur, was evidently less impressed than Belmont. He described the senator as "garrulous, chattering and gabby, conceited, unread, nothing but a facility of talk, no depth or extent of acquirement, no solid training except that which he has picked up in the Senate—that is all—and great affectation and pomp of patrician importance." Brewster to Simon Cameron, July 20, 1884, Simon Cameron Papers, Library of Congress. I am indebted to Professor Robert D. Marcus for this source.

[7] *New York Times*, July 11, 15, 1872; *New York World*, July 13, 1872.

Perry Belmont, circa 1877. (Courtesy of Mr. August Belmont)

circumstances dictated otherwise: a respected public official, with a revered and distinguished family name and tradition. In any event, their relationship grew more intimate in the winter of 1874–1875, when Belmont's oldest son, Perry, just graduated from the Columbia University Law School, went to live with Bayard and served as his assistant during the entire second session of the Forty-Third Congress. Both Belmonts regularly observed Bayard's activities, paying particular attention to his public statements on major issues of the day. Before long they were caught up in a drive to secure Bayard the next presidential nomination. That the Delaware lawmaker possessed neither the extensive party organization nor the personal fortune of Governor Tilden did not deter Belmont, who, after all, had gotten accustomed to backing underdogs.[8]

In March, 1875, Belmont conceived the idea of assembling all Democratic senators at a Manhattan Club affair in honor of their accomplishments during the current session of Congress. Acting in his capacity as club president, he issued invitations, through Bayard, for a reception to be held immediately following the Senate's imminent adjournment. Belmont's purpose was not only to increase the club's prestige among the party's elected lawmakers but to introduce Bayard to as many influential New York Democrats as possible, especially those men who might mobilize a stop-Tilden drive. Bayard consented, but the reception never materialized. Marble inadvertently upset the plans by announcing in the *World* that the affair was intended only for freshman Democrats. Belmont hurriedly attempted to correct this contretemps, but an unexpected prolongation of the session scuttled the whole proceeding.[9] Bayard regretfully telegraphed Belmont that his senatorial colleagues dashed for homeward-bound trains just after adjournment, leaving so few in Washington that "I felt it was better not to put the Manhattan Club to the trouble of entertaining the mere handful of us." [10]

In October, Belmont's daughter, Jeannie, died, and this personal tragedy drove all thoughts of politics from his mind. Belmont's depression continued into 1876, leading his son, Perry, to express his concern to Bayard: "If he would only interest himself in politics, it would be a great thing." Almost as if to order, Belmont roused himself. A friend, former General Fitz-John Porter, serving as an interim New York City Commissioner of Public Works, found his confirmation to the post attacked by several aldermen who criticized his lack of concern

[8] Belmont to Bayard, Jan. 24, Feb. 7, 1875, Thomas Francis Bayard Papers, Library of Congress.

[9] Marble to Bayard, March 14, 1875, Belmont to Bayard, March 15, 1875, Bayard papers. Interestingly, Marble did not know of Belmont's pro-Bayard commitment. As late as the fall of 1875 he tried to draft Belmont—despite the known grudge—into the Tilden ranks. Marble to Belmont, Sept. 31, 1875, private Belmont collection.

[10] Bayard to Belmont, March 25, 1875, Bayard Papers.

for the working man. Belmont appeared before the Board of
Aldermen, testified to Porter's good standing as a Democrat,
and defended the commissioner's recent action lowering the
wages of city laborers from $2 to $1.60 a day on economic
grounds: "If I was in Mr. Porter's place, I would have done the
same. . . . There is no reason why laborers' wages should not
be reduced in times of depression." Newspapermen cornered
Belmont and questioned him about local politics. Belmont answered bluntly and unhesitatingly, conscious of his role as an
"elder statesman."

Perry Belmont and Bayard were overjoyed at this renewed
interest. Bayard invited the banker to the capital to discuss financial issues being debated in Congress. Belmont's acceptance
formally spelled the end of the period of mourning and political
withdrawal, and after his return, Perry could happily report to
Bayard that "my father's trip to Washington seems to have
done a great deal of good. He takes much more interest in public affairs than before." [11]

Active again, Belmont joined the ranks of a burgeoning stop-
Tilden movement in New York. He attended several secret
conferences of "high-grade" Democrats and in March joined
Kelly, Congressman Fernando Wood, and national chairman
Schell as signers of a widely circulated statement opposing
Tilden for the presidency. In April Belmont traveled to the
Democratic State Convention at Utica and was designated a
Tammany delegate to St. Louis in June. Assessing the probable
anti-Tilden strength within the delegation, he worked to line up
Bayard support among uncommitted Democrats in the conven-
tion-bound group, constantly reiterating his conviction that the
senator could carry New York "better than Tilden."

To Belmont's discomfiture, he soon discovered that not every
Tilden opponent preferred Bayard as an alternative, and that all
kinds of political deals were being discussed. Kelly reportedly
leaned to Governor Hendricks of Indiana some days and to
General Hancock on others. "Old Boss Whore" Schell, accord-

11 *New York Times*, Oct. 21, 1875, Jan. 11, 1876; Perry Belmont to Bayard,
Jan. 11, Feb. 14, 18, 1876, Bayard Papers.

ing to the Washington lobbyist, Sam Ward, flirted with everyone, though mostly with the Hendricks crowd. Other undecided New Yorkers favored Senator Allen G. Thurman of
Ohio. This New York fascination for a midwestern candidate
reflected a belief that the Empire State would go for any Democrat in November, and that a standard-bearer from the Midwest would attract much needed strength in the pivotal states
of Ohio, Illinois, Missouri, and Indiana, whose combined electoral votes totaled 40 percent of the necessary majority.[12]

Belmont's advocacy of Bayard for the presidential nomination could only lead to another parting of the political ways between himself and Marble. Marble, a Tilden enthusiast and
speech writer since 1874, fervently believed that the New York
governor possessed "ability transcending that of any other
Democratic statesman living," and he worked hard and long for
his nomination. Even Tilden's refusal to lend Marble enough
money to reverse the *World*'s recent financial losses did not
succeed in shaking the publisher's faith. Forced to sell the paper
in May, 1876, to William Henry Hurlbert, another Democrat,
Marble went to Albany to assist the governor in administrative
and literary capacities. From the state capital, he carried on a
correspondence with out-of-state Democrats, pointing to reform as the "dominant issue overriding every other" and to
Tilden as "the man who chances to be its foremost champion." [13] Nor could Belmont count on the usually steadfast
Barlow who was friendly to both Bayard and Tilden. Barlow
refused to commit himself to one for fear of offending the
other, leading supporters of both to think he really favored
their man.[14]

Unable to rely on help from his two old cronies, Belmont

[12] Barlow to Bayard, March 25, April 26, 1876, Sam Ward to Bayard, May
2, 1876, John Hunter to Bayard, May 5, 1876, Bayard Papers; Sanford E.
Church to Belmont, May 20, 1876, private Belmont collection; Flick, *Tilden*,
283; *New York World*, April 27, 28, 1876.

[13] Phelan, *Manton Marble*, 90–92; Marble to William H. English, May 8,
1876, William Hayden English Papers, Indiana Historical Society; *New York
World*, May 22, 1876; *New York Tribune*, May 23, 1876; Belmont to Marble,
June 12, 1876, Marble Papers.

[14] Barlow wrote Bayard in May that "I believe we shall win," while to Marble he claimed modest credit for smoothing Tilden's path. Barlow to Bayard,

worked closely with Tilden's leading upstate opponent, Judge Church, who as a former lieutenant governor still had eyes for the top rung at Albany. Church favored Hendricks or Hancock for the nomination but did not consider this difference with Belmont half so important as their mutual desire to thwart Tilden. By early June the two had dispatched agents on missions to Michigan, Indiana, Illinois, and Missouri in an effort to convince midwestern Democrats that Tilden would never carry his home state in November. Two weeks before the convention, Belmont himself traveled to Baltimore and Washington, conferring with Maryland and Virginia delegates and with those congressmen in the capital who were acknowledged political leaders in their home states. What he learned did not please him. Tilden's strategists were infiltrating the same territories and were successfully squashing pro-Bayard sentiment by denigrating the national chances of any Democrat from a former slaveholding state.[15]

If all this caused Belmont's optimism to wane, he did not betray this in his letters to Bayard. He assured the senator that, though he lacked commitments from the necessary two-thirds of convention-bound delegates, he still remained the "second choice of almost every member" en route to St. Louis. If a Tilden stampede could be prevented for three ballots,

your nomination is in my opinion a certainty. . . . Of your triumphant election, if nominated, I have not a moment's doubt. . . . You are sure to command the suffrages of a great many prominent men not in politics & who have not heretofore voted our ticket. I have seen a great many men of that stamp, who openly profess their preference for you.[16]

Dispassionate observers could sense the irresistible tug of a Tilden tide by the time delegates started arriving in St. Louis during the preconvention week of June 20. Pro-Bayard dele-

May 9, 19, 1876, Bayard Papers; Barlow to Marble, June 8, 1876, Marble Papers.

15 Church to Belmont, May 29, 31, June 1, 12, 1876, private Belmont collection; Belmont to Bayard, June 9, 1876, Bayard Papers.

16 Perry Belmont to Bayard, June 2, 1876, Belmont to Bayard, June 9, 1876, Bayard Papers; Bayard to Belmont, June 16, 17, 1876, Church to Belmont, June 19, 1876, private Belmont collection.

gates despaired on discovering that so many fellow Democrats viewed Tilden as politically the stronger man around the nation. Belmont, however, had not lobbied in Baltimore and Washington, sent couriers to the West and South, and come all the way to St. Louis to yield before the event. He steadfastly urged Bayard's candidacy upon old colleagues and new acquaintances.

When the convention opened on June 27, Belmont secured permission to address the assembled throng. Propriety forbade him from mentioning any candidate by name prior to the nominating speeches and forced him to rely upon the perspicacity of his listeners. For the Democrats to gain the presidency the party must nominate that man "whose private character and public record will infuse that enthusiasm and that confidence into our ranks which alone can insure success." He received a hearty round of applause for his efforts, indicating, if anything, that the backers of each contender read support for their own favorite in the former chairman's words.[17]

Little is known of Belmont's endeavors at St. Louis other than his unflagging "loyalty" to the Bayard cause. Perhaps his hopes rose when Kelly stood before the convention and announced that a "respectable minority" within the New York delegation opposed Tilden, convinced he could not win his home state in the general election. But such flurries failed to obstruct the Tilden avalanche. He received 417½ out of a total of 738 delegate votes on the first ballot, just 75 short of the two-thirds requirement. Bayard ran a poor fifth, with only 23 votes. On the second and final tally, Tilden's 535 votes gave him the presidential nomination, and the second place on the ticket was awarded to his runner-up, Hendricks.[18]

Belmont originally intended to sit out the campaign just as he

[17] J. S. Moore to Bayard, June 25, 1876, Perry Belmont to Bayard, June 29, 1876, Bayard Papers; *Official Proceedings of the National Democratic Convention, Held in St. Louis, Mo., June 27th, 28th, and 29th, 1876* (St. Louis, 1876), 64–66.

[18] John Hunter to Bayard, July 6, 1876, Bayard Papers; Church to Belmont, July 7, 1876, private Belmont collection; *Official Proceedings of the National Democratic Convention*, 77–78, 131–35, 145–46.

had done four years earlier. He sent a $1,000 check to the national committee along with a note announcing he was "done with politics." But as the contest's tempo accelerated, most signs pointed toward a Democratic victory. The Republican presidential nominee, Governor Rutherford B. Hayes of Ohio, lacked the heroic aura of the incumbent Grant. The alluring aroma of political success proved more than the sulking Belmont could withstand. In addition, Marble, Prince, and Edward Cooper of New York all pleaded that the former chairman was too valuable a leader to stand aloof. Prince, still secretary of the national committee, notified his old chief that

If we succeed in this election the Administration will want your aid in carrying on the Government. . . . The services you have rendered the party in the past are generally recognized & appreciated & have put the party under such obligations to you, as to justify any demand upon it you may make.[19]

Such flattering appeals achieved their desired effect. Before long Belmont extended the olive branch to Tilden; the governor, in turn, readily acknowledged "the handsome terms in which your congratulations are conveyed." In a letter to the *New York World*, Belmont conceded that, notwithstanding his earlier choice of Bayard, he "concur[red] heartily" in the St. Louis nominations and platform. "And this I do the more unhesitatingly for the reason that I have long believed Governor Tilden to be one of the few statesmen in any party capable of fulfilling the pledges of our masterly platform." He denied a Republican statement that he had once criticized Tilden as "counsel for all the broken-down corporations with which New York has been afflicted for a long term of years" and charged its perpetrator with "slovenly inaccuracy." In August the banker contributed another $1,000 to the national committee, along with the advice that a "local finance committee," composed of wealthy New York Democrats, be established "to make more efficient the flow of contributions." By September he notified Bayard, who had also become more conspicuous on

[19] Marble to Belmont, July 2, 1876, Edward Cooper to Belmont, July 2, 1876, Prince to Belmont, July 12, 1876, private Belmont collection.

the hustings, that "I shall do my best to prevent the misfortune of a Republican victory." [20]

Opposition statements that Tilden's election would impair the country's credit exasperated Belmont, particularly an "official" Washington statement in the pro-Hayes *New York Evening Post* that a Democratic victory would mean federal assumption of old Confederate debts and a halt in the sale of United States Government bonds in London. The Wall Street financier rejected these "base fabrications," declaring that the success of either Tilden or Hayes "would not any more affect the intrinsic and market value of our bonds than the advent of a Conservative or Liberal Ministry in England would jeopardize the security and quotation of English consols." [21]

Belmont's renewed appearances at Democratic rallies invited a revival of Republican charges about the "behind-the-scenes Rothschild power." In response to these "nauseating" attacks, the banker volunteered to address a huge Tilden-Hendricks Ratification Meeting in New York City. There, Belmont sarcastically alluded to having "read that after the election it is the intention of Mr. Rothschild and myself to buy up the whole United States." He confided he had not heard from Rothschild yet, and for his own part had discovered that "Uncle Sam . . . has different plans for farming out the country. He is going to sign a lease of it to his namesake, Uncle Samuel J. Tilden." The ample laughter and clapping of the friendly crowd failed, however, to halt the "fearfully abusive" assaults against Belmont.[22]

[20] Tilden to Belmont, July 14, 1876, Cooper to Belmont, Aug. 23, 1876, private Belmont collection; *New York World*, July 15, 1876; *New York Tribune*, July 17, 1876; Belmont to Bayard, Sept. 13, 15, 1876, Bayard Papers.

[21] Abram S. Hewitt to Belmont, Oct. 18, 1876, Marble Papers; *New York Tribune*, Sept. 8, Oct. 21, 1876; *New York World*, Oct. 20, 1876; Belmont, *Letters, Speeches and Addresses*, 223–26.

[22] Belmont to Perry Belmont, Oct. 22, 1876, in Perry Belmont, *An American Democrat*, 179–81; Belmont to Marble, Oct. 26, 1876, Marble Papers; Belmont, *Letters, Speeches and Addresses*, 205–06. In Ohio Hayes received "reliable information" that the Rothschilds, through Belmont, had contributed $2 million "to carry the election for Tilden, under the promise that they should have the exclusive agency & control of United States finances in Europe for the next four years." John Livingston to Hayes, Nov. 11, 1876, Rutherford Birchard Hayes Papers, Hayes Memorial Library, Fremont, Ohio. Of course, if such

With the October state elections near in Indiana and Ohio, Belmont sent Tilden twenty $500-bills "as my contribution [for use] . . . where decisive battles are now being fought." He apologized for not affording "a bigger bundle," but he still felt the effects of the Panic of 1873. This substantial evidence of Belmont's cooperative spirit so pleased Tilden that he summoned the banker to his Gramercy Park residence for a chat and sounded him out on a possible position within a Democratic administration. Belmont, despite his well-known effusiveness, did not commit himself but allowed Tilden to dominate the two-hour conversation.

The following day Belmont confided his thoughts to Marble. Tilden had assumed that the banker's ambition lay in public finance and intimated that a high spot in the Treasury would follow a Democratic victory. But the presidential candidate had guessed wrongly. "If I have any ambition at all," the former minister to the Netherlands admitted, "it is entirely confined to diplomacy. . . . If I am not good there, I am certainly of not much good anywhere else." With a restraint hardly resembling that with which he had applied for the Naples mission a quarter century earlier, Belmont continued:

If it should embarrass our friend [Tilden] to promote my aspirations in that direction then I have to renounce the rest. Of course I know the difficulties by which he is surrounded & I most likely place an undue value upon my qualifications & my claims on the party. Still, I wish you would, when you find a suitable chance, make my position & my views clear to him so that there may be no misunderstanding on his part.[23]

Whether due to Belmont's lubrication or not, the results of the October elections were encouraging. In Indiana, Democrat James D. Williams defeated Republican Benjamin Harrison, grandson of the country's ninth President, for the governorship. In Hayes' home state of Ohio, the Republican candidate for secretary of state, the only statewide office being contested,

---

had been Belmont's intention, he would have done better by becoming a Republican during the Civil War.

[23] Belmont to Tilden, Oct. 1, 3, 1876, Tilden Papers; Belmont to Marble, Oct. 2, 3, 1876, Marble Papers. No additional material on what "President" Tilden had in store for Belmont has been found.

squeaked through to victory by less than 7,000 votes—a fact which alarmed the G.O.P.

Brightened by prospects for November, Belmont spoke to an overflow crowd at Cooper Union on October 13 and assured his listeners that a Tilden administration would never assume any part of the Confederate debt. Friends praised the talk, and the *World* and the *Herald* carried flattering editorial comments. As the campaign neared its climax, Belmont presided over a Manhattan Club rally on October 30, with Tilden and other distinguished members present. He exulted: "Victory is in the air! That mighty orb of our political system—Democracy—is passing out of its long eclipse. . . . One more week of toil and we will deck the banner of 'Tilden and Reform'." In a letter to Marble the day before the election, Belmont discussed the kind of cabinet and advisers Tilden would need in Washington and quipped: "The only fear is that we might do so well [in office] that the people would insist upon a second & third term." Then, he finished off excitedly: "Shall vote tomorrow morning, & be back in the evening to join in a grand Hallelujah!" [24]

The popular votes cast on Election Day fulfilled Democratic hopes by giving Tilden a quarter-million margin, but Democratic jubilation had to be postponed when the electoral vote division became the subject of partisan controversy. The Democrats won New York, New Jersey, Indiana, and Connecticut in the North and claimed the entire South, awarding Tilden the Electoral College vote, 203-166. Republican headquarters disputed this and reported Hayes pluralities in the states of Florida, South Carolina, and Louisiana, which meant a Hayes electoral vote margin of 185-184. The Democratic governor of Oregon complicated matters further by disqualifying one of the Republican electors in his state and certifying a Democrat in his place—even though Hayes unquestionably carried the state—be-

[24] *New York World*, Oct. 14, 31, Nov. 1, 1876; *New York Herald*, Oct. 14, 1876; Belmont, *Letters, Speeches and Addresses*, 213–22; Sam Ward to Belmont, Oct. 18, 1876, Alfred Gilmore to Belmont, Nov. 1, 1876, William D. Shipman to Belmont, Nov. 1, 1876, Leroy Pope Walker to Belmont, Nov. 3, 1876, private Belmont collection; Belmont to Tilden, Nov. 1, 1876, Tilden Papers; Belmont to Marble, Nov. 3, 6, 1876, Marble Papers.

cause the elector also held a postmastership in violation of an Oregon law. These disputes laid the groundwork for a lengthy and bitter battle over rival claims to the presidency. On December 6 two sets of electoral returns from the four disputed states greeted Congress, which was itself divided into a Republican Senate, 45-29, and a Democratic House, 169-109. The Constitution offered no clear guide to resolve the discrepancies.[25]

No Democrat—not even Tilden—was more anxious about the outcome of the electoral crisis than Belmont. When he learned in November of Republican attempts to "steal" the election he was furious. Bad enough that it would prevent another chance at a diplomatic role or even, as some of his friends suggested, the Treasury Department.[26] But to see the Democratic Party shunted aside after a popular mandate was unbearable. Two days after the election, as confusion over the results increased, Belmont went to national committee headquarters to ascertain what positive steps the national chairman, Congressman Abram S. Hewitt of New York City, planned to insure Tilden's claims. Hewitt, momentarily unsure, reminded Belmont that any possible disturbance to political stability would injure federal credit at home and abroad. To this Belmont replied:

I am as much interested in the credit of the country as any gentleman present. I would sooner see every bond I hold sink in the ocean before consenting to the loss of what has been gained by the Democratic Party.[27]

Disgusted with Hewitt's "timidity," Belmont sent a quick note to Tilden urging "a public meeting this afternoon or evening to denounce this outrage. . . . Prompt and vigorous ac-

[25] The Twelfth Amendment provided that "the President of the Senate shall, in the presence of the Senate and House of Representatives, open all the certificates and the votes shall then be counted." But counted by whom? If by the Republican Senate, then the Hayes electors would be sustained; if by the Democratic House, then Tilden would be counted in.

[26] James O'Connor, a Baltimore banker, urged Belmont to accept the Treasury "when tendered." O'Connor to Belmont, Nov. 9, 1876, private Belmont collection.

[27] *Washington Star*, Nov. 29, 1890.

tion seems necessary." But Tilden shied away from mass demonstrations and held that the American people should "work
their own way out of the crisis." In turn, he suggested to Belmont that prominent, respected men of both parties be persuaded to investigate election returns in the disputed southern
states. Belmont conferred with Hewitt and hurriedly telegraphed Bayard:

Can you make it possible to comply with request National Comm. to go
at once to N. Orleans. Situation there very grave. Powerful aid and advice like yours invaluable to protect law & prevent fraud.

Bayard begged off for reasons of health, but well-known Democrats such as Marble, Watterson, Trumbull, Doolittle, House
Speaker Samuel J. Randall of Pennsylvania, and former Congressman George W. Julian of Indiana did go.[28]

Meanwhile, Belmont tried to shore up Tilden's confidence
and keep him informed about the developing situation. On one
day he warned the candidate that "no other solution but your
election can end the agony of the country and prevent the most
disastrous consequences." On the next, he notified the governor
of secret Republican conferences. The following day he transmitted a "*Herald* bulletin" claiming South Carolina for the
Democrats by 1,000. "This seems official and I hasten to send it
to you."

On November 22 a long article appeared in the *New York
Sun* suggesting that the only constitutional redress available to
Tilden's supporters, in the event of Hayes' ultimate victory,
was to appeal to the people at the next election. Belmont suspected George Ticknor Curtis, a lawyer and historian, of writing the piece. The banker had a long talk with Curtis, a Democrat, and got him to admit his authorship of the article. Using
great delicacy, Belmont informed the well-meaning Curtis that
"all our friends viewed the question differently" and that perhaps another "explanatory" article was called for. When Curtis
stalled, Belmont brought the situation to Tilden's attention:

[28] Belmont to Tilden, Nov. 9, 10, 1876, Bayard to Hewitt, Nov. 10, 1876,
Tilden Papers; Tilden to Belmont, Nov. 9, 1876, private Belmont collection;
Flick, *Tilden*, 338, 351; Belmont to Bayard, Nov. 10, 1876, Bayard Papers.

Curtis is a *vain* man, who likes to be made something of. I think some little notice of him by you or your friends in the way of seeking his legal *advice* . . . would relieve his constitutional [doubts]. . . . No pains ought to be spared to get him to undo, as far as he can, the mischief.[29]

Business attitudes toward the electoral crisis naturally concerned Belmont. When Republican National Chairman Zachariah Chandler claimed a Hayes victory the day after the election, the banker assured Tilden by telegram that "Government bonds [were] strong. . . . Wall Street evidently not frightened by the Republican bugbear." Belmont felt that mercantile and financial pressure should be brought to bear on Congress for a just settlement. Unfortunately Congress, convening the first week of December, did little to reassure the business community. In the midst of the electoral debate, the House passed a bill, introduced by Missouri Democrat Richard P. Bland, providing for free and unlimited coinage of silver at a ratio of sixteen to one with gold. To Belmont this "blunder" could only play into Republican hands by alienating "conservative businessmen." He warned Marble that if national chairman Hewitt could not "ably & firmly impose" discipline on fellow Democratic congressmen, "we are gone. We want now the support & sympathy of the commercial & financial classes more than before the election." Belmont warned that such legislation would only make business leaders less eager to see a Democratic administration in Washington. He promised to do what he could to quiet their apprehensions, but the party's elected officials must back him up with "sane" legislation.[30]

Belmont helped arrange a number of high-level conferences at his and Tilden's homes to effect greater coordination between Democratic legislative leaders and the national organiza-

[29] Belmont to Tilden, Nov. 11, 12, 13, 1876, Tilden Papers. Eventually Belmont arranged a meeting between Curtis, Tilden, and Charles A. Dana, owner-editor of the *Sun*. Belmont to Tilden, Nov. 23, 1876, Curtis to Tilden, Dec. 10, 1876, Tilden Papers.

[30] Belmont to Tilden, Nov. 8, 1876, Tilden Papers; Belmont to Marble, undated [probably Dec. 13, 1876], Marble Papers. The banker's complaint over the Bland bill was temporarily stilled when the Forty-Fourth Congress adjourned before the Senate could vote on the measure.

tion. On one such occasion, Belmont's dinner guests included Tilden and Marble; Bayard, Thurman, and John B. Gordon of Georgia from the Senate; and Speaker Randall and Lucius C. Q. Lamar of Mississippi from the House. The banker thought Tilden made a "very favorable impression" but remained disappointed that, for all the talk of firmness and determination, no concrete plans for mobilizing the nation's most efficacious pressure—the people—had been formulated.[31]

As soon as the Washington contingent left New York, Belmont pleaded with Marble to get Tilden to assert his cause in two ways. First, he must impress upon the public mind, by calling mass meetings and rallies, that the Democratic rank-and-file would not countenance any fraudulent handling of electoral votes. Second, the governor should publish a pamphlet "embodying the history of the proceedings in the Electoral count of all former Presidential elections. . . . It ought to be published at once and sent broadcast in large numbers all over the North & West." As he had immediately after the election, Tilden again rejected Belmont's urging that he carry his case to the people. He preferred that the debate be confined to Congress and maintained at a high level. Belmont's other suggestion struck a responsive chord. Tilden, assisted by Marble and John Bigelow, the author-diplomat, promptly prepared a long list of precedents governing the tally of electoral votes.[32] With the New Year approaching and Congress paralyzed by indecision, Belmont pressed a third time for positive action by the people to counteract "Radical boldness and recklessness. . . . A vigorous agitation in & out of Congress can alone rouse the people to

[31] Belmont to Marble, Dec. 15, 1876, undated [probably Dec. 24, 1876], undated [probably Dec. 25, 1876], Marble Papers; Belmont to Bayard, Dec. 19, 1876, Bayard Papers; Bayard to Belmont, Dec. 21, 1876, private Belmont collection; Belmont to Tilden, Dec. 22, 1876, Tilden Papers.

[32] The compilation was published in January, 1877, under the title, *The Presidential Counts*. It sought to disprove the contention of some Republicans that the President of the Senate traditionally controlled the Congressional count of electoral votes. Belmont to Marble, undated [probably Dec. 24, 1876], Marble Papers; Allan Nevins, *Abram S. Hewitt, With Some Account of Peter Cooper* (New York, 1935), 344–45; Flick, *Tilden*, 354–55; Barlow to Bayard, Jan. 11, 1877, Bayard Papers.

the gravity of the situation. . . . Public meetings should be held in every Northern State & city, and the impulse ought to be given from Headquarters." But Tilden, once again frustrating Belmont, stood firmly against taking the issue into the streets.[33]

In mid-January a joint Senate-House committee gave preliminary approval to a fifteen-member Electoral Commission consisting of five senators, five representatives, and five Supreme Court judges. As soon as Belmont learned of this he notified Marble, and the two men went to Tilden's house. The three agreed to oppose the establishment of any commission and to urge Bayard, one of the joint committee's members, to block the scheme. Belmont telegraphed the senator that, "having the whole right & three-quarters of the People on our side, we give away too much under the desire to compromise." With the Republicans "scared to death," there was no necessity for "dangerous departure from Constitutional precedent. . . . We have only to stand firm to win." When the banker asked Tilden whether he wanted to add a personal message, the governor replied: "Mr. Belmont, individually I do not care the snap of my fingers for the Presidency and will not consent to raffle for it."[34]

Bayard's return telegram upheld the commission as the most practical compromise still available and indicated that he would support its establishment. "Have no fear," he wrote Belmont, "that 'dangerous departures' from the Constitution will be sanctioned by me." Belmont quickly apologized for "a presumption on my part" and voiced "high appreciation of the patriotic motives & the sound legal & constitutional doctrines which have ever been the guides of your political course." But to Marble the banker expressed his genuine feelings: "I am afraid the mischief is done."[35] As if sensing Belmont's reservations, Bayard

33 Belmont to Marble, undated [probably Dec. 27, 1876], Marble Papers; Belmont to Tilden, Jan. 6, 1877, Tilden Papers.
34 Belmont to Bayard, Jan. 17, 1877, Sam Ward to Bayard, Jan. 17, 1877, Bayard Papers; H. W. Potter to John Bigelow, Feb. 22, 1879, Tilden Papers.
35 Bayard to Belmont, Jan. 18, 1877, Belmont to Bayard, Jan. 19, 1877, Bayard Papers; Belmont to Marble, Jan. 18, 1877, Marble Papers. Unknown to his

assured his New York champion that most Democrats in Washington supported the bill, while most Republicans, believing it increased Tilden's chances, opposed it. "I believe Mr. Tilden's induction to office is by this bill made not only possible, but probable." [36]

By the end of January both houses approved the Electoral Commission, and Grant signed it into law. The Senate selected three Republicans and two Democrats, the House three Democrats and two Republicans. The tacit understanding was that the justices were to number two Democrats, two Republicans, and the independent David Davis. But Davis resigned to fill a United States Senate vacancy from Illinois, leaving only four Republican justices from whom a successor could be chosen. Ultimately, Joseph P. Bradley became the final judge to join the commission.

In the midst of these events Tilden requested Belmont to attend a private conference in Gramercy Park. Belmont replied with alacrity, only to discover that Tilden, a millionaire several times over, wanted him to help defray the huge debt incurred by the Democratic National Committee since Election Day. Belmont asked for time to consider the matter. On January 26 he sent his regret that, notwithstanding his *"earnest & sincere* desire" to help out, "entirely personal, imperative & painful" reasons blocked him from consenting. Not satisfied simply with refusing Tilden, the banker launched into an angry attack on the committee's "heavy expenditures." He criticized the high rent for "keeping up the committee rooms" as "unnecessary." Neither Tilden nor Hewitt should have permitted such large disbursements in the absence of available campaign funds. "I have heard, incidentally, since I saw you, of retainers of $10,000 to Western lawyers for services which would have been well paid with one-tenth of that sum." In conclusion, Belmont offered Tilden a counter-proposal:

---

father, Perry Belmont wrote Bayard on January 18 not to fret over those people in New York who "are allowing themselves to become excited." A "general feeling of relief" prevailed there. Perry Belmont to Bayard, Jan. 18, 1877, Bayard Papers.

[36] Bayard to Belmont, Jan. 27, 1877, private Belmont collection.

Have a statement made out at some early day of all the expenditures incurred since the election, & then see to what extent your friends will be ready to bear their share. My personal attachment to you & my fealty to the party will make me respond to the extent of my ability.[37]

Proceedings before the Electoral Commission began the first week of February, and Bayard, one of the three Democratic senators on the commission, invited Belmont to visit the capital for the historic occasion. The banker could not get away, but he sent his son Perry who was promptly employed again as Bayard's secretary for the remainder of the commission's existence. On February 9, in an eight-seven decision along straight party lines, the commission awarded Florida's four votes to Hayes without finding it necessary to "go behind the returns." Any hope Belmont still harbored now vanished as he foresaw identical eight-seven decisions for each remaining dispute.[38]

Belmont lost no time in warning Tilden and his advisers of "the danger of the situation" and then submitted his own opinion on the way out of the Republican trap. "We have been deceived & hoodwinked in the formation of this Commission, because it does not carry out either the letter or the spirit of the law which created it." Tilden should ask the seven Democrats on the commission to resign on the ground that "it is good, sound reasoning for a judge or arbitrator to withdraw from a case which he is to judge upon evidence when that evidence is withheld." The only consequence would be that the electoral count would remain suspended, and "we will have to have a new election next autumn. This may be considered revolutionary, but it is better to fight now than to lie down & have our liberties trampled upon."

Charles O'Conor, the chief Democratic counsel before the commission, told Belmont he still had hope that Justice Bradley would swing Louisiana for Tilden. But Belmont, less sanguine, derided such beliefs as "the shallowest illusions of confiding humanity. As well might you now expect the wolf to allow the

37 Belmont to Tilden, Jan. 25, 26, 1877, Tilden Papers.
38 Bayard to Belmont, Jan. 27, 1877, private Belmont collection; Belmont to Marble, undated [probably Jan. 28, 1877], undated [probably Jan. 29, 1877], Marble Papers; Belmont to Bayard, Jan. 30, 1877, Bayard Papers; Perry Belmont, An American Democrat, 183–84.

lamb to escape unharmed from its clutches as hope for a right-ful decision from the radical majority which has got us at the throat." Tilden "must give the signal & take the management of affairs in Washington into his own hands." But again Tilden hesitated to translate Belmont's suggestions into action, relying on a policy of watchful waiting. Belmont, scornful of Tilden for his inaction and seeming acquiescence in the "frauds," broke openly with the defeated candidate. He began referring to him contemptuously as "Our Leader" and apparently never wrote or spoke to him again.[39]

Time confirmed Belmont's misgivings. On February 16, 23, and 28, the commission gave Louisiana, Oregon, and South Carolina to Hayes. Southern Democratic threats to filibuster against official Congressional acceptance of the commission's findings were quieted by Republican promises to withdraw fed-eral troops from the South, appoint at least one southerner to the cabinet, and make substantial appropriations for southern internal improvements.[40]

Strangely, Tilden, who had the most to lose, maintained his composure and became reconciled to a Hayes administration, while Belmont, who had so vehemently opposed the governor's nomination, became more and more impassioned as Inaugura-tion Day neared. He roundly denounced the Republican com-mission members for their brazen partisanship, singling out the three Republican justices for complicity in "dragging the Er-mine of the Supreme Court to the lowest strata of political filth & corruption." To Bayard he expressed the wish that every Democrat who had a son would emulate the Carthaginian gen-eral, Hasdrubal, and make him swear "eternal hate to those who have torn down the pillars of the best & freest government."

Belmont did not submit Bayard's performance in the electoral crisis to the same critical scrutiny. He expressed "profound ap-preciation" for the senator's motives and actions. The broad

[39] Belmont to Marble, Feb. 11, 1877, Marble Papers; Belmont to Perry Bel-mont, Feb. 12, 1877, quoted in Perry Belmont, *An American Democrat*, 200–01; Belmont to Tilden, Feb. 15, 1877, Tilden Papers.

[40] Hayes made good on the first two pledges, but the third, ironically, was thwarted by a Democratic House throughout Hayes' four years in office.

land of America held no "truer & more enlightened patriot & no more honest a man." Bayard's "righteous" and "principled" conduct contrasted sharply with opposition "robbers." From now on, no matter what party or personal considerations stood in the way, Belmont pledged to toil as unceasingly and energetically to promote Bayard's presidential prospects as he would to destroy any chances Tilden conceivably possessed for a renomination: "You were the leader of my choice in our last campaign against corruption & sectionalism. You are still so to me." [41]

41 Belmont to Marble, Feb. 28, March 9, 1877, Marble Papers; Belmont to Perry Belmont, Feb. 29 [sic], 1877, quoted in Perry Belmont, *An American Democrat*, 201–02; Belmont to Bayard, Feb. 28, March 9, 1877, Bayard Papers; Bayard to Belmont, March 1, 1877, private Belmont collection.

13

★ ★ ★

Championing Bayard's Candidacy

The nation had no sooner regained its equilibrium after Hayes took office in March, 1877, when passions were aroused by a reinvigoration of the monetary debate. The depression of 1873 had left as its legacy a strong demand by certain farm and labor groups for an increase in the money supply, one of the more popular remedies being similar to Pendleton's idea of issuing more greenbacks. The inflationists met with little success during Grant's second term. Then, western silver-mine operators, faced with declining market prices and upset that an 1873 act had "demonetized" silver in the United States, began advocating "easy money"; silver, not greenbacks, would be the agency for monetary inflation. Midwesterners and sizeable interests in the South and East joined the mine operators and prepared once more to strike at the monetary policies prevailing in the nation's financial and governing circles.

Such movements gathered political strength which cut across party lines and alarmed Belmont, who held to the traditional Democratic position of hard, or "sound," money. In his capacities as foreign exchange dealer and international investment banker, he believed he was entitled to offer his advice to the Treasury Department. Though its new chief, former Senator John Sherman of Ohio, had come under Belmont's censure during the recent electoral crisis, the banker felt the present issue was "above party" and sought to cultivate the Republican Secretary.[1] Shortly after Sherman joined the cabinet, Belmont

[1] In March, 1877, the Senate displeased Belmont by confirming Sherman, "the man who was the staunchest defender of the rascalities of the Louisiana

warned him of the disquieting national atmosphere. Two "here-sies," silver and inflation, confronted American society. The first was worse than the second, although both attempted to defraud public creditors. The conflict essentially boiled down to one of "honesty and dishonesty—the difference merits no other name."

In the first session of the new Forty-Fifth Congress, Bland revived his currency measure of the previous session, and the House again passed it. Belmont, stirred to further protest, wrote Sherman how the bill's enactment must appear "to the whole civilized world" as "an act of repudiation" and a "stain upon our National credit." It behooved the Senate leaders of both parties to check the "blind & dishonest frenzy" taking hold in the House. Sherman's response to this exhortation was sympathetic and left Belmont grateful "that no measure of the character now pending" could obtain "executive sanction."[2]

Assured that midwesterners Hayes and Sherman disapproved of the Bland bill, Belmont moved to hinder its prospects in the Senate. Bayard happened to be a member of the Senate Finance Committee to which the measure had been sent, and this enabled Belmont to keep abreast of day-to-day activities.[3] The senator, in turn, frequently wrote of his need "for a long conversation" and hoped that Belmont might testify before the Finance Committee. Though flattered by the invitation to appear at Congressional hearings, Belmont declined the offer, recalling the "discouraging" treatment he had received some time earlier before the House Ways and Means Committee. Besides, he complained, "I am a 'Bondholder' & have the misfortune to represent large 'foreign Bondholders'." He did counter with an

---

Returning Board" and the "most bitter assailant & defamer of the down-trodden people of that State." Belmont to Bayard, March 9, 1877, Bayard Papers; Belmont to Marble, March 9, 1877, Marble Papers.

[2] Belmont to Sherman, June 14, Nov. 7, 9, 1877, copies, private Belmont collection.

[3] On November 16 Bayard confided: "We discussed the silver bill in committee today, but came to no conclusion & I do not think we will meet again until next Tuesday." Bayard to Belmont, Nov. 16, 1877, private Belmont collection.

offer to send running commentaries on the Senate debates which might be helpful to Bayard and the "sound" money coterie around him.[4]

Senate Finance Committee Chairman William B. Allison, an Iowa Republican opposed to Bland's "extremism," thought it more expedient to water down the legislation with restrictive amendments rather than try to bury it entirely. The result, as reported out of committee on November 21, was a bill limiting government silver coinage to a monthly maximum of 4 million dollars and clearly thwarting Bland's purpose of unlimited purchase and coinage. Bayard promptly sent Belmont an official version of the new Bland-Allison bill and, in anticipation of a rough debate on the Senate floor, accompanied it with a précis of his own prepared remarks for such time.[5]

On the same day the upper house took up the revised silver bill, Senator Stanley Matthews, an Ohio Republican, having just received instructions from his home legislature, introduced a concurrent resolution providing that the interest on government bonds be paid in silver. Bayard denounced the resolution from the Senate floor, and Belmont quickly responded with praise. "Every day renders you dearer to your friends. . . . You have demolished this miserable petty-fogging attempt to commit the Senate to his rascally scheme to dishonor the country." Opinion from sources closer to the action cast doubt on whether Bayard's floor speech had any effect on the resolution's chances. Matthews boasted that over two-thirds of the Senate, more than the number required to override a presidential veto, would vote for his resolution. Sherman, in a trip to New York, underlined the seriousness of the situation in a conference with Belmont. The Secretary, "very much exercised about the Bland bill," voiced his fear that the Senate would easily support it.[6]

---

[4] Belmont to Bayard, Nov. 18, 1877, Bayard Papers.

[5] Bayard to Belmont, Nov. 22, 1877, private Belmont collection; Belmont to Bayard, Nov. 26, 1877, Bayard Papers. Sherman later reported in his memoirs that Allison's amendments "completely revolutionized" the Bland bill. John Sherman, *Recollections of Forty Years in the House, Senate and Cabinet: An Autobiography* (2 vols., Chicago, 1895), II, 621.

[6] Belmont to Bayard, Dec. 18, 30, 1877, Bayard Papers.

Congress recessed over the Christmas and New Year holidays, and Bayard utilized the break to visit Belmont, who offered him the hospitality of his Fifth Avenue residence. There the two men had "good long talks" on the financial questions agitating the country. Despite the Allison amendments, the banker had not altered his conviction that the "iniquitous bill" would yield "fatal results" to the country and the Democratic Party alike. Bayard concurred, and together they decided to bring pressure on several Democratic senators whose views on the money question were known to be moderate, hoping that the Bland-Allison bill's victory margin could be reduced to below two-thirds. Voorhees of Indiana, Thurman of Ohio, James B. Beck of Kentucky, and Matt W. Ransom of North Carolina had already fallen prey to "dishonest or ignorant demagoguery," but others, such as George R. Dennis of Maryland, Eli Saulsbury of Delaware, Matthew C. Butler of South Carolina, and Benjamin H. Hill of Georgia, were known to be wavering and might be won over in time.[7]

Belmont hastily wrote Maryland Governor John Lee Carroll a long, congratulatory letter on his recent "excellent" message to the state legislature, expounded on how southern prosperity was tied up with the North and East, and wondered if "an expression of opinion" by the legislature might influence Dennis in the "right direction." Dennis proved unwilling to cooperate, but efforts directed toward the others succeeded. Saulsbury came around to the views of his Delaware colleague. Butler, a cousin of Mrs. Belmont, adopted "the line of good sense" after "a quite encouraging short conversation" with Bayard and "a few friendly lines" from the banker.

Hill "seemed on the right track," though Bayard requested Belmont to get other New York bankers to write him. Belmont complied and even took a short trip in late January to Washington to further the cause. Hill finally agreed to oppose Bland-Allison, but the visit to the capital, unfortunately, contained a less desirable side effect. The *Washington Telegram*, up to now

[7] Belmont to Bayard, Dec. 30, 1877, Bayard Papers; Bayard to Belmont, Jan. 14, 1878, private Belmont collection.

a Democratic organ, seized upon Belmont's presence in the Senate gallery as "proof" that the "European Shylocks—the Rothschild Jews" were directing the bondholders' fight against a "starving Nation of people." From now on, the *Telegram* asserted, it would cease supporting the Democratic Party.[8]

On January 25 the Senate took up the Matthews resolution and passed it easily with bipartisan support, 45-20. Far from conceding the uselessness of continuing to combat Bland-Allison, Belmont opposed the silver heresies whenever he had the opportunity.[9] In the first week of February, former Governor Hendricks, Tilden's running mate, addressed a rally in Indianapolis at which he urged full Democratic backing for the Bland-Allison bill. Belmont composed a lengthy reply to the arguments used by Hendricks, and several major New York papers reprinted it. The answer included the banker's now familiar arguments against repudiationists and "shinplaster inflationists." Compared with Hendricks' invidious silver doctrines, "the assumptions of the Paris Commune were but clumsy attacks on the rights of property." Belmont ended, however, on a slightly more constructive note. The way to achieve a stable bimetallic currency was not to "talk so flippantly about remonetizing silver." Only an international conference between the United States and the world's leading commercial nations, followed by concerted legislation, could accomplish that end. It may be, the banker concluded, that "If Congress will only do nothing, we shall obtain [bimetallism] in due time."[10]

Congratulations for Belmont's "admirable exposition" came from a number of bankers and public officials. Isaac T. Smith, president of the Metropolitan Savings Bank in New York City, begged Belmont to reprint the letter as a tract and send copies

[8] Belmont to John Lee Carroll, Jan. 10, 1878, Perry Belmont to Bayard, undated [probably Jan. 18, 1878], Sam Ward to Bayard, Jan. 22, 1878, Belmont to Bayard, undated [probably Jan. 23, 1878], undated [probably Jan. 24, 1878], clipping from *Washington Telegram*, late Jan., 1878, Bayard Papers.

[9] William Graham Sumner to Belmont, Feb. 1, 1878, Theodore F. Randolph to Belmont, Feb. 5, 1878, Henry W. Blair to Belmont, Feb. 5, 1878, private Belmont collection.

[10] *New York Times*, Feb. 9, 1878.

to western bankers and congressmen, particularly to those "purblind" on the subject of a double coinage. Belmont's words would do more "to clear their mental vision than a barrel full of windy speeches" by those unsophisticated and untutored in finance. Congressman Henry W. Blair, a New Hampshire Republican, praised Belmont's "profound forecast" of the radical calamities—communism and anarchy—which would follow on the heels of the silver heresy. Thanks to honest men like Belmont, repudiationist delusions would be buried under "the fertilizing flakes of truth." [11]

The Senate ignored these truthful "flakes." A week after the letter to Hendricks, the upper house voted on and passed the Bland-Allison bill by a comfortable margin of 48-21, six more votes than were needed to override a veto. The House immediately concurred in the amendments, and the bill went to the White House for executive approval. Faced with a *fait accompli*, Belmont hoped Hayes would sign the measure or at least allow it to become law by the lapse of time. He feared that a veto would only prolong the uncertainty of the monetary situation and perhaps prove even more disturbing to financial stability.[12] But, just as Sherman had promised Belmont, Hayes vetoed the bill on the last day of February. Congress promptly passed the bill with the required two-thirds majority in both chambers. Belmont learned to live with the new law, though he regretted that his party's split in the proceedings weakened Democratic claims to be the "honesty" party. At least he could assure Bayard that "your noble & unwavering stand" by the side of "right & justice" earned the "approbation of every honest American." [13]

With these words as a keynote, Belmont started his drive to

11 Smith to Belmont, Feb. 9, 1878, Blair to Belmont, Feb. 11, 1878, private Belmont collection.

12 Harry Barnard, *Rutherford B. Hayes and His America* (Indianapolis, 1954), 463. According to Hayes' diary, sixteen anti-silver Republican congressmen from New York shared Belmont's attitude toward a veto. Charles R. Williams, ed., *Diary and Letters of Rutherford Birchard Hayes: Nineteenth President of the United States* (5 vols., Columbus, Ohio, 1922–26), III, 461, 465–66.

13 Belmont to Bayard, Sept. 15, 1878, Bayard Papers.

nominate Bayard in 1880. Since the previous nominee is almost always a potential candidate for renomination, Belmont tried to measure what strength Tilden still had in the party; he found little to worry him. True, many Democrats sincerely believed that the former governor deserved renomination if for no other reason than the "fraud of '76." But a significant portion of the party, particularly in the East, felt that Tilden's conduct during the electoral crisis set a dismal model for party leadership. In addition, his poor health since the crisis had removed him from public view.[14]

The proceedings of the Democratic-inspired Potter Committee did little to help Tilden's cause. In May, 1878, the Democratic-controlled House of Representatives set up a special investigating committee to examine the corruption surrounding the recent election and designated Tilden's friend, Representative Clarkson N. Potter of New York, as its chairman. Unfortunately for the progenitors, who intended to use the findings for 1880 campaign propaganda, their efforts boomeranged. The committee uncovered a huge batch of ciphered telegrams which, after decoding, indicated that Tilden's agents in the disputed southern states—particularly Marble—had tried almost as eagerly as the Republicans to "buy" the needed electoral votes. Tilden's testimony before the committee denied either complicity or knowledge of his agents' actions, but the damage was done. Many Democrats suspected Tilden's credibility, and a number of party newspapers stopped demanding his renomination in 1880.[15]

Though Belmont's name never came up during the hearings, Whitelaw Reid, the *New York Tribune*'s editor since 1872, sent one of his staff to get a statement regarding the ciphered telegrams. The reporter found Belmont dining at the Manhattan Club with a few friends and revealed the purpose of his visit. Belmont replied angrily:

[14] Perry Belmont, barely four months after Hayes' inauguration, happily noticed during a dinner with a number of other young New York Democrats "what little interest is generally taken in Mr. Tilden's movements." Perry Belmont to Bayard, July 31, 1877, Bayard Papers.

[15] Flick, *Tilden*, 427–38; Nevins, *Hewitt*, 399.

The editor sent you, did he? He couldn't have sent you. He knows better than to send anybody to me. That paper has told too many lies about me for him to send anybody to interview me. That's all I have to say.

Reid struck back several days later by pronouncing Belmont a "boor" who "should at least learn to put a restraint upon his natural propensities and imitate, as well as he can, the manners of a gentleman." [16]

Though Belmont foresaw little danger of a popular upsurge for the titular leader Tilden, the road to 1880 was far from clear for Bayard or, indeed, any Democratic aspirant. An unpredictable factor had entered the picture with the formation in February, 1877, of the Greenback Labor Party, which announced its intention to compete for national and state offices in the 1878 elections. In 1866 and 1870 Belmont had welcomed cracks in the solid wall of Republicanism and the possibilities for fusion which resulted from them. But this new movement, calling for redemption of Civil War bonds in greenbacks, free coinage of silver on a parity with gold, and the suppression of national bank notes, was anathema. Belmont looked with "dismal foreboding" at the inclination of many Democratic candidates to court Greenback Labor support.

Belmont had been cognizant of this political intruder when he delivered a "state of the party" address to the Manhattan Club in January, 1878. In a call for party unity, Belmont warned that western and southern "jealousy" of the East, combined with the "distressing confusion" over party principles displayed in the Bland-Allison debates, might "abort" the coming struggles against "our common enemy." The legitimate issue, "fraud," had been shunted aside by current intraparty dissension. In view of the party's regional acrimony, Democratic divisions in New York State were especially unfortunate.[17] In

16 *New York Tribune*, Oct. 10, 14, 1878. Reid had been with the *Tribune* since 1868 and succeeded Greeley as editor-in-chief in 1872.

17 *New York Times*, Jan. 26, 28, 1878. On the other hand, Charles Nordhoff, Washington correspondent for the *New York Herald*, suspected that western Democrats believed one of their own men, perhaps Senator Thurman of Ohio, could win the West and South on an out-and-out greenback platform, "so

New York City Tammany leader Kelly continually feuded with the "Irving Hall Democracy" and the "County Democracy." Even the local newspaper situation was discouraging, as Democratic journals seemed more intent on bandying abuse than on disseminating the "wisdom" of Jefferson and Jackson.[18]

In August, 1878, Bayard visited Belmont at Newport to confer on political strategy. They decided that the senator, by virtue of his seniority in Congress and his leadership of the sound-money wing, should initiate a public dialogue with western Democrats like Thurman, Hendricks, and Voorhees, in an effort to disabuse them of their "new Gospel of American finance." Bayard returned to Delaware and in a widely reprinted speech of August 29 delivered a stinging rebuke to the "Greenback craze." Democrats in the West and South thought his exposition would finish Bayard politically, though many eastern friends welcomed the senator's reaffirmation of their beliefs. Belmont, of course, had only praise for the address:

It is my firm conviction that sound financial principles, such as you so ably advocate, will in the end prevail. . . . The Demagogues who have so recklessly misled their followers for their own selfish ends are sure to be left high and dry when the tidal wave of the good common sense of the American people will sweep over the land.[19]

The fall elections illustrated that Belmont's optimism on the efficacy of Bayard's speech was at best premature, while his earlier assessment as to the dangers of the new movement had been well founded. In the September races in Maine, two of the five

---

as to make New York & the East needless for success." Nordhoff to Belmont, Feb. 23, 1879, private Belmont collection.

[18] Perry Belmont, in a fit of anger, had recently written Bayard that "it is a pity there is not a more pronounced newspaper which can be called a Democratic organ, or mouthpiece for the Democrats in New York, for the *Sun* is edited by [the pro-Tilden] Dana, and the influences of the *World* are rather more Republican than mysterious." Perry Belmont to Bayard, Aug. 7, 1877, Bayard Papers. Rumors, later substantiated, abounded that Jay Gould, a nominally Republican transportation and communications magnate, controlled Hurlbert, the *World*'s editor.

[19] Belmont to Bayard, Aug. 13, Sept. 3, 1878, Bayard Papers; Bayard to Belmont, Aug. 31, 1878, private Belmont collection.

Republican congressmen lost in re-election bids. One of the upset victors, Democrat George W. Ladd, had accepted Greenback Labor backing, while the other, Greenback Laborite Thompson H. Murch, beat both the Republican incumbent and the Democratic challenger. Bayard passed off the Maine results as sharpening the battle for "those of us who mean to 'defend the pass'." But Belmont bemoaned the fact that a Republican defeat was not in this case a cause for Democratic joy, and he lashed out at "demagogues in our party" who were becoming "still more reckless in their cowardice." [20] Complete election results confirmed the seriousness of the Greenback Laborite challenge. Democratic confidence at regaining the Senate, 42-33, their first majority there since the Buchanan years, was undermined by results in the House where Greenback Laborites won fourteen seats.

While Belmont had found no reservoir of party feeling for another Tilden nomination, the banker's Bayard strategy had to take into account that the former governor still controlled the New York organization. An amendment to the state constitution, adopted in 1874, had lengthened the governor's term from two to three years beginning in 1876. With 1879 approaching, party leaders still had no idea whether Tilden would again seek the governorship or endorse his protégé, incumbent Governor Lucius Robinson, for a second term. The victory of either man would insure Tilden's control of the seventy-vote New York delegation to the 1880 national convention. Such a situation posed a considerable threat, but Belmont saw two alternatives. Anti-Tilden Democrats could withhold their support in the gubernatorial contest and allow a Republican victory to kill off further Tilden presidential pretensions, or both sets of New York Democrats could settle for a compromise candidate who would unify the party's warring elements and select a harmonious, not necessarily pro-Tilden, delegation to the Cincinnati convention the following year.

Each alternative contained elements of danger. A Republican

[20] Bayard to Belmont, Sept. 12, 24, 1878, private Belmont collection; Belmont to Bayard, Sept. 15, 27, 1878, Bayard Papers.

victory in 1879, producing a New York delegation shorn of its usual national convention prestige and unable to flex its mighty political muscles, would play directly into the hands of those Democrats who constantly clamored for a westerner's nomination. But Belmont saw no potential Stephen Douglases beyond the Alleghenies, only Democrats "tainted with unsound records on the financial question. It would be madness to believe that inflation and repudiation can be supported at the polls in a presidential election." [21] On the other hand, a victorious compromise candidate would not be worth much as New York's governor unless he himself harbored presidential ambitions. It would do Bayard's chances for 1880 no good to have one obstacle—Tilden—replaced by another.

Belmont's solution, at once brilliant and impractical, depended on the person of former governor, former presidential nominee, and elder statesman of the New York Democrats, Horatio Seymour, now living quietly as a gentleman farmer in Utica. Seymour was the only person whom both sides might accept, and at sixty-nine he posed no threat to Bayard. But would Seymour agree to run? He was not well, and in 1876 he had spurned a similar request. Besides, he had lost his last two attempts at political office and had been out of public life for eleven years.[22]

Before approaching Seymour directly, Belmont consulted with the leading anti-Tilden malcontents in New York City and upstate: Augustus Schell, whom Tilden had removed as national chairman in 1876 in favor of Hewitt; Kelly of Tammany; William Dorsheimer of Buffalo, Tilden's lieutenant governor who had been alienated over his failure to get the 1876 gubernatorial nomination; Sanford Church, also frustrated in a desire for the 1876 gubernatorial designation; and Amasa J. Parker, one-time congressman from Albany, state judge, and ubiquitous in New York politics for the preceding forty-five years. Dorsheimer, Church, and Parker were old Seymour

[21] Belmont to Horatio Seymour, April 19, 1879, August Belmont Papers, Collections of The New-York Historical Society.
[22] Mitchell, *Seymour*, 522–26.

friends of long standing, and they assured Belmont that the former governor "is very much opposed to Tilden & that he will, when the time comes, aid us."

Belmont sounded out Seymour, referring to the general situation confronting the Democratic Party in state and nation and to certain machinations by "Tilden's agents." Seymour's reply was a model of evasiveness. He didn't "think it wise to say much at this time as to the next Presidential election, candidates, etc." Slightly annoyed, but not too surprised, Belmont sensed how little could be expected in the way of Seymour's "active support." Still, he hoped that broader party pressure could persuade Seymour to run.[23]

With the Democratic State Convention only five months away, Belmont moved swiftly. He sent out private invitations to every prominent Democrat in the state, except Tilden and Governor Robinson, to meet at 109 Fifth Avenue, on Saturday afternoon, April 5. A postscript enjoined the "strictest secrecy" upon the participants. Forty-six people turned up at the Belmont mansion, which satisfied both the ego of the host and the curiosity of the guests about who else had been invited. The party stalwarts in attendance included Barlow, Kelly, Schell, Parker, former Governor John T. Hoffman, and Congressman Benjamin A. Willis of Manhattan.

The proceedings got under way with virtually unanimous agreement on the need for a compromise gubernatorial candidate. Kelly and Hoffman warned bluntly that a Democratic failure to unite in 1879 would not only cost the party the state house that year but the White House the next. The anti-Tilden conferees brought up Seymour as the most suitable harmony candidate. The Tilden group felt such a conclusion "too immature" in view of the uncertain wishes of Tilden and Robinson. Besides, one of them queried, would Seymour come out of retirement to make the race? Belmont, Hoffman, and others answered that if Seymour "really thought that he was the only

23 Perry Belmont to Bayard, Feb. 16, 1879, Belmont to Bayard, March 11, 1879, Bayard Papers; Seymour to Belmont, March 6, 1879, private Belmont collection.

person who could unite his party, he would sacrifice his personal feeling to that end." The reply was disputed, and at this point, an upstate politician, William Purcell, rose to read excerpts from a recent Seymour letter to him:

> I see that you suggest my name as a candidate for the office of Governor. . . . I cannot be a candidate for any office nor can I accept any nomination if made.

Further discussion seemed futile as long as the status of the former governor's availability remained unclear, so the conference appointed a committee of seven, headed by Belmont, to secure a clear-cut answer from Seymour.[24]

Belmont sent Seymour a brief note that a committee would soon "await upon you and ascertain whether you will consent" to a gubernatorial nomination. Seymour's polite answer confirmed what Purcell had read at the conference. He was, of course, "grateful" for such expressions of "good will & confidence" but quickly came to the point. Why go to the trouble, he inquired, of "making a long journey" regarding "a matter which *was disposed of*?" The only possible effect of the committee's trip to Utica would be to "occasion idle and mischievous comments." Seymour did not think he could contribute much to solving the party's current impasse, but should he come up with any ideas he would go to New York and call upon Belmont.[25]

Belmont stubbornly declined to recognize the obvious. In a more lengthy letter, Belmont used flattery, persuasion, and exhortation. He admitted to having known for some time "your determined wish" not to reenter public life and, "having no personal or selfish end to gain, certainly should not have given consent to the movement so enthusiastically at my house of the *leading men of our party* had I not been convinced, *then as I am now*, that in your hands lies at this moment the destiny of the Democratic Party." Belmont listed all the objections to Tilden's renomination in 1880 and stressed point by point the

---

[24] *New York Times*, April 7, 1879; Seymour to [Purcell], Feb. 24, 1879, Seymour Papers; John Hunter to Bayard, April 7, 1879, Bayard Papers.

[25] Belmont, et al., to Seymour, April 7, 1879, Seymour Papers; Mitchell, *Seymour*, 536; Seymour to Belmont, April 16, 1879, private Belmont collection.

latter's weaknesses and inability to lead a great party, much less a great nation. Unless Seymour, the only man in New York State capable of unifying all dissident factions in the party, rose gloriously and nobly to the grand challenge, "I fear the Democratic Party is doomed to perish & our beloved country will be given up to centralization & sectionalism, with nothing left of Republican institutions but their name." [26]

Belmont's redoubled efforts came to naught; Seymour was touched but adamant. With no other New York Democrat of comparable stature left to rally Belmont's group, the anti-Tilden movement ground to a halt. The banker's old nemesis, the *Tribune*, noted this standstill and poked fun at the "unknown fate of Mr. August Belmont and his gallant companions who started out, recently, in search of a candidate, and have not been heard of since." Recent "incendiary" speeches by Republicans like Senator Roscoe Conkling of New York and Representative James A. Garfield of Ohio, reviving the "bloody shirt" issue and aimed "only at producing infinite mischief," contributed further to Belmont's pessimism. Democrats, he wrote Bayard, might as well adopt France's motto, " 'Dieu protege la France.' I see no hope or help except for Him." [27]

Fate relieved Belmont from additional participation in the gubernatorial charade. On April 22 his carriage collided with a heavy grocery wagon, upsetting Belmont's light vehicle and jamming him between the wheels. His two frightened horses dragged Belmont a block before a pedestrian halted them. The sixty-five-year-old banker miraculously escaped without serious injury but suffered shock and extensive bruises. A few days later, he assured a worried Bayard that "I expect to be all right again, though my beauty will be marred for a little while yet by all the beautiful colors of the rainbow, sadly out of place around my eyes & forehead." [28]

26 Belmont to Seymour, April 19, 1879, Belmont Papers, New-York Historical Society; Perry Belmont, *An American Democrat*, 210–12.

27 *New York Tribune*, April 15, May 2, 1879; Robert G. Caldwell, *James A. Garfield: Party Chieftain* (New York, 1931), 268–69; Belmont to Bayard, April 25, 1879, Bayard Papers.

28 Bayard to Belmont, April 22, 1879, private Belmont collection; Belmont to Bayard, April 25, 1879, Bayard Papers; *New York Times*, April 23, May 1, 1879.

Belmont spent the summer recuperating, and the fight at the coming gubernatorial convention passed him by. Tilden announced that he "did not think it fit to run for Governor" and endorsed the incumbent Robinson, paving the way for the clash that erupted in September at Syracuse. The Tilden men backed Robinson for renomination. The anti-Tilden forces, unable to unite, scattered their support, with Kelly's powerful Tammany delegation pushing General Henry W. Slocum, a former congressman from Brooklyn. The contending sides debated and wrangled for eight hours before deciding to ballot. By then, Robinson's renomination seemed assured. During the roll call Augustus Schell rose from his seat next to Kelly, announced that he could not support Robinson, and to a chorus of cheers and hisses proceeded to walk out of the hall, followed by seventy-one other anti-Tilden delegates. The remaining Democrats renamed Robinson; that same evening the seceders held a rump convention and nominated Kelly as their gubernatorial candidate. The Republicans benefited from this Democratic rupture, and two months later, to no one's surprise, Alonzo B. Cornell easily outdistanced the two Democrats, though their combined vote exceeded his.[29]

Belmont had not been idle while the New York gubernatorial race worked itself out. To prevent Tilden's control of the New York delegation to the national convention was only part of his larger plan to put Bayard in the White House. At the same time he had been urging Seymour to come to the rescue of state Democrats, he was rounding up additional New York backers for Bayard. Belmont attempted to focus the amorphous anti-Tilden feeling into a solid pro-Bayard bloc, telling Parker, Seymour, and others that it did not suffice merely to take a negative stance when conditions required a positive one. Bayard united "in the highest degree the moral & intellectual qualifications" required of a President and was the "strongest & least assailable" candidate, while Tilden, Hendricks, and Thurman would be forced into futile, defensive campaigns. Belmont

[29] John Hunter to Bayard, Sept. 21, 1879, Perry Belmont to Bayard, Oct. 3, 1879, Bayard Papers; *New York Times*, Sept. 11-13, 1879; Flick, *Tilden*, 445-46.

urged the senator to "declare" for the nomination or at least authorize his New York friends to advance his cause openly. He warned how Tilden's "agents" fabricated popular enthusiasm for their man and simultaneously attacked Bayard's 1877 performance on the Electoral Commission.

It is unjust & unfair to you to have you a target for the attacks not only of the Republican press, but also of the Tilden organs. . . . You are too young & have too high a destiny before you either in the Senate or the White House to have this equivocal position of a *would be* candidate.[30]

The banker's call for boldness was met with hedging by the anti-Tildenites. Parker thought an "announcement" for Bayard would be "premature." Seymour felt it "injurious" for any name to be presented before the gubernatorial election. John Hunter, a New York lawyer and socialite whose friendship with Bayard dated from the 1850s, also disagreed with Belmont's sense of timing, as did Dorsheimer and Church. The banker suspected the latter two of demonstrating more interest in their own political prospects than Bayard's, "even willing to let the Presidency slide" if they could advance themselves locally. The powerful Kelly kept his own counsel, although rumors linked him with Hendricks' managers in Indiana.[31]

Bayard, in Washington, weighed the opposing views carefully and then adopted Belmont's, seeing "nothing to be gained by a suppression of an avowed intention & desire" to nominate him. As a political veteran, Bayard realized that rival claimants and their followers would stoop to "all the forms of misrepresentation & defamation." But that was to be expected and, in fact, might serve to gauge his actual strength among the rank and file.

If I really possess their confidences & good will, such attacks, if unjust, will not weaken me; if they should show me to be really assailable, then it will be better I should be gotten out of the way.

30 John Hunter to Bayard, Feb. 12, 1879, Belmont to Parker, Feb. 27, 1879, Belmont to Seymour, March 3, 1879, Belmont to Bayard, March 3, 1879, Bayard Papers.
31 Belmont to Bayard, March 3, 1879, Hunter to Bayard, March 4, 1879, Seymour to Belmont, March 6, 1879, Parker to Belmont, March 9, 1879, Perry Belmont to Bayard, March 9, 1879, Bayard Papers.

Putting the situation into words that Belmont the equestrian
would appreciate, Bayard admitted that "if I cannot stand the
trial gallops, how could I be relied upon for the race itself?"
Bayard's official entry into the presidential sweepstakes fifteen
months before the Cincinnati convention of 1880 and Belmont's
assumption of the managerial reins pointed to the probability
that a Bayard nomination would find Belmont assigned again to
the national chairmanship; a Bayard election would find Belmont in a major governmental post.[32]

Belmont went to work immediately, his perennial fascination
with the art of President-making stimulated by Bayard's faith in
his political judgment. His first efforts were directed toward lin-
ing up major New York newspaper support. Dana's *Sun* continued to champion Tilden; the *Tribune* and the *Times* refused
to desert the Republican banner. But Belmont and his son,
Perry, cultivated young James Gordon Bennett, who had succeeded his late father as editor of the independent *Herald*.
Their pressure, combined with the high recommendation of the
paper's Washington correspondent, Charles Nordhoff, resulted
in a November, 1879, editorial advocating Bayard for the presidency. The *World*, which Belmont had usually been able to
rely on, pursued an erratic course. That Hurlbert opposed
Tilden was certain, but whom he preferred remained unclear.
At times, his editorials spoke favorably of Thurman and Associate Supreme Court Justice Stephen J. Field. Still, the Belmonts, father and son, hoped that by convention time Hurlbert
could at least present Bayard's case more favorably than those
of his opponents. As Belmont confided to Bayard, "He is like a
woman, & a very attractive one at that. He used to love you &
'nous revenons toujours a nos premieres amours.' So I think it

[32] Bayard to Belmont, March 7, 1879, private Belmont collection; Belmont to
Bayard, March 11, 1879, Bayard Papers. Bayard honored Belmont with a visit
to New York soon after. Their correspondence attests to the senator's high
regard for Belmont's counsel: "Whether success shall attend my political
fortunes or no, I shall always be proud to have gained . . . the good opinion
& regard of a man so honorable, able, courageous, and patriotic as yourself."
"You have drawn me to you by your kindness & high qualities." Bayard to
Belmont, March 7, April 22, 1879, private Belmont collection.

will prove now." Events confirmed these hopes, although Hurlbert delayed open endorsement of Bayard until the very eve of
the national convention.[33]

Belmont could do little more in New York until the state
convention to select Cincinnati delegates, and he used the inter-
val to try to steer the South and Midwest into Bayard's camp.
Surprisingly, southern Democrats, while acknowledging Bayard
as the Senate's foremost defender of "states' rights" and white
supremacy, did not jump at the chance to nominate one of their
own. Senator Hill of Georgia told Belmont that part of this reticence could be attributed to the "dishonest money craze"
sweeping much of the region. Southerners had "allowed themselves to indulge in a most infatuated dalliance with the senseless
harlot of inflation" and being "political adulterers" they were
incapable of respecting Bayard's goodness. The Delaware senator would be lucky to get five of Georgia's twenty-two convention votes. Bradley T. Johnson, a former Confederate general and now a leading member of the Virginia state legislature,
believed Bayard might secure half of Virginia's twenty-two
votes, but spoke pessimistically of general southern reliability at
the coming convention: the South "has become timid and fear-
ful of responsibility [which] has made her distrustful and even
has deprived her of political sagacity and forecast. . . . Lack
of experience, lack of success, and lack of education have reduced her to this extremity." [34]

A quick trip through some southern states and confidential
talks with other Democratic leaders showed Belmont there was
a more serious reason for southern inertia toward Bayard.
Agents of other presidential hopefuls, particularly those representing Tilden, Speaker Randall of Pennsylvania, and General
Hancock, had already ploughed the ground, and Bayard could
count on no more than forty percent of the southern delegates.

[33] Belmont to Bayard, Feb. 5, March 11, May 16, 1879, Perry Belmont to
Bayard, undated [probably March 9, 1879], Nov. 8, 1879, May 26, June 11,
1880, Bayard Papers; *New York Herald*, Nov. 8, 1879.
[34] Hill to Belmont, Nov. 1, 1879, private Belmont collection; Johnson to
Belmont, Nov. 6, 1879, Belmont to Hill, Nov. 9, 1879, Belmont to Bayard, Nov.
10, 1879, Bayard Papers.

Undaunted, Belmont assured the senator that in the hour of decision Democratic leaders would rally around him, if not for reasons of "patriotism & statesmanship," at least because of the instinct for self-preservation. "There is no salvation without you & the sooner the South can be made to comprehend this the better." [35]

Midwestern prospects for Bayard appeared no more hopeful. Illinois' bloc of forty-two votes backed favorite son William R. Morrison, a congressman, and no wavering could be detected. The "inflationist" Thurman apparently had all of Ohio's forty-four votes. Indiana's thirty votes seemed headed for Hendricks, whose currency views resembled Thurman's. But Hendricks' grip on the delegation was far from solid; even Indiana men admitted that his candidacy owed more to sentiment—he had been Tilden's luckless running mate—than conviction. William H. English of Indianapolis, a banker and former four-term congressman, led a sound-money faction among Hoosier Democrats. This split indicated a possible vein of support for Bayard though, because of the Indiana unit-rule system, one which the senator could not tap until the second ballot at Cincinnati.[36]

Early in 1880 Belmont asked John Hunter and other allies to help raise a $50,000 campaign fund, the banker himself pledging $10,000. In the course of his rounds Hunter approached Kelly for support. Kelly responded sympathetically and suggested an alliance between Bayard and Tammany. Belmont, hearing of Kelly's plan, objected and spelled out his arguments in a long

[35] Perry Belmont to Bayard, Nov. 8, 1879, Belmont to Bradley T. Johnson, Nov. 10, 1879, Belmont to Bayard, Feb. 1, March 8, 1880, Belmont to John Hunter, Feb. 19, 1880, Belmont to Perry Belmont, Feb. 19, 1880, Bayard Papers; Bayard to Belmont, Nov. 19, 1879, private Belmont collection.

[36] As early as September, 1878, English requested authorization to lead the Bayard boom in Indiana, but Bayard and Belmont managed to avoid any commitments at that time. Bayard to Belmont, Sept. 12, 1878, private Belmont collection; English to Bayard, Sept. 8, 1878, Nov. 19, Dec. 3, 1879, Bayard Papers; Edward F. Madden to English, Nov. 14, 15, 1879, Bayard to English, Nov. 23, 1879, English Papers. Unknown to Belmont, English, attempting a political comeback, didn't intend putting all his eggs in the Bayard basket and simultaneously negotiated with Tilden. J. J. Cahill to English, Feb. 16, 1880, William H. Barnum to English, Feb. 29, 1880, English Papers.

letter to Hunter. It would be folly for Bayard's New York friends to align themselves openly with the avowed enemies of Tilden. The former governor's influence dominated the state Democratic organization and, if he so desired, could get the New York delegation instructed for him under the unit rule. Even if Tilden should then decide not to run, his influence with the delegates would be paramount. "I have good reason to believe," Belmont continued,

that Tilden, seeing that he cannot get the nomination himself, will not permit, if he can help it, any other New Yorker to get it. He cannot consistently with his record on finance go for Hendricks or Thurman; for the same reason he will not saddle himself with Randall, and therefore Bayard could certainly be the most available and in fact the *only* choice left for him.

In a letter to his son Perry the same day Belmont warned it would do the senator no good to antagonize those Tildenites who preferred Bayard as their second choice and might come over to him when Tilden gave up. Though Bayard might yet be nominated without Tilden's assistance, "he cannot win against Tilden's pronounced opposition." [37]

No sooner did Belmont articulate this strategy than Tilden's most sympathetic New York paper, the *Sun*, delivered a stinging attack on Bayard. On February 18 Dana mentioned a Bayard speech, delivered at Dover, Delaware, in June, 1861, in which Bayard advocated permitting the South to secede peacefully from the Union. Six days later Dana printed the entire speech, accompanied by adverse editorial comment.

These developments forced Belmont to admit the failure of his earlier tactics. Since Tilden was now "plainly hostile" to Bayard, nothing could be gained by attempting to appease "that arch-intriguer of Gramercy Park." Belmont managed to extract some consolation from the fact that Tilden and his "henchmen" had irrevocably "thrown down the mask" by shooting off their "great 'Dover' shell." Had they kept it back for a month or

37 Belmont to Bayard, Feb. 1, 1880, Hunter to Bayard, Feb. 16, 1880, Belmont to Hunter, Feb. 19, 1880, Belmont to Perry Belmont, Feb. 19, 1880, Bayard Papers.

two longer, Bayard might have been hurt materially. But, as Belmont assured the senator, the disclosure would have no adverse effect "or in any event only with a few blind fanatics who never vote the Democratic ticket anyhow." [38]

Belmont no longer had any reason to oppose an alliance with the Kelly forces. But Kelly had reconsidered and decided to avoid any firm commitment to Bayard. Instead, he joined the group Belmont had tried to convert—the confirmed anti-Tildenites who let their energies evaporate rather than channel them into constructive support for another candidate. The Tammany leader announced that under no conditions would he support Tilden for President again. He repeated this threat at the Syracuse state convention in 1880, but, as Belmont predicted, his undirected obstreperousness failed to sway the majority. Tilden received unit-rule support of the New Yorkers chosen to attend the national meeting. For Belmont and his son, both designated delegates to Cincinnati, the unit-rule decision was especially distasteful. It meant that their first-ballot votes would go, willy-nilly, to the man they had sworn to defeat.[39]

In May, 1880, the New York Chamber of Commerce invited Bayard to speak on the currency question at its monthly dinner. Hunter learned that Treasury Secretary Sherman had also been asked to address the group that day and urged Bayard to accept: "You certainly hold a position not second to Sherman's in financial views & I cannot see how it can do any harm." Belmont, however, disagreed on the ground that Bayard's record on currency matters was so well known to "these princes of finance" that "it is neither necessary nor politic" to enlarge on them at such a late date. The senator concurred in Belmont's judgment and turned the chamber down.

[38] *New York Sun*, Feb. 18, 24, 1880; Belmont to Bayard, March 8, 1880, Bayard Papers. Perry Belmont blamed Congressman Robert M. McLane of Maryland for misrepresenting Tilden's strategy to his father. Perry Belmont to Bayard, March 8, 1880, Bayard Papers.

[39] Charles O'Conor to Belmont, March 17, 1880, private Belmont collection; *New York Tribune*, March 17, April 24, 1880; *New York World*, April 22, 1880; Perry Belmont to Bayard, March 24, April 17, 23, 24, 1880, Bayard Papers.

Belmont continued to prove indispensable to Bayard in the short time remaining before the convention. He and Perry helped prepare and distribute pamphlets denouncing the "unrepresentative" character of the New York state convention. The elder Belmont joined two other Bayard men and contributed $1,500 to print an "official" biography of the Delaware legislator. Belmont also collected pro-Bayard testimonials from prominent people to pass around at the convention. One of the men he approached, Charles O'Conor, provided Belmont with a lengthy and laudatory letter in which the veteran Democrat explained that, notwithstanding his "repugnance to interfering in elections," Bayard was the "most desirable candidate." As a bonus, O'Conor threw in the unsolicited information that Charles Francis Adams, "wearing a name among the most illustrious in American history," shared his predilection for Bayard.[40]

Filled with the experience of five previous national conventions and armed with the pro-Bayard endorsements, Belmont, accompanied by Perry, prepared to do battle with fellow Democrats in Cincinnati over the choice of a nominee to oppose the Republican candidate, James Garfield.[41] He arrived on June 20, several days before the official opening, and worked so hard to increase Bayard's strength among the remaining uncommitted delegates that by the time the convention was called to order he was "quite used up . . . , suffering perfect tortures of headache & general prostration."

The outcome of Belmont's efforts remained in doubt up to the eve of the voting, for Tilden had kept his own counsel regarding renomination. With the suspense at fever pitch, Daniel Manning, Tilden's lieutenant in the Empire State delegation, released a letter from the former candidate declaring that for rea-

40 Perry Belmont to Bayard, April 26, May 26, June 4, 11, 1880, Hunter to Bayard, April 27, 29, 1880, Belmont to Bayard, April 27, 1880, O'Conor to Belmont, June 17, 1880, Barlow to Bayard, June 28, 1880, Bayard Papers; O'Conor to Belmont, June 10, 1880, private Belmont collection.

41 On June 2, 1880, the National Greenback Labor Party selected Representative James B. Weaver of Iowa, a former Union general, as its presidential candidate.

sons of impaired health he must decline to be the 1880 nominee. The New Yorkers went into caucus and by a close margin of 36-34 elected to throw all seventy votes to Tilden's preference, former Congressman Henry B. Payne of Ohio, now a Standard Oil Company executive. The result angered Belmont, as it confirmed that Tilden had not withdrawn his influence along with his candidacy and would continue to thwart Bayard. On the afternoon of the 23rd, names of contenders were placed in nomination. The applause following Bayard's nomination, while warm, disturbed the banker, because it didn't approach the ovation that greeted the naming of General Hancock.[42]

By the end of the first ballot late Wednesday night, Belmont knew that Hancock posed the greatest threat. The general led all rivals with 171 votes; Bayard, a close second, had 153½. Payne could only garner eleven additional votes besides New York's seventy, and Thurman was fourth with 68½. The convention adjourned until Thursday, allowing time for pressures, deals, and compromises. With Payne's chances obviously impossible, the New York delegation switched to Tilden's next choice, House Speaker Randall. Belmont and Perry tried frantically to push Bayard but, instead, encountered a reverse trend, with Bayard delegates slipping away to Hancock. By early Thursday morning Belmont was so desperate that he dashed off a telegram to Marble in New York, begging him to try to change Tilden's attitude toward Bayard. He assured his old friend that a word from Tilden to the New York delegation could insure a Bayard victory. Marble's prompt reply ended Bayard's last and only hope for New York; Tilden would go all the way with Randall. Belmont retired for the night, with no idea how to push Bayard up to the magic figure of 486 required for nomination.[43]

The balloting resumed at 10:30 Thursday morning with many delegates convinced that the struggle would be decided

[42] Belmont to August Belmont, Jr., June 23, 1880, private Belmont collection; Flick, *Tilden*, 455–58.

[43] Belmont to Marble, June 24, 1880, Marble to Belmont, June 24, 1880, Marble Papers.

before lunch. Intimations of Hancock's burgeoning strength came when a handful of delegates in Alabama and California switched to him, but the decisive break occurred as Illinois transferred Morrison's forty-two favorite-son votes to Hancock. The tension dissolved into an uncontrollable bedlam, as the galleries yelled "Hancock! Hancock!" Indiana surprised everyone by staying steady with Hendricks, but Hancock maintained his forward momentum. By the end of the second ballot the general's total, almost doubled, stood at 320. Bayard, down to 111, had been pushed into third place behind Randall. The only full delegations which had maintained their loyalty to Bayard's standard were those of Delaware, South Carolina, and Florida.

No sooner did the convention chairman announce the second ballot's totals than the galleries howled, shrieked, and cheered over and over for Hancock. No business could be transacted for some time, since voices on the floor were inaudible. Even as the disorder mounted, hurried consultations ensued between delegations. By the time the sergeant-at-arms restored order, a stampede psychology had taken over, with states begging for recognition from the rostrum so that they could join the Hancock bandwagon. Wisconsin succeeded in getting the floor and threw ten more votes to the general. The bedlam that followed, according to a journalist present, was "an exhibition of the noise and confusion which can be caused by a mass of people confined by four walls, a floor, and a roof." When the sounds subsided and the additional states had recorded their changes, Hancock's final total was 705 out of a possible 738½ votes. To balance the ticket with a westerner—Hancock hailed from Pennsylvania—English of Indiana was unanimously given the vice-presidential nomination.[44]

Belmont was bitterly disillusioned with the convention result, despite what one observer called his "unremitting efforts." As soon as he returned home, he unburdened his heart to Bayard.

[44] *New York Times,* June 25, 1880; *New York Herald,* June 25, 1880.

I am sorry for the country. . . . I regret . . . the folly & ingratitude of a party you have served so well & faithfully. You are today more than ever the foremost Statesman not only of your party but of the Country at large & at a comparative early age you have already secured for yourself a name in American history along with that illustrious trio of Calhoun, Webster & Clay.

There was no need to dwell upon Hancock's modest "intellectual capacity," nor to describe the madness during which "an organized mob in the galleries" had forced the nomination. Half in truth and half in frustration Belmont criticized the operations of national party conventions as a "severe strain upon popular institutions," making self-government a "tragical farce." However, even Hancock would be better than a Tilden "legatee" or "Republican misrule," and there was always the possibility that after his election Hancock would surround himself "with statesmen possessing all the qualifications which he so sadly needs." To Belmont, of course, "statesman" was synonymous with "Bayard," who he hoped (in Hunter's words) would "father the new administration" by becoming the chief of the State Department.[45]

Belmont spent most of the summer at Newport but followed closely news of the national committee's activities. Chairman Hewitt had resigned in March, 1877, and former Senator William H. Barnum of Connecticut, another Tilden man, had been temporarily installed in the post.[46] Barnum resigned at the convention, and the national committee put off the naming of his successor until July 14. Belmont personally favored Pennsylvania Senator William A. Wallace, Hancock's campaign manager, for the chairmanship, and a Hancock aide assured the

[45] Barlow to Bayard, June 28, 1880, Belmont to Bayard, June 27, 1880, Hunter to Bayard, June 28, 1880, Bayard Papers. Bayard's reply to Belmont betrayed less disappointment with the convention: "Whatever may be the results . . . , I have secured some things I value more. To have such letters as your own, so full of affection and regard, so warm and generous in praise, is surely a more secure and valuable possession than the shouts of an unthinking and excited crowd and the fickle praise and the fluctuating favor of the populace." Bayard to Belmont, July 2, 1880, private Belmont collection.

[46] Nevins described Barnum as a "political hack of low reputation." Allan Nevins, *Grover Cleveland: A Study in Courage* (New York, 1932), 160.

banker that the general also preferred Wallace. But Belmont and Hancock notwithstanding, the national committee met and designated Barnum to continue as chairman. On the same day Barnum was renamed, Belmont received an invitation from Wallace to join the Democratic Congressional Campaign Committee. He formally accepted the place but, in a private note accompanying his letter, lambasted the Tilden sentiment still prevailing on the national committee and implored Wallace to help rid the Hancock campaign of the "old regime" influence. The Pennsylvanian advised Belmont to disregard Barnum's selection and promised that "Genl. Hancock is *utterly and absolutely uncommitted to anyone* as to the future." Indeed, Wallace added, the Congressional Campaign Committee "in its present form" expressly intended to counteract the intriguing hand of Tilden. Such assurances mollified Belmont.[47]

Belmont's perennial optimism regarding Democratic chances led him to lend an occasional hand in behalf of the national ticket. In September he addressed a rally of German-Americans, speaking to the audience in what he called "my rusty German," and presided at a Tammany Hall rally at which Bayard and Kelly also spoke. In October, the feature of a "Wall Street Business Men's Meeting" was a letter from Belmont pleading Hancock's cause on purely economic grounds. The general had rejected opposition charges that he would use federal funds to aid "rebel war claims." Furthermore, a Democratic administration would save taxpayers millions by ending the "extravagant appropriations squandered" by Republican congresses. Belmont even tried to persuade Hancock's old comrade from Civil War days, McClellan, now governor of New Jersey, to come to New York and say a few kind words for the national ticket. "Nothing would give me greater pleasure than to oblige you in any way in my power," answered McClellan. But official duties at Trenton prevented his departure from the state house.

Occasionally, the one-time chairman wandered into national

47 *New York Times,* June 25, 1880; Belmont to Bayard, July 14, 1880, Hunter to Bayard, July 17, 1880, Bayard Papers; Wallace to Belmont, July 13, 17, 1880, private Belmont collection.

committee headquarters, offering advice here and an encouraging word there. When a telegram arrived at national headquarters from the Ohio State Democratic Committee begging the East for support in the October state elections, Belmont volunteered to wire Bayard; he asked him to "make two or three speeches there," figuring that the senator's visit might be worth 3,000 additional Democratic votes. Bayard did not make the trip, but even if Belmont's figures were accurate, the senator could not have done much good. The Republicans swept Ohio by almost twenty thousand votes.[48]

Like clockwork the "Rothschild agent's" wealth came up as an issue, only this time the Republican press had two Belmonts to attack. Perry, with sound political and legislative experience as Bayard's assistant, decided to run for Congress after the incumbent from New York's First District, Democrat James W. Covert, declined renomination. The day of the party primary had yet to come; delegates from each political precinct within the district met in convention in October and selected the younger Belmont as their candidate. The pro-Garfield *New York Times* attributed Perry's designation not to "personal popularity" (as the Democrats claimed) but "wholly and solely to the fact that his father . . . is the agent of the Rothschilds and a rich man, and is expected to bleed handsomely in his son's behalf." Republicans in the district estimated that the senior Belmont would go as high as $25,000 to insure Perry's election in November. Belmont ignored the attacks, at least in public, though New York friends noticed his strong concern for Perry's success, even at the expense of the national ticket.[49]

On Election Day the story of the five previous presidential campaigns repeated itself. The Republican candidate, Garfield,

---

[48] *New York Tribune*, Sept. 13, Oct. 1, 1880; *New York Times*, Sept. 24, 25, 1880; Belmont to Bayard, undated [probably Sept. 24, 1880], Sept. 29, 1880, Bayard Papers; Belmont, *Letters, Speeches and Addresses*, 223–29; clipping from the *New-Yorker Staats-Zeitung*, Sept. 11, 1880, McClellan to Belmont, Oct. 30, 1880, private Belmont collection.

[49] *New York Times*, Sept. 24, Oct. 21, 1880; Hunter to Bayard, Oct. 23, 1880, Bayard Papers.

topped Hancock in the Electoral College, 214-155.[50] Most of the Bayard stalwarts were not unduly depressed by Hancock's defeat, and, in fact, Belmont emerged with a delightful consolation prize—Perry's easy election to the House of Representatives.[51] Belmont and other Bayard friends attributed the party's defeat to voter unfamiliarity with Hancock's views on significant issues due to the "weakness" of the general's candidacy. With "Tildenism" on the wane in the East and midwestern party leaders like Thurman and Hendricks out of public office, the prospects for Bayard's nomination the next time around looked bright. The fifty-two-year-old senator's long legislative career—he was now dean of Senate Democrats—would make him a formidable contender. Certainly, if anyone deserved the title "Mr. Democrat" at the start of the 1880s, it was Bayard, and his New York supporters vowed to make him "Mr. President" as well.[52]

[50] General James B. Weaver, the Greenback Labor candidate, got no electoral votes and only 3.4 percent of the total popular vote. Though their strength had declined politically since 1878, Greenback Laborites managed to elect eleven men to the House of Representatives.

[51] Perry Belmont established a creditable record while in the House. He was re-elected without Republican opposition in 1882, again in 1884, and, without precedent in his district, for a fourth term in 1886. In his last two terms he was made chairman of the Committee on Foreign Affairs. He refused to seek a fifth term, and Democratic President Grover Cleveland, on the advice of Secretary of State Bayard, appointed him Minister to Spain in November, 1888. Perry Belmont, *An American Democrat*, 375–78; *New York Times*, Oct. 22, 1882, May 26, 1947; *Biographical Directory of American Congress*, 837–38.

[52] Barlow to Bayard, Nov. 5, 1880, Belmont to Bayard, Jan. 28, 1881, Bayard Papers.

14

★ ★ ★

An Elder Statesman of His Party

BELMONT AND BAYARD maintained contact and often exchanged ideas on political subjects in the years following the 1880 election. When outgoing President Hayes appointed fellow Ohioan Stanley Matthews to a United States Supreme Court vacancy in January, 1881, Belmont commented to Bayard: "Of course, I do not want or expect to influence your vote [for confirmation] in any way." But the temptation to do exactly that proved too strong, and the New Yorker denounced Matthews for the "dirty work he did during the fraud of 1876." Bayard, far from annoyed at his friend, revealed his opposition to Matthews and his resentment at the amount of "button-holing and lobbying" for Senate approval as if the election were for county sheriff.[1]

In March, President Garfield became involved in a patronage fight with New York's senior Senator Roscoe Conkling over the appointment of William H. Robertson to be Collector of the New York Port. Again Belmont confessed to Bayard that "I could not refrain from writing you" that "all our friends" supported the appointment. Not only was Robertson qualified and fit, but any political slap at the "selfish & arrogant" Conkling, even by another Republican, would please New York Democrats. Bayard heeded the advice and subsequently spoke

[1] Belmont to Bayard, Feb. 7, 1881, Bayard Papers; Bayard to Belmont, Feb. 8, 1881, private Belmont collection. The Senate Judiciary Committee killed the appointment by refusing to act on it until the end of Hayes' term. Garfield, another Ohioan, resubmitted Matthews' name when he entered the White House in March, and the Senate, by one vote, confirmed him. Bayard led the opposition. Barnard, *Hayes*, 498–99; *New York Times*, May 13, 1881.

out in the Senate in Robertson's favor. To Belmont's satisfaction, Robertson's victory spelled the beginning of the end of Conkling's power in New York politics.[2] When the newly elected Congress was about to meet, Belmont wrote the senator how Perry looked forward to his prospects as a legislator and bade Bayard "lend him a helping hand" for the sake of a father "who values & cherishes your friendship as one of the brightest treasures of his life."[3]

August Belmont soon after his 70th birthday. (Courtesy of Mr. August Belmont)

[2] Belmont to Bayard, March 27, 1881, Bayard Papers; Tansill, *Bayard*, 297–98. Conkling and his junior colleague, Thomas C. Platt, dramatically resigned their Senate seats when they realized that Robertson would be confirmed. The New York legislature refused to re-elect them to their own vacancies, and Conkling never again held public office.
[3] Belmont to Bayard, Nov. 12, 1881, Bayard Papers.

Belmont, now in his late sixties, gradually curtailed strenuous political activity, though he still observed politics closely and contributed what money and time he could afford to elect Democratic candidates. When the Democratic Congressional Campaign Committee discovered it had spent more money in 1880 than it had received through donations, Belmont gladly helped pay off the deficit. But such contributions were due more to an ingrained spirit of party loyalty than to any expectation of party reward.

From London, Sir Nathaniel de Rothschild asked Belmont to comment on rumors in English newspapers that the next President, if Democratic, would appoint him Minister to the Court of St. James. Belmont downgraded the reports as coming from someone "wrongfully informed." He considered himself out of politics "absolutely & irrevocably. . . . No office at home or abroad can induce me to leave the quiet walks of private life." When Sir Nathaniel insisted that Belmont's appointment to the London mission would be a "pleasure" to his many English friends, Belmont, with an obviously heavy heart, elaborated:

While some eight or ten years back it would have been the height of my ambition . . . , my age & my failing health both preclude the possibility of my accepting this or any other office at home or abroad in the gift of the Government or people. Nothing would give me even now a greater pleasure & gladden my old days more than residence of a couple of years in good old England. . . . However, all these are fairy visions, never to be realized & I can only say "it might have been." [4]

Belmont's reflection on what "might have been" revealed an understandable sadness, but it also indicated how much his eyes and mind turned toward the past. This introspection, combined with his advancing years and his inflexibility on the subject of Bayard's candidacy, had taken its toll and so marked him that when a bright new Democratic prospect appeared, Belmont failed to rise to the occasion.

The fresh personality was Grover Cleveland, catapulted into

[4] William A. Wallace to Belmont, May 8, 1881, Belmont to Rothschild, Dec. 11, 1882, Jan. 5, 1883, Rothschild to Belmont, Dec. 19, 1882, private Belmont collection.

national prominence by his victory in New York's 1882 gubernatorial contest. Cleveland, previously mayor of Buffalo, immediately became the leading contender for the 1884 Democratic
presidential nomination and a threat to Belmont's plans for Bayard. Former followers of Tilden rushed into line behind Cleveland, while Kelly, Dorsheimer, and other anti-Tilden men kept
aloof. Tammany finally broke openly with the new governor in
the fall of 1883 over Kelly's determination to renominate corrupt State Senator Thomas F. Grady to the legislature. With
the renomination tantamount to election, Cleveland communi-
cated to Kelly his wish that Grady "not be returned to the Senate." The Tammany leader ignored the governor's plea and
moved ahead to get Grady renamed. Cleveland next appealed to
Belmont—the two had met at a Manhattan Club reception—who he heard "had much influence" with Kelly. "I don't
know," the governor wrote on October 20,

Thomas F. Bayard (Courtesy of
Georgetown University Press)

Grover Cleveland (Library of Congress)

but it seems to me that Mr. Grady should not come back to the Senate. He is personally very distasteful to me, and I should regard his presence in the Legislature next winter as a slight or an insult. . . . Besides this . . . , I deem him utterly untrue and untrustworthy in his relations to the people and his party. . . . I do not see how the Democratic Party can secure or retain the support and confidence of the people, if such men are sent to the front as its representatives.

Cleveland ended with a request that Belmont persuade Kelly to withdraw Grady's name from the coming canvass.

The governor's letter placed Belmont in a quandary. He knew Cleveland to be an able, honest official, handicapped in carrying out reforms by just such professional patronage-dispensers as Grady. But to assist Cleveland was to weaken Kelly, and in the long run, Bayard; every victory over Tammany's "machine" endeared the governor more to Tilden men and to "silk-stocking" and independent Democrats and Republicans. Not willing to exert himself for "honest government" at Bayard's expense, Belmont used his advancing years to excuse his inaction. His response to Cleveland praised the governor's abilities and public record, but at the same time he denied having influence with Kelly and emphasized his retirement from active politics. Cleveland hastily apologized for his inconsideration and any "annoyance" that may have resulted from the exchange. In the end, Kelly's own district leaders vetoed Grady's renomination as a sop to local dissident Democrats.[5]

Belmont, along with Perry and Kelly, attended the 1884 national convention at Chicago as a delegate. Once there, he discovered that Cleveland already controlled over forty percent of the committed delegates and was an odds-on favorite. Belmont was skeptical about the chance to unite all non-Cleveland forces behind Bayard, for a number of the minor candidates were merely favorite sons waiting to switch to the most likely victor. Events bore out this traditional convention truth. On the first roll call, Cleveland comfortably led the field with 392 votes; Bayard, in second place, trailed with 168. Most of the favorite

[5] Nevins, *Cleveland*, 134–36; Cleveland to Belmont, Oct. 20, 25, 1883, private Belmont collection; Belmont to Cleveland, Oct. 23, 1883, Grover Cleveland Papers, Library of Congress.

sons now hopped onto the Cleveland bandwagon, and the New York governor concluded the second ballot with well over the required two-thirds figure. Bayard, with his first-ballot total cut in half, was a poor second. To balance Cleveland, a sound-money easterner, the convention again nominated Hendricks to the second place on the ticket. By then, the Belmonts and Kelly had already left Chicago, accustomed to conventions with unhappy endings.

Belmont felt that the convention had erred in choosing new-comer Cleveland over nationally known Bayard, particularly since the Republicans had nominated veteran Congressman and former Secretary of State James G. Blaine of Maine. Besides, Belmont believed it was "madness" to put up the New York governor with "the Irish so deeply opposed to him," and he feared that Irish defections in Perry's normally Democratic district would even lead to a Republican victory there. But this situation alone did not account for Belmont's post-Chicago depression, which became pronounced only when no appeals for his aid came from the Democratic National Committee and other campaign organizations.[6]

Belmont's two oldest sons tried everything to draw their father back into the political stream and prevent him from sitting out the campaign in their summer home at Newport. August, Jr., who had entered his father's banking firm upon graduation from Harvard, rallied behind Cleveland and Hendricks and helped establish a Democratic campaign headquarters in Nassau County immediately after the convention. Letters to his father spoke of the political club's "flourishing growth" and of the excitement engendered in the county by the ticket. The older man was pleased to hear of his namesake's interest, but he remained unmoved. Perry took time out from his own re-election campaign to go to Newport and address a large Cleveland-Hendricks rally in August. The proud father attended—the first time he ever heard Perry speak before an audience—and was "astonished" at the young man's "quick self-

6 Belmont to August Belmont, Jr., July 29, 1884, private Belmont collection.

August Belmont's Newport summer estate, "By-the-Sea," as it appeared in the 1870's. It was demolished in the 1940's. (Courtesy of the Newport Historical Society)

possession"; but he took no part in the festivities. September came and went. August, Jr., stepped up his efforts. He informed his father that Kelly, Dorsheimer, and nearly all of the old anti-Tilden group had come over to Cleveland's side. So also had thousands of prominent Republicans, such as Schurz, Benjamin H. Bristow, Henry Ward Beecher, and Charles Francis Adams, along with numerous Republican newspapers like the *New York Times,* the *New York Evening Post,* and the *Springfield* (Massachusetts) *Republican.* Everyone, it seemed, spoke out for Cleveland but August Belmont, Sr.[7]

Nettled, the older Belmont thanked the younger for "your kind advice about my own action" and then explained his grievance:

The conduct of the men, who have the campaign in charge, toward me, . . . has been & is absurd as it would be humiliating if I cared at all

[7] Belmont to August Belmont, Jr., July 27, 29, Aug. 21, Oct. 10, 1884, private Belmont collection.

Mrs. August Belmont and her son, August, Jr., outside "By-the-Sea," Newport, circa 1859. (Courtesy of Mrs. Eleanor Robson Belmont)

for what comes from that quarter. I have been for 40 years an active & for more than 30 years a prominent man in the party, have been 12 years Chairman of the Natl. Committee & have spent $500,000 if I have spent one dollar in the service of the party. What do I get in return? Because I was in favor of the foremost man in the party & in the country, I have not even had the recognition of being asked to speak or to preside at any meeting—a thing which has not happened in more than a quarter of a century!

Having exposed the root of their father's injury, the two sons renewed their attempts. Young August passed on some anti-Belmont gossip which, in previous years, would have roused the former chairman to a public defense. He reminded his father of the harsh words he had leveled at Cleveland's candidacy at the convention and told of a Wall Street broker who suspected the senior Belmont of backing "Ben" Butler of Massachusetts, now a presidential nominee of the Greenback Labor Party. Belmont responded immediately:

You are in complete error. I never was hard or harsh on Cleveland at Chicago . . . & *never uttered a disparaging word against him.* This his friends & the managers of the campaign . . . know full well & have told me so themselves.

But he saved his real fire for the pro-Butler canard:

You may tell the Broker . . . *that he is an ass,* & I wish you would tell him so in my name. The idea of some ignorant fool, probably a new fledged neophyte from the Republican ranks, to dare & sit up in judgment over a man who has served unswervingly & zealously the Democratic Party for more than 40 years & has brought *heavier pecuniary sacrifice for it, during its darkest hours, than any man living in the United States.* I wish you had not written me this. It makes my very blood boil & has spoiled this quiet bright Sunday for me.[8]

Meanwhile, Perry contacted Senator Arthur P. Gorman, Maryland's national committeeman and the brains behind titular chairman Barnum, and described his father's despondency. A few days later, Belmont, Sr., received Gorman's letter requesting his thoughts on the current campaign and his estimate of Cleveland's strength in New York State. The banker reacted positively. He deplored intermittent attacks by certain "Cleveland journals" upon the "Irish element," which normally supplied a heavy Democratic vote in the Empire State. "Of course," he continued, "these elements are bad, pernicious, & loathsome, but you have to take things as they are & not as they ought to be." The Democratic press would be better off mounting a sensible, effective onslaught against Blaine, who as a newspaperman in the 1850s advocated "Know-nothingism & proscription of Irish & Catholics. . . . This ought to be taken hold of & repeated every day by every anti-Blaine paper throughout the land." His reserve broken, Belmont was caught up once more in the quadrennial excitement of a national election. His presence was noted at party rallies, and his checks went out to people who could put them to good use. Gorman received $3,500 for national committee expenses, while Kelly and his lieutenants were given $2,800 to help secure a solid New York City Irish vote.[9]

[8] Belmont to August Belmont, Jr., Oct. 10, 12, 14, 1884, private Belmont collection.

[9] Gorman to Belmont, Oct. 16, 1884, Oct. 12, 1888, Belmont to Gorman, Oct. 17, 1884, various checkbook stubs, private Belmont collection; John R. Lambert, *Arthur Pue Gorman* (Baton Rouge, La., 1953), 202–12.

Election Day, November 4, turned out to be a rainy one in New York, but the results coming in over the telegraph wires brightened many a Democratic household. Cleveland swept the South—henceforth to be called the "Solid South"—Indiana, New Jersey, and Connecticut. The electoral vote, however, was close enough to make victory hinge upon the outcome in New York, where the returns showed such a neck-and-neck race that many Democrats had nightmares of another " '76." Cleveland, however, demonstrated he was no Tilden by issuing a telegram on November 6, stating: "I believe I have been elected President, and nothing but grossest fraud can keep me out of it, and that we will not permit." Yet in a letter to Gorman on the 10th, a cautious Belmont warned that Republican managers in New York

are still confident to count their man in. Vast sums of money have been spent & are being spent all over the State in order to falsify the returns. . . . I need not assure you & your colleagues on the national committee to the utmost watchfulness. . . . A firm & decided stand and *no possible compromise of unconstitutional tribunals* must be our watchwords.[10]

The Associated Press eventually reported Cleveland's victory in New York by less than 1,200 votes, and those Republican newspapers which had declared the result in doubt soon conceded. "Thank God you are triumphantly elected," Belmont wired to the President-elect in Albany. The "falling off" in the New York vote, he explained, was due to rival Democratic slates having been put forward in the mayoralty race, notwithstanding "all efforts of mine, as well as of Senator Gorman, to prevent this fatal policy."

The bipartisan New York Merchants' and Business Men's Association, which had endorsed Cleveland in July, called for a mammoth victory celebration at the Academy of Music and invited Belmont to preside. He accepted and sat on the dais exchanging hearty jokes with fellow businessmen, Democratic and Republican alike. In his joyful speech of welcome, Belmont hailed the fruits of a "hard fought" battle in which loyal Demo-

10 Nevins, *Cleveland*, 186; Belmont to Gorman, Nov. 10, 1884, private Belmont collection.

crats overcame federal corruption, an entrenched bureaucratic machine comprising "more than 130,000 office-holders," and a party "strengthened by rich and powerful monopolies which placed millions of money at the disposal of unscrupulous leaders." He acknowledged the large number of erstwhile opponents gracing the platform by praising "the powerful aid given our cause by the Independent Republicans." [11]

No sooner did Cleveland's election become a certainty than the press began its perennial guessing games over the names of Democrats most likely to obtain posts within the coming administration. Belmont wrote Nathaniel de Rothschild that "Some of our Journals have already made free with my name in connection with the English mission." But he personally could not believe that Cleveland, besieged with twenty applicants for every office, "will step out of his way to tempt me." Belmont's surmise proved correct.[12]

The administration, however, invited Bayard to enter the cabinet. At first, Cleveland and his shrewd, young political strategist, William C. Whitney, did not think the senator could be persuaded to leave Capitol Hill, but a talk between Whitney and Perry convinced the President-elect otherwise. Cleveland wanted to offer Bayard the Treasury, which, in view of his tenure on the Senate Finance Committee and his many speeches on money and banking, seemed plausible enough. Two obstacles prevented this. Tilden, though in semi-retirement, objected to Bayard's gaining control of a position which handled many lucrative patronage appointments. Other advisers persuaded the President-elect that the senator's intimacy with Belmont and Kelly would enable "such men to have their way with him." Whitney again approached Perry to inquire whether Bayard would accept the State Department and was told that the senator should be asked the same question directly. Bayard traveled twice to Albany—in January and February, 1885—to confer

[11] Belmont to Cleveland, Nov. 13, 1884, Cleveland Papers; Oscar S. Straus, *Under Four Administrations: From Cleveland to Taft* (Boston, 1922), 39–40; Belmont, *Letters, Speeches and Addresses,* 230–31.
[12] Belmont to Rothschild, Nov. 18, 1884, private Belmont collection.

with Cleveland and Whitney. At the second meeting he accepted the State portfolio and promised to allow the Chief Executive the privilege of releasing the names of the cabinet to the public.[13]

That so many political conferences and decisions were going on without the need for his services saddened Belmont, but Bayard's reticence over his own dealings with the incoming administration was intolerable. The banker, though he knew of Perry's role and the senator's two visits to Albany, had yet to hear of them directly from Bayard. Two weeks before the inauguration, Belmont wrote Bayard a lengthy "epistle," scolding him for having passed through Gotham twice without stopping off at "109." The banker rambled on about his long service to the party and how now, because of his stand for Bayard at Chicago, "against the choice of the machine politicians of my own State . . . , I am virtually laid on the political shelf." Still, he would put aside all considerations of wounded pride, out of "warm & unwavering love for my country & party," in order to prevent Cleveland from any great blunders in the selection of cabinet officers. *"Mind, I do not wish to know before it is announced to the public, whether you take the State Dept. or not."* But if the cabinet were to become a "homogeneous whole," no midwestern Democrat of the "Thurman stripe" with "dangerous" views on currency should be admitted; Bayard's influence must prevent this "fatal mistake."

Unfortunately, the senator's prompt reply only exasperated Belmont further. Effusive with flattery but short on detail, Bayard's letter refused to take up any discussion of the cabinet on the ground that Cleveland "must be allowed to take his own way and time to announce his determinations." Not until Inauguration Day did Belmont, along with the rest of the public, learn that Bayard would be the new Secretary of State, and that no soft-money midwesterner would occupy a cabinet position. Thereafter, relations between Belmont and Bayard cooled. In

13 Anonymous letter to Bayard, Nov. 29, 1884, Perry Belmont to Bayard, Nov. 30, 1884, Bayard to Sidney Webster, Dec. 1, 1884, Bayard Papers; Horace White to Carl Schurz, Jan. 24, 1885, Schurz Papers; Flick, *Tilden*, 489.

July, Perry, who still idolized Bayard and as chairman of the House Committee on Foreign Affairs worked closely with him, intervened and reconciled the two men, though Bayard's growing preoccupation with foreign policy decisions and patronage distribution left them little common ground.[14]

Cleveland's inauguration marked Belmont's withdrawal from all active political participation, though he told an old friend from national committee days in April that his "allegiance & devotion to our great National party" would never lessen. Occasionally, he wrote a few letters of recommendation for acquaintances interested in federal appointments, placing one as chargé d'affaires in Mexico City, another as consul in Mannheim, Germany, and a third as a clerk in the Navy Department under Secretary Whitney.[15] The *New York World* reported his presence at a Democratic rally during the Congressional campaign of 1886. In 1888 he sent the Democratic National Committee $10,000 to help Cleveland's re-election campaign, partly out of loyalty to the party and partly to smooth Perry's pending appointment as Minister to Madrid. Such gestures as these were appreciated but no longer really expected.[16]

That Belmont had become an elder statesman of his party was evident not only by the appearance of so many new faces in important Democratic Party posts, but also by the funerals of a number of long-time political associates. O'Conor and Augustus Schell died in 1884. Seymour, Kelly, and Tilden passed away in 1886—all within the space of six months—and Barlow in 1889. These losses, coupled with the fact that he was now in his seventies, produced more than a tinge of mellowness in Belmont and a keen desire to forgive and forget the hoary quarrels of the political past. On March 18, 1888, he joined a group of thirty-six other "friends and admirers" of the late Tilden in pre-

14 Belmont to Bayard, Feb. 20, 1885, Bayard Papers; Bayard to Belmont, Feb. 22, July 24, 1885, private Belmont collection.

15 Belmont to Henry D. McHenry, April 27, 1885, Eleanor Belmont Papers; Daniel S. Lamont to Belmont, March 12, 1885, J. C. Monaghan to Belmont, June 18, 1885, William C. Whitney to Belmont, Sept. 5, 1885, S. H. B. Mason to Belmont, May 29, 1889, private Belmont collection.

16 *New York World*, Oct. 15, 1886; Matthew C. Butler to Belmont, Sept. 13, 19, 1888, Gorman to Belmont, Oct. 12, 1888, private Belmont collection.

senting a portrait of the former governor to the State of New
York. The following month he learned that former Senator
Conkling was near death, the result of exposure to the "Blizzard
of '88." Belmont visited the one-time vehement Republican,
cheered him with "consoling recollections," and presented him
with a bottle of wine. Conkling's grateful letter to Belmont was
his last. Two years later, the banker contributed $1,000 to help
erect a memorial statue to Conkling, the man he had excoriated
only twelve years earlier for having revived the "bloody shirt"
issue against the Democratic Party. Belmont even patched up
his differences with Whitelaw Reid of the *New York Tribune*.[17]

On January 1, 1890, Belmont sent a note to his son, August,
Jr., asking him and his wife to "come & dine. . . . There are
not many years in store for your loving old father." The sad
words turned out to be prophetic. Belmont suffered more and
more from dyspepsia, rheumatism, and the soreness of his lame
knee. Neighbors noticed him hobbling painfully as he walked
his dachshund along Fifth Avenue. His trips down to Wall
Street became infrequent. In November sponsors of a horse
show at Madison Square Garden persuaded Belmont to become
a last-minute substitute for a judge who had withdrawn. He
perspired freely in the drafty arena and, while still drenched,
went out into the cold night air to summon his carriage. He
spent a restless night and the next morning complained of fever
and a cough. The family doctor visited him and found incipient
pleurisy. The following day, Saturday, a lung specialist called
in for consultation diagnosed pneumonia. By nightfall Belmont
was unconscious. His condition steadily deteriorated on Sunday, and the attending physicians told the family around his
bedside that there remained little hope for recovery. He died at
3 A.M., Monday, November 24, without ever regaining con-
sciousness.

The funeral service at the Church of the Ascension, the same

17 Flick, *Tilden*, 506–07; Alfred R. Conkling, *The Life and Letters of Roscoe
Conkling: Orator, Statesman, Advocate* (New York, 1889), 703; Conkling to
Belmont, April 5, 1888, August Belmont, Jr., to Clarence A. Seward, Dec.
11, 1890, Reid to Belmont, April 25, 1889, private Belmont collection.

church where he had been married forty-one years earlier, was
attended by a large crowd of dignitaries, including Republican
Vice President Levi P. Morton. Former President Cleveland
and New York Governor David B. Hill, who had been feuding
over leadership of the state organization, sat side by side in a
front pew, leading the *Brooklyn Citizen* to editorialize that
even in death Belmont had rendered the Democratic Party a
service "no living leader had been able to accomplish." To
those familiar with the arduous problems he faced as Democratic National Chairman during the Civil War and Reconstruction, this was a fitting epitaph.[18]

There was a certain tragic course to the life of August Belmont.
A success in the worlds of international finance, society, and
culture, he chose to venture deeply into a different world—politics—where he was thwarted at almost every turn. Though he
gave unstintingly of his time and money and brought a superior
talent for organization to the tasks at hand, he never attained
the results or recognition commensurate with the magnitude
of his efforts. As a foreign-born Jew in a heyday of nativism
and a wealthy banker in a period of anti-capitalist agitation and
recurrent economic depression, his motives were often suspect
and his activities hampered by unfavorable publicity. As chairman of the Democratic National Committee during a time of
intraparty crisis, his inability to unite key party factions and
imbue them with a cohesive vision militated against his success.
Even had he been able to surmount the handicaps of personal
identity and party divisiveness, it was highly improbable that he
(or any other Democrat) could have been the architect of electoral victories. His most significant work coincided with the
convulsive years of war and reconstruction when no strategy,
no action could have staved off the erosion of loyal leadership
and faithful rank and file. Taking all these circumstances into
account, it was inevitable that Belmont, intrepid though he was,
would be rebuffed by forces beyond his control.

[18] Obituaries in various New York City newspapers, Nov. 25, 1890; *New
York Times*, Nov. 30, 1890; clipping from *Brooklyn Citizen*, Nov. 30, 1890,
found in private Belmont collection.

Ironically, Belmont's most substantial party achievement might not have occurred had he been blessed with the victories he coveted. When he assumed the chairmanship, it was a position previously occupied by political unknowns who used it only a few months every four years, and then solely as a fundraising instrument. But constant political setbacks meant fewer public forums for the Democratic viewpoint, tighter Democratic pursestrings, and a closed door for Democratic patronage seekers. Belmont's efforts to arrest party atrophy and to counteract, or at least neutralize, Republican dominance gradually transformed the nature of his national committee post.

He originated a variety of methods to attract funds—never an easy job for a weak opposition party—and supervised the publication and distribution of political propaganda. He coordinated the national committee's functions with those of Democratic state committees and of the Congressional campaign organizations. He even reached out directly to the voters through periodic public addresses and exhortations. Most strikingly, he used his official capacity to speak for the party and "negotiate" not only with prospective presidential nominees, but with other fledgling parties and movements as well. The fact that he was a notable figure outside politics further publicized his work on the committee and made his political endeavors "must" stories for Democratic and Republican newspapers alike. By 1872, when Belmont stepped down, the chairmanship had become an eagerly sought post within the party hierarchy, one with formidable power and prestige.

Belmont's administrative evolution paralleled a personal one. He rose to power early, and an impatience to get to the top characterized his career in the 1850s. But once his political course spiraled downward, eagerness turned into a stubbornness to hold on despite the unlikelihood of immediate success and concomitant reward. Perhaps his youthful drive was due to an inflated opinion of himself plus a belief that human behavior was as predictable as international finance. But after 1860 he underwent too much financial sacrifice, personal abuse, and political reversal for personal factors to be the rationale behind such lifelong persistence.

What, then, is the explanation? What made Belmont, against all odds, all hope, almost all reason, continually pick up the shards of defeat and try to put the Democratic Party together again? The most probable answer is his passionate concern for the survival of that party. Naturally he took some missteps, but the seeming inconsistencies and about-faces that dot his career either diminish in importance or take on a new reasonableness when related to this political goal. If he could not win with the Democratic Party, he was determined to keep it alive, by almost any means, until he could. Belmont's identification with the loyal opposition during the war years; his struggle to patch up party dissension and broaden its base after the war when the Democratic label was equally burdensome; his tentative consideration of a merger with the National Union movement; his initiation of a dialogue with the Liberal Republicans which culminated in a coalition candidate and platform; his all-out effort to turn a popular mandate into an electoral majority after the 1876 election—all these were cogent decisions consonant with his dedication to the continuing existence of a Democratic entity.

Selected Bibliography

I. *Manuscripts*

Samuel Latham Mitchill Barlow Papers, Henry E. Huntington Library.

Thomas Francis Bayard Papers, Library of Congress.

John Bell Papers, Library of Congress.

August Belmont Papers (private collection of Mrs. Eleanor Robson Belmont), New York City.

August Belmont Papers, Library of Congress.

August Belmont Papers, Collections of The New-York Historical Society.

August Belmont Papers, New York Public Library.

Eleanor Robson Belmont Papers, Columbia University.

Blair Family Papers, Library of Congress.

James Buchanan Papers, Historical Society of Pennsylvania.

Salmon Portland Chase Papers, Historical Society of Pennsylvania.

Grover Cleveland Papers, Library of Congress.

Samuel Sullivan Cox Papers, Brown University.

John Givan Davis Papers, Indiana Historical Society.

Stephen Arnold Douglas Papers, Illinois State Historical Library.

Stephen Arnold Douglas Papers, University of Chicago.

William Hayden English Papers, Indiana Historical Society.

Simon Gratz Collection, Historical Society of Pennsylvania.

Andrew Johnson Papers, Library of Congress.

Herschel Vespasian Johnson Papers, Duke University.

Abraham Lincoln Papers, Library of Congress.

Manton Malone Marble Papers, Library of Congress.

William Learned Marcy Papers, Library of Congress.

George Brinton McClellan Papers, Library of Congress.

George Nicholas Sanders Papers, Library of Congress.

Carl Schurz Papers, Library of Congress.

Horatio Seymour Papers, Collections of The New-York Historical Society.

William Henry Seward Papers, University of Rochester.

Henry Hastings Sibley Papers, Minnesota Historical Society.
Samuel Jones Tilden Papers, New York Public Library.
Thurlow Weed Papers, University of Rochester.

II. *Published Documents, Correspondence, Memoirs,
and Other Primary Sources*

[Armstrong, William]. *The Aristocracy of New York: Who They Are
And What They Were.* . . . New York, 1848.
Annual Report of the American Historical Association, 1902. Two vols.
Washington, 1903. Second volume contains Diary and Correspondence
of Salmon P. Chase.
*Annual Report of the American Historical Association for the Year
1911.* Two vols. Washington, 1913. Second volume contains corre-
spondence of Robert Toombs, Alexander H. Stephens, and Howell
Cobb.
Bancroft, Frederic, ed., *Speeches, Correspondence and Political Papers
of Carl Schurz.* Six vols. New York, 1913.
Barnes, Thurlow Weed. *Memoir of Thurlow Weed.* Boston, 1884.
Basler, Roy P., ed. *The Collected Works of Abraham Lincoln.* Eight
vols. New Brunswick, N. J., 1953.
[Beach, Moses Yale]. *Wealth and Biography of the Wealthy Citizens of
New York City.* . . . Sixth ed. New York, 1845.
Belmont, August. *A Few Letters and Speeches of the Late Civil War.*
New York, 1870.
——. *Letters, Speeches and Addresses.* New York, 1890.
Belmont, Eleanor Robson. *The Fabric of Memory.* New York, 1957.
Belmont, Perry. *An American Democrat: The Recollections of Perry
Belmont.* Second ed. New York, 1941.
Bigelow, John, ed. *Letters and Literary Memorials of Samuel J. Tilden.*
Two vols. New York, 1908.
Biographical Directory of the American Congress, 1774–1949. Washing-
ton, 1950.
Blaine, James G. *Twenty Years of Congress: From Lincoln to Garfield.*
Two vols. Norwich, Conn., 1884–86.
Breen, Matthew P. *Thirty Years of New York Politics: Up-to-Date.* New
York, 1899.
Brooks, Noah. *Washington in Lincoln's Time.* New York [1958].
Butler, Benjamin F. *Butler's Book: Autobiography and Personal Reminis-
cences of Major-General Benjamin F. Butler.* Boston, 1892.
Clews, Henry. *Fifty Years in Wall Street.* New York, 1908.
Coleman, Ann Mary Butler Breckenridge, ed. *The Life of John J.
Crittenden, with Selections from His Correspondence and Speeches.*
Two vols. Philadelphia, 1871.

Conkling, Alfred R. *The Life and Letters of Roscoe Conkling: Orator, Statesman, Advocate.* New York, 1889.

Diamond, Sigmund, ed. *A Casual View of America: The Home Letters of Salomon de Rothschild, 1859–1861.* Stanford, Calif., 1961.

Halstead, Murat. *A History of the National Political Conventions of the Current Presidential Campaign: Caucuses of 1860.* Cincinnati, 1860.

Hammond, Harold E., ed. *Diary of a Union Lady, 1861–1865.* New York, 1962.

Haswell, Charles H. *Reminiscences of an Octogenarian of the City of New York (1816 to 1860).* New York, 1896.

Hesseltine, William B., and Rex G. Fisher, eds. *Trimmers, Trucklers & Temporizers: Notes of Murat Halstead from the Political Conventions of 1856.* Madison, Wisc., 1961.

Johannsen, Robert W., ed. *The Letters of Stephen A. Douglas.* Urbana, Ill., 1961.

Locke, David Ross. *The Struggles (Social, Financial and Political) of Petroleum V. Nasby.* Boston, 1893.

McAllister, Ward. *Society as I Have Found It.* New York, 1890.

McPherson, Edward. *A Political Manual for 1868. . . .* Washington, 1868.

Moore, John Bassett, ed. *The Works of James Buchanan: Comprising his Speeches, State Papers, and Private Correspondence.* Twelve vols. Philadelphia, 1908–11.

Nevins, Allan, and Milton H. Thomas, eds. *The Diary of George Templeton Strong.* Four vols. New York, 1952.

Nevins, Allan, ed. *The Diary of Philip Hone, 1828–1851.* New York, 1936.

Official Proceedings of the National Democratic Convention. . . . Different cities, 1856–1884.

Russell, William Howard. *My Diary North and South.* Boston, 1863.

Sanborn, Alvan F., ed. *Reminiscences of Richard Lathers: Sixty Years of a Busy Life in South Carolina, Massachusetts and New York.* New York, 1907.

[Sanders, George N.]. *The Political Correspondence of the Late Hon. George N. Sanders. . . .* New York, 1914.

Schappes, Morris U., ed. *A Documentary History of the Jews in the United States, 1654–1875.* New York, 1950.

Schuckers, Jacob W. *The Life and Public Services of Salmon Portland Chase.* New York, 1874.

[Scoville, Joseph A.]. *The Old Merchants of New York City.* Five vols. New York, 1864–70.

Seward, Frederick W. *Seward at Washington as Senator and Secretary of State: A Memoir of His Life, with Selections from His Letters, 1861–1872.* New York, 1891.

Sherman, John. *Recollections of Forty Years in the House, Senate and Cabinet: An Autobiography.* Two vols. Chicago, 1895.

Straus, Oscar S. *Under Four Administrations: From Cleveland to Taft.* Boston, 1922.

Train, George Francis. *Young America in Wall-Street.* New York, 1857.

Williams, Charles R., ed. *Diary and Letters of Rutherford Birchard Hayes: Nineteenth President of the United States.* Five vols. Columbus, Ohio, 1922–26.

III. *Books and Articles.*

Albion, Robert G., and Jennie B. Pope. *The Rise of New York Port, 1815–1860.* New York, 1939.

Alexander, De Alva Stanwood. *A Political History of the State of New York.* Four vols. New York, 1906–23.

"Antipathy of Race and Religion." *Harper's Weekly,* VII (Feb. 28, 1863), 130–31.

Auchampaugh, Philip G. "The Buchanan-Douglas Feud." *Journal of the Illinois State Historical Society,* XXV (April, 1932), 5–48.

"August Belmont." *Harper's Weekly,* XXXIV (Dec. 6, 1890), 951–52.

Benton, Josiah H. *Voting in the Field: A Forgotten Chapter of the Civil War.* Boston, 1915.

Bonham, Milledge L., Jr. "New York and the Election of 1860." *New York History,* XV (April, 1934), 124–43.

Bowen, Croswell. *The Elegant Oakey.* New York, 1956.

Brummer, Sidney D. *Political History of New York State During the Period of the Civil War.* New York, 1911.

Coben, Stanley. "Northeastern Business and Radical Reconstruction: A Re-examination." *The Mississippi Valley Historical Review,* XLVI (June, 1959), 67–90.

Coleman, Charles H. *The Election of 1868: The Democratic Effort to Regain Control.* New York, 1933.

Cox, Lawanda, and John H. Cox. *Politics, Principle, and Prejudice, 1865–1866: Dilemma of Reconstruction America.* Glencoe, Ill., 1963.

Cronau, Rudolf. *Drei Jahrhunderte Deutschen Lebens In Amerika: Eine Geschichte Der Deutschen In Den Vereinigten Staaten.* Berlin, 1909.

Curti, Merle E. " 'Young America'." *The American Historical Review,* XXXII (October, 1926), 34–55.

Destler, Chester M. *American Radicalism, 1865–1901: Essays and Documents.* New London, Conn., 1946.

Dorpalen, Andreas. "The German Element and the Issues of the Civil War." *The Mississippi Valley Historical Review,* XXIX (June, 1942), 55–76.

Duberman, Martin B. *Charles Francis Adams, 1807–1886.* Boston, 1961.

Encyclopaedia Judaica: Das Judentum in Geschichte und Gegenwart. Ten vols. Berlin, 1928–34.

Ettinger, Amos A. *The Mission to Spain of Pierre Soulé, 1853–1855: A Study in the Cuban Diplomacy of the United States.* New Haven, Conn., 1932.

Fite, Emerson D. *The Presidential Campaign of 1860.* New York, 1911.

Flick, Alexander C. *Samuel Jones Tilden: A Study in Political Sagacity.* New York, 1939.

Flippin, Percy S. *Herschel V. Johnson of Georgia: State Rights Unionist.* Richmond, 1931.

Foner, Philip S. *Business & Slavery: The New York Merchants & the Irrepressible Conflict.* Chapel Hill, N. C., 1941.

Glanz, Rudolf. "The Rothschild Legend in America." *Jewish Social Studies,* XIX (January–April, 1957), 3–28.

Gottheil, Richard J. H. *The Belmont-Belmonte Family: A Record of Four Hundred Years.* New York, 1917.

Gray, Wood. *The Hidden Civil War: The Story of the Copperheads.* New York, 1942.

Gunderson, Robert G. *Old Gentlemen's Convention: The Washington Peace Conference of 1861.* Madison, Wisc., 1961.

Hendrick, Burton J. *Lincoln's War Cabinet.* Boston, 1946.

Henry, Robert S. *The Story of the Mexican War.* Indianapolis, 1950.

Heslin, James J. " 'Peaceful Compromise' in New York City, 1860–1861." *The New-York Historical Society Quarterly,* XLIV (October, 1960), 349–62.

Hirsch, Mark D. *William C. Whitney: Modern Warwick.* New York, 1948.

"History of Democratic National Conventions." *The American Monthly,* LXIV (October, 1864), 353–59.

House, Albert V. "The Speakership Contest of 1875: Democratic Response to Power." *The Journal of American History,* LII (September, 1965), 252–74.

Hyman, Harold M. *Era of the Oath: Northern Loyalty Tests During the Civil War and Reconstruction.* Philadelphia, 1954.

Kirkland, Edward C. *The Peacemakers of 1864.* New York, 1927.

Klein, Philip S. *President James Buchanan: A Biography.* University Park, Pa., 1962.

Krug, Mark M. *Lyman Trumbull: Conservative Radical.* New York, 1965.

Lambert, John R. *Arthur Pue Gorman.* Baton Rouge, La., 1953.

Lindsey, David. *"Sunset" Cox: Irrepressible Democrat.* Detroit, 1959.

Luthin, Reinhard H. "The Democratic Split During Buchanan's Administration." *Pennsylvania History,* XI (January, 1944), 13–35.

McKitrick, Eric L. *Andrew Johnson and Reconstruction.* Chicago, 1960.

Markens, Isaac. *The Hebrews in America: A Series of Historical and Biographical Sketches*. New York, 1888.

Merrill, Horace S. *Bourbon Democracy of the Middle West, 1865–1896*. Baton Rouge, La., 1953.

Milton, George F. *The Eve of Conflict: Stephen A. Douglas and the Needless War*. Boston, 1934.

Mitchell, Stewart. *Horatio Seymour of New York*. Cambridge, Mass., 1938.

Murphy, Charles B. "Samuel J. Tilden and the Civil War." *The South Atlantic Quarterly*, XXXIII (July, 1934), 261–71.

Myers, William S. *General George Brinton McClellan: A Study in Personality*. New York, 1934.

Nevins, Allan. *Abram S. Hewitt, With Some Account of Peter Cooper*. New York, 1935.

——. *The Emergence of Lincoln*. Two vols. New York, 1950.

——. *Grover Cleveland: A Study in Courage*. New York, 1932.

——. *Ordeal of the Union*. Two vols. New York, 1947.

——. *The War for the Union*. Two vols. New York, 1959–60.

Nichols, Roy F. *The Democratic Machine, 1850–1854*. New York, 1923.

——. *The Disruption of American Democracy*. New York, 1948.

——. *Franklin Pierce: Young Hickory of the Granite Hills*. 2nd ed. Philadelphia, 1958.

Nicolay, John G., and John Hay. *Abraham Lincoln: A History*. Ten vols. New York, 1886–90.

Oates, Stephen B. "Henry Hotze: Confederate Agent Abroad." *The Historian*, XXVII (February, 1965), 131–54.

Phelan, Mary C. *Manton Marble of the New York World*. Washington, 1957.

Potter, David M. *Lincoln and His Party in the Secession Crisis*. New Haven, Conn., 1942.

Randall, James G., and Richard N. Current. *Lincoln the President*. Four vols. New York, 1946–55.

Rauch, Basil. *American Interest in Cuba, 1848–1855*. New York, 1948.

Rawley, James A. "Financing the Fremont Campaign." *The Pennsylvania Magazine of History and Biography*, LXXV (January, 1951), 25–35.

Redlich, Fritz. *The Molding of American Banking: Men and Ideas*. Two vols. New York, 1947–51.

Ross, Earle D. *The Liberal Republican Movement*. New York, 1919.

"The Rothschilds and the Union." *Harper's Weekly*, VII (April 25, 1863), 258.

Sears, Louis M. "August Belmont: Banker in Politics." *The Historical Outlook*, XV (April, 1924), 151–54.

——. *John Slidell*. Durham, N. C., 1925.

———. "Slidell and Buchanan." *The American Historical Review*, XXVII (July, 1922), 709–30.

Sharkey, Robert P. *Money, Class, and Party: An Economic Study of Civil War and Reconstruction*. Baltimore, 1959.

Shenton, James P. *Robert John Walker: A Politician from Jackson to Lincoln*. New York, 1961.

Smith, Justin H. *The War With Mexico*. Two vols. New York, 1919.

Smith, William E. *The Francis Preston Blair Family in Politics*. Two vols. New York, 1933.

Spencer, Ivor D. *The Victor and the Spoils: A Life of William L. Marcy*. Providence, 1959.

Stebbins, Homer A. *A Political History of the State of New York, 1865–1869*. New York, 1913.

Tansill, Charles C. *The Congressional Career of Thomas Francis Bayard, 1869–1885*. Washington, 1946.

Unger, Irwin. *The Greenback Era: A Social and Political History of American Finance, 1865–1879*. Princeton, N. J., 1964.

Watterson, Henry. *History of the Manhattan Club: A Narrative of the Activities of Half a Century*. New York, 1915.

Wilson, Charles. "McClellan's Changing Views on the Peace Plank of 1864." *The American Historical Review*, XXXVIII (April, 1933), 498–505.

Woolfolk, George R. *The Cotton Regency: The Northern Merchants and Reconstruction, 1865–1880*. New York, 1959.

Zornow, William F. *Lincoln & the Party Divided*. Norman, Okla., 1954.

Index

Adams, Charles Francis, aids Belmont, 102; 1868 campaign, 166; Liberal Republican candidacy, 198-200; favors Bayard, 255; backs Cleveland, 268

Albany Evening Journal, 53-54

Albert, Prince, 102

Allison, William B., 236-39

Anti-Catholicism, 18, 270

Anti-Semitism, in 1852 *Times* and *Tribune* editorials, 19; Gibson case, 39; 1860 election, 82; Civil War, 113; 1864 campaign, 138, 143-46; Belmont-Kemble correspondence, 165-66; 1868 election, 172; Tammany press, 188-89

Astor, John J., 77

Astor, William B., 71, 77

August Belmont and Company, viii, 51; formation and activities, 7; temporarily renamed, 33; Belmont's income, 34n; 1873 panic, 210, 223

Austria-Hungary, 7, 29

Baltimore Sun, 183

Bancroft, George, 57, 90

Banks, Nathaniel P., 121-22

Barlow, Samuel L. M., viii, 213; 1856 election, 51; joins Democratic group, 62; aids *World*, 117-18; Belmont Congressional nomination, 119-20; Delmonico's meeting, 121; McClellan candidacy, 122, 124, 127, 129, 131, 135, 148, 151; sees Andrew Johnson, 153; National Union movement, 156; 1868 campaign, 168, 176n; aids Belmont, 187, 189-90; 1876 candidates, 218; at 1879 conference, 245; death, 274

Barnum, William H., 258-59, 270

Bate, William B., 202

Bayard, Thomas F., viii; Belmont friendship, 214; 1876 campaign, 215-21; electoral crisis, 226-29, 231-33, 249; currency issue, 235-37, 239; 1880 campaign, 239-44, 247-61; Republican patronage, 262-63; 1884 race, 264-67; cabinet appointment, 272-74

Beck, James B., 237

Beecher, Henry Ward, 268

Bell, Isaac, 119-20

Bell, John, 73, 78, 80-81, 83

Belmont, August, Jr., 33, 275; father's letter, 212; 1884 campaign, 267-70

Belmont, August

— banking activities: viii, 51; forms August Belmont and Company, 7; Christmas, Matthiessen and Company, 33; annual income from, 34n; Kemble correspondence, 165-66; 1873 panic, 210, 223

— diplomatic role: Austrian consul general, 7-8; Cuban issue, 21-26, 40-45, 49, 55, 57-60, 85; desires appointment, 25-31; Minister to The Hague, 31-51; Gibson case, 37-39, 45-47; consular treaty, 37, 45-47; extradition treaty, 47-49; resignation, 55-56; seeks Madrid post, 58-60; Civil War activities, 92-112, 114-15; rumored appointment, 221, 223, 264, 272

— Judaism: 276; background, 1, 4-5; 1852 editorials, 19; Gibson case, 39; 1860 election, 82; Civil War, 113; 1864 campaign, 138, 143-46; Kemble allusion, 165-66; 1868 elec-